The Arrogance o  er

Editorials by William J. Lawrence
Member, Red Lake Ojibwe

1988-2009

Foreword by Gerald Vizenor

Edited by E. R. Thompson

Assisted by Sara Lawrence

Assembled and Edited by E.R. Thompson
Editorials by William J. Lawrence
Published Under the Auspices of
The Native American Press, LLC
Minneapolis, Minnesota
Permission of Sara Lawrence and Amy Lawrence Wolf
All Rights Reserved

ISBN-13: 978-1-7325518-0-0
ISBN-10: 1-7325518-0-4
First Edition
Printed in the United States

William J. Lawrence   1939-2009

Education:

1957   Diploma - Bemidji High School, Bemidji, MN.

1957   Attended University of Minnesota; Scholarship. [Football, Baseball] Minneapolis, MN.

1962   B.A. Business, Accounting & Economics – Bemidji State University; Bemidji, MN.

1972   Juris Doctor – University of North Dakota School of Law; Grand Forks, ND.

Military Service:

1962-1966 Lieutenant – United States Marine Corp, service in Viet Nam.

1966-1982 Captain – USMC Reserve.

Work Experience:

1988-2009 Publisher/Owner - *The Native American Press/Ojibwe News.* Bemidji and St. Paul, MN.

2003-2004 Legal advisor - Red Lake Band of Chippewa; Red Lake, MN.

1984-1992 Senior Contract Negotiator - Honeywell, Inc.; Minneapolis, MN.

1978-1984 Business Manager – Fort Mojave Indian Tribe; Needles, CA.

1975-1978 Superintendent – Bureau of Indian Affairs, Colorado River Agency; Parker, CA.

1969-1975 Administrator - Indian Adult programs; Minnesota Department of Education.

1968-1969 Director - Economic Development & Planning; Red Lake Reservation, MN.

1958-1959 Starting pitcher/Championship team – Detroit Tiger Farm Team; Valdosta, GA.

Publications:

2002 "In Defense of Indian Rights," *Beyond the Color Line: New Perspectives on Race and Ethnicity in America.* Thernstrom, Abigail and Stephan, editors. Hoover Institute Press: Stanford, CA.

1988-2009   Weekly editorials and news articles for *The Native American Press/Ojibwe News.* Discussed Federal Indian Policy, treaty rights, denial of civil rights on Indian Reservations, Tribal Sovereign Immunity, tribal corruption, mismanagement and non-accountability by tribal officials.

Presentations:

1997 "Tribal Casinos Must Share the Wealth." Testimony, Minnesota Joint House/Senate Tax Committee.

1997 "Investigating in Indian Country: Tribal Governments and the Agencies that Oversee Them." Investigative Reporters and Editors National Convention.

1998 "The American Indian Equal Justice Act." Testimony, U.S. Senate Committee on Indian Affairs.

2002 "Rules of Procedure for the Recognition of Tribal Court Orders and Judgments." State of Minnesota Supreme Court.

2007 "Discrimination Against Native Americans in Border Towns." United States Civil Rights Commission.

Community Service:

1970-1973 Member, Minnesota State Advisory Council for Vocational Education.

1974-1975 Member, Board of Education, Bemidji Public Schools, Bemidji, MN.

1981-1982 Member, President, Board of Trustees, Mojave Valley Elementary School, Mojave Valley, CA.

1998-2009 Member, Minnesota Minority Media, Coalition President 1992, 1996, 2000, 2004.

Awards:

1997 Nominated for Pulitzer Prize in Journalism for investigative reporting and editorial writing.

2003 Recipient of the Freedom of Information Award given by the Society of Professional Journalists "For aggressive defense of the people's right to know and consistent support for the First Amendment," St. Paul Chapter.

2005 Inductee, Bemidji High School Athletic Hall of Fame.

2008 Inductee, Bemidji State University Athletic Hall of Fame.

Personal:

Private pilot, over 1200 logged hours, pilot in-command.
Father of three; grandfather of four.
Enrolled member of the Red Lake Band of Chippewa Indians.
Deceased 3-2-09. Buried with full military honors - US Marine Corp.

Table of Contents

- Washington's "Noble Savage" mentality.
- Corruption, oppression – not reporting it – jeopardizes sovereignty.
- Federal Indian policy is the problem not the solution.
- The Justice system in Indian Country needs new strategies.

Chapter VI. Introduction Tribal Sovereignty.
- Tribes' abuses of sovereignty will kill the goose that laid the golden egg.
- Mystic Lake's CEO's conduct could prove to be the arrow that pierces the veil of tribal sovereign immunity.
- Congress can't see forest of civil rights for trees of sovereign immunity.
- Giving tribal sovereign immunity a run for its money.
- Future bright for Indian people on reservations, only if tribal sovereign immunity limited.
- State needs to develop clear policy for review of tribal court decisions.
- Minnesota Indian gambling: an unregulated, unaccountable, monopoly with nearly unlimited cash, hiding behind tribal sovereign immunity.

Chapter VII. Introduction: Tribal Corruption.
- Candidate seeks Presidential assistance.
- Mismanagement, fraud and improvident deals have cost the Native Community nearly $100 million.
- Everything the Tribal Establishment doesn't want you to know about Tribal courts.
- Red Lake's financing of Water Park Project made public in round-about way.
- Buying the status quo is killing us.

- Wrongful Termination suit: Another test of the rule of law at Leech Lake.
- *Press/ON* to publish financial information on twelve Minnesota tribal entities.
- Anishinabe! Elections approach, take up your burden, choose wisely.
- Leech Lake Leadership to do list: 1. Reorganize under rules that will serve and protect the people.

Note: The Lawrence editorials are reprinted exactly as they appeared in *The Native American Press/Ojibwe News.*

Introduction: Letters to the Editor.
- "Writer critical of *The Native American Press.* . .
- "Agree non-members take home tribal money. . .
- "Leech Lake Vote Buying. . .
- "Basic human rights not for all. . .
- "Red Lake Students hungry. . .
- "Mr. Bill Lawrence. . .
- "We have our own 'Katrina'. . .
- "The 'Buck' stops here. . .
- "Father of slain Red Lake Security guard responds…

Bibliography

Appendix

The Native American Press/Ojibwe News series on Fetal Alcohol Spectrum Disorder.

Dedication

For our families, our children, our grandchildren, and our great grandchildren; and for all others who care about such things.

ACKNOWLEDGEMENTS: Many individuals deserve recognition and gratitude for their contribution to this collection. Thank you to all my family members for your love, support and polite attention to my alternating tales of jubilation and tribulation throughout the length of the project.

Special thanks also goes to Bill Lawrence's family, Sara Lawrence and Amy Lawrence Wolf, for their ongoing acceptance of my presence in their lives and for their total support of this work.

Deep appreciation to Gerald Vizenor, probably the most published Native American writer of our day, for agreeing to write a Foreword for Bill's book. His contribution is especially valued as he interrupted his own work to pay tribute to Bill, his long time friend. He has earned our gratitude also for his unfailing courtesy and support.

Reviewers David E. Wilkins and Catherine C. Robbins earn kudos for acknowledging the value and depth of Bill's work; they saw the need in the broader society for education in this area that has been largely ignored.

Louise Mengelkoch, recognizing that *The Native American Press/Ojibwe News* is a unique body of work, deserves credit for taking the initiative to see that the paper is preserved in the Minnesota Digital Newspaper Hub/Minnesota Historical Society, thus assuring that this body of work will long be available as a resource for those who desire to know truths that have escaped notice by the mainstream.

Judge R.A. "Jim" Randall, a special friend, legal advisor and ally, for his enthusiastic support of the project. Lawrence was especially grateful for the articulation of

Randall's legal opinions in *Cohen vs Little Six* (Dissent) and *Granite Valley vs Jackpot Junction* (Concur) that coincided with his own educated opinions.

Bob Nelson, Bill's long time friend, provided many anecdotes about their time together.

A big thank you to all my friends who kindly asked about the progress of the book and, in listening to the report, inadvertently learned more than they ever wanted to know about the project, yet remained supportive. Their interest was an encouragement to me. In short anyone who knows me deserves thanks for the courteous interest I received throughout the process of completing *The Arrogance of Tribal Power.*

Regretfully, not everyone can be named, but these individuals should be acknowledged: Mark Boswell-cartoons, Tony Evans-editorial advice, Adrienne Leugers-cover, Diana Anderson-manuscript preparation, Patty Healy and Mike McKenna-proof readers, Narda Pitkethly-consultant.

Finally, because I believe Bill's spirit has lingered to facilitate this project, we acknowledge the inspiration we received from him.

Forward by Gerald Vizenor.

William Lawrence, the resolute founder and editor of *The Native American Press/Ojibwe News*, never hesitated to denounce the corruption of reservation leaders, or to expose the deceit and chicanery of casino politics. His primary motivation as an editor, however, was to defend the civil rights of natives on reservations, and to arraign the pretense of absolute treaty sovereignty.

Lawrence was rightly admired for his integrity, persistence and persuasion as an editor, and most of his detractors, Chip Wadena, Skip Finn, and others, were exposed for malfeasance and indicted for serious crimes. After fifteen years as an editor and investigative writer Lawrence received the 2003 Minnesota Society of Professional Journalists Freedom of Information Award in recognition of his editorial dedication to native rights and the freedom of information.

He was a courageous advocate and plucky editor for the rights of natives on federal reservations, and he carried out his advocacy in the great tradition of *The Progress* and later *The Tomahawk*, the first two independent native newspapers published by Augustus Hudon Beaulieu on the White Earth Reservation in Minnesota. The federal agent ordered the removal of the publisher and editor, Theodore Hudon Beaulieu, both native citizens of the reservation, and arbitrarily confiscated the actual rotary press. The second edition of the newspaper was published more than a year later after a federal court decision in favor of the publisher and editor.

The first edition of *The Progress*, March 25, 1886, declared on the front page, "We shall aim to advocate constantly and withhold reserve, what in our view, and in the view of the leading minds upon this reservation, is best for the interests of the residents. And not-only for their interests, but those of the tribe wherever they now are residing." Lawrence clearly carried out that declaration and much more, and he might have proclaimed similar stouthearted maneuvers on the masthead of *The Native American Press/Ojibwe*

1

News.

Most native newspapers were initiated and sponsored by reservation governments. Obviously the underwriters managed the news and easily censored critical stories about federal policies, contracts, or most recently the management and distribution of money from casinos.

The *Red Lake Times*, for instance, was started by Roger Jourdain, then the notorious chairman of the Red Lake Band of Chippewa, and the reservation government, but after a year of crude content management the newspaper was dead but not buried, and two former writers contacted Lawrence to support a new and independent weekly named the *Ojibwe News*.

Mike Mosedale reported in *City Pages*, "From the outset, the *Ojibwe News* was an in-your face publication—or, more accurately, an in-Roger Jourdain's-face publication. The first issue, published in May of 1988, led with an exposé of financial shenanigans at Red Lake. Subsequent editions featured similar stories, along with stinging editorials authored by Lawrence denouncing everyone from the 'dictatorial' Jourdain (and 'his ten little Indians' on the tribal council) to the "bureaucrats" of the Bureau of Indian Affairs.

Lawrence conveyed a manner of confidence, not courtly or suave, but casual, poised and cordial, and with a great sense of humor. His friends recognized a signature smile that preceded a tease, a familiar native practice in most families. And, of course, he could easily turn a tease of his own serious moments around to share a generous sense of humor. He teased me many times, as an activist, journalist, poet, and as a private in the army. I teased him as a muckraker of traditional tribal corruption, and he turned that around with an ironic gesture that Chip Wadena, the chairman of the White Earth Reservation, who was convicted in federal court of embezzlement, money laundering, and other acts of corruption, only diverted casino money because he had a huge family to support. Some natives, with intended irony, characterized Chip Wadena as

2

the Robin Hood of White Earth. The tease countered the medieval legend because the tribal outlaw stole from the losers, the game money at the casino, and seldom shared the loot with the native poor. Lawrence named the malfeasance "Chippygate."

Mosedale pointed out in *City Pages* that "Lawrence's demeanor stands in contrast to his maverick sensibilities and sometimes inflammatory rhetoric." He "seldom raises his voice, instead offering his complaints as though he were reading a grocery list aloud."

David Lillehaug, the United States Attorney for Minnesota, for instance, told Mosedale that Lawrence came to his office in Saint Paul and said, "I'm here to tell you there's a serious problem with corruption on Indian reservations in Minnesota, and that I and my publication hope and expect that you will make that a high priority. And if you don't, we will point that out." Lillehaug recalled that Lawrence was obviously forward, but "he didn't come in with a grudge or assuming that he wouldn't be listened to. We hit it off pretty well."

Lawrence was impressed with Minnesota Appeals Court Judge Jim Randall who had questioned the notion of absolute tribal sovereignty and argued that natives on federal reservations were denied the civil rights of ordinary citizens. Reservation governments were not obligated to provide the same civil rights and protections of the Constitution of the United States.

Judge Randall told Mosedale that Lawrence arrived at his courthouse chambers with no notice and said, "I'm Bill Lawrence, publisher of *The Native American Press*, and I've been waiting for your opinion for 28 years." Those who heard and then read the story in *City Pages* were not surprised because the editor and the judge had expressed similar concerns about native civil rights and critiques of treaty reservation sovereignty.

Lawrence had read about Judge Randall's dissent to an appeals court decision that Sylvia Cohen, who was not native, should have the right to pursue a case for personal injuries against the Mystic Lake Casino. Mosedale wrote that Judge Randall and Lawrence "shared the same birthday, they are both ex-Marines, both love sports, and both had concluded the notion of tribal sovereignty was a sham." Randall told Mosedale, "The more I learned about what he was doing, how he feels, the more I became convinced that he was on the right track. And he has the clearest mind of any writer working today on what are the problems in Indian country."

Lawrence was born on the Red Lake Reservation, and graduated from Bemidji State University with a degree in business administration. He served as a Captain with the United States Marines in Vietnam, and returned to law school but interrupted his studies a second time to become the first industrial and economic development officer for the Red Lake Reservation.

He had developed an impressive and ambitious five-year economic and industrial development program for the reservation that concentrated mostly on private enterprise or entrepreneurialism. The program, for instance, proposed a native owned liquor store, motel, restaurants, service station, fuel oil distributor, and larger developments of a golf course, water and power companies.

In a few months' time Lawrence had obtained federal funds to establish a bulk fuel oil dealership, an industrial park on the reservation, improvements in telephone services and communications, reforestation programs, construction of a utility building, and home construction. Moreover, he sponsored a native entrepreneur to obtain a small business loan from the federal government to build the very first coin-operated laundromat on the reservation. Previously natives traveled some thirty miles to use automatic washers.

Lawrence was determined to create an economic system independent of the federal government, and to support entrepreneurial services that would provide a basic exchange of money, goods, and services on the reservation. Some of these practical entrepreneurial developments, however, were sidetracked by politics. Roger Jourdain, the elected chairman of the reservation government, was more responsive to outside corporate operations that would exploit native labor and reduce the number of people unemployed. These distinct economic philosophies, native entrepreneurs and limited partnerships, and corporate exploitation of reservation labor were not easily reconciled in an authoritarian government.

Lawrence was educated and determined to change the reservation government, from authoritarian to egalitarian, and the conditions of dependency and poverty. He decided to enter politics and ran for chairman of the reservation. Roger Jourdain defeated Lawrence and was elected to his fourth term. The politics of favoritism continued and the enthusiasm for changes in the economic development were diverted to corporate and federal dominance. Jourdain was beholden to his good friends Hubert Humphrey, Walter Mondale, and the political favors of the Democratic Farmer Labor Party.

Jourdain had also defeated Leon Cook, another young native who was born on the Red Lake Reservation. Cook wanted to return to the reservation as a progressive chairman with promises of economic change. Cook, like Lawrence, wanted to move aggressively for independent economic development to reduce the dependency on the federal government. The people, however, apparently were not ready for change. There were no distinct party lines in the reservation election, or a clear division of political factions. The arguments and ideas were usually between the old and new ideas, and the young and the older candidates. Lawrence and Cook were the new and the young, and Jourdain was established as the old and familiar, and the most traditional.

Lawrence announced in a press release that he had decided to become a candidate for chairman "so that the Red Lake people will have a clear choice between the dictatorial and irresponsible leadership that presently exists, and the leadership that would frugally and conscientiously manage tribal affairs and be responsible

5

to the people's needs." And, "the people of the reservation deserve a better fate than we are now enduring." He clearly conveyed that natives must trust the energy and counsel of the younger educated natives as well as the older tribal members on the reservation. "The people are afraid of change," he said, and "they know most of the time what they can expect from Jourdain."

The *Minneapolis Tribune* described the election as a "contest between those who have stayed on the sprawling community held reservation and those who have left to seek their fortunes in white urban society."

Lawrence was always forthright about an ethos of egalitarian governance and advocated for the democratic doctrine of a balance of power on reservations, and these concepts of governance were the necessary revisions in native constitutions and reservation governments. He directed native education programs for several years and then edited the *Ojibwe Press*. Later he founded *The Native American Press*. He continued his dedication to reservation government reform and advocacy of native civil rights as an investigative journalist and editor.

I was a staff writer for the *Minneapolis Tribune* and prepared a series of articles on economic development on native reservations in Minnesota. Lawrence was clearly the most dedicated, educated, and articulate about economic development on the Red Lake Reservation. Our friendship started with those two or three days of conversations about money and entrepreneurs on the reservation. I wrote more fully about his economic programs for the Federal Reserve Bank in Minneapolis, and in *The Everlasting Sky: New Voices from the People Named the Chippewa*.

"I am proud of my heritage as a member of the Red Lake Band, and share the desire for the Indian people to preserve their languages, their cultures, their customs and their traditions. But in a world of accelerating change globally, to believe that the Indian people can isolate themselves on small parcels of land on this earth and defy the winds of change is a prescription for economic failure and cultural elimination," Lawrence wrote in an editorial entitled *Do Indian Reservations Equal Apartheid?* His critical comments were both personal and ironic, of course, that natives "have no access to federal courts for redress of wrongs done to them by tribal government. Because tribal government all too often controls the tribal courts, directly, or through the power of appropriations, there is no oversight and control of tribal councils. The result is rampant, continuous and ongoing problems with corruption, abuse, violence or discord. Most tribes do not give their members audited financial statements of tribal funds or casino funds, which may represent thousands of dollars per tribal member. It is literally impossible for tribal members to find out where all of the money is going."

I once asked my good friend if he had ever whistled in the dark. He smiled, puckered his lips, and said, "I never learned how to whistle for anything."

Gerald Vizenor   February 3, 2016

Chapter I. Nothing Has Changed.
"We served an important service shining light on the misdeeds
of those in power."[1]

Conditions on many American Indian reservations remain dismal for many natives[2] despite the best intentions and two decades of attention paid to the issues by William J. "Bill" Lawrence, owner/publisher of the Minnesota-based *Native American Press/Ojibwe News,* 1988-2009.

In an address at the American Indian Law and Policy Symposium in 1998, Lawrence explained, "... we started the newspaper ten years ago to try to fill... [the need] in Indian country for a free press. Our mission is to expose tribal corruption, defend civil rights, demand accountability, and promote a better way of life for tribal people."[3]

Proof that nothing has changed since then lies in the poor living conditions that natives continue to endure on many of America's reservations, i.e.: pervasive poverty, unemployment of 50-80 percent,[4] inadequate and overcrowded housing,[5] accompanied by illness, addiction, crime and violence.[6] If that isn't the worst, add the fact that some natives are consistently denied most of the elements of a democratic society: civil rights protections, separation of powers, due process, governmental accountability, fair elections and a free press.[7]

Lending support to the opening statement that conditions remain unchanged is this headline from the lead story of the first issue: "Red Lake Housing overpays tribal per diem [by $38,340]."[8] It introduces the lead story in the first issue of *The Native American Press/Ojibwe News (Press/ON),*[9] and details how tribal leaders rewarded their attendance at Minnesota Housing Finance Agency meetings with per diems of $250. The allowable charge was $35 per day. The tribal officials made restitution, using the tribe's general fund, thus preserving the overpayments to their personal accounts. Such stories were common throughout the 21-year life of the paper.

A review of editorials will show innumerable incidents of this kind.

Similar acts are lead stories in other publications. The April 14, 2010 edition of the *Florida Sun Sentinel* reported, "Former Seminole Councilman [David Cypress] Guilty of Tax Fraud" is one example. The article reported the paper had looked "into the spending while [he] was in charge of the ... reservation. They found he had spent more than $160 million in tribal funds between 1999-2007, more than all the other council members combined... [He] spent tens of millions of dollars on himself, family members and other tribal members as he represented [the reservation] on the Council... Tribal members tried to oust Cypress for misspending in 2005, but the Council dismissed the recall petition. Cypress continued to be elected to his Council seat."[10]

Other news stories discuss a situation involving a former two-time President of the National Congress of American Indians: [Tex] "Hall is no longer in the [chairman] race as of September 16, [2014] amid a scandal involving his 'unethical business deals' associated with the oil and gas industry. Yesterday members of the tribe protested outside of the tribal administration building .... the protestors demanded more transparent government, citing years of allegations of impropriety by the chairman."[11]

"Mr. Hall's self-assurance belied the fact that his grip on power was slipping. After six years of dizzyingly rapid oil development, anxiety about the environmental and social costs of the boom, as well as about tribal mismanagement and oil-related corruption, had burst to the surface ... Mr. Hall, a once-seemingly untouchable leader, was under investigation by his tribal council ...[12]

"A request by the Three Affiliated Tribes council for a federal investigation into former tribal chairman Tex Hall took another step forward Tuesday... The resolution calls for the U.S. Attorney to investigate Hall's financial relationship with a man facing federal murder-for-hire charges and the former chairman's potential abuse of tribal trust.

"... the group wants follow up on a year-old report... that spells out instances of Hall using his office to divert funds to his oil field partnership... "[13]

The fine detail may be different but the overall content, tribal authorities abusing power, is similar. (See Annotated Bibliography of Relevant, Current Articles for more recent, but similar articles.)

*   *   *   *   *

The publisher is gone; the last issue of the paper has been distributed. It would be easy to believe that Lawrence's free-press-in-Indian-country experiment has flopped.

Although no longer in publication, the paper has not disappeared. *The Native American Press/Ojibwe News* is still accessible through the Minnesota Digital Newspaper Hub, at the Minnesota State Historical Society. Digitization removes the publication from the archives, assuring that accounts of the concerns and needs of native peoples will not be forgotten.

Robert G. Hays in his book, *A Race at Bay, New York Times Editorials on the "Indian Problem," 1860-1900*, describes the editorial function: "... in a free society, where newspapers are readily available, the editorial pages serve as an irrefutable guide to the things that matter... and at the same time, those things that rightfully should be of concern may go unnoticed until the editorial writers call them to the public's attention... [the editorials] stand as a valid record of what people care about—or should care about."[14]

Lawrence's editorials, of another time and circumstance, function similarly. *Press/ON's* editorials offer insights and increase the available information about past and ongoing problems on reservations.

"In American Mythology, a government is a democratic government."[15]

Holding that their country is the godparent of democracy, Americans feel compelled to support those who aspire to obtain its benefits. Many countries have asked for and received support,[16] but America's savior complex is selective in its application. This

11

country goes abroad, subject to foreign policy considerations, to assist oppressed peoples elsewhere in their struggles for freedom.

But America is unfamiliar with the details of compelling problems here at home.

"There is a democracy deficit in Indian Country."[17]

Those caring Americans, who decry civil rights violations elsewhere, would probably be stunned to learn there are approximately one million U.S. citizens in this country, living without the "privileges enumerated by the Bill of Rights, which are enjoyed by all other citizens of this country."[18] These citizens live under political, social and economic conditions that are essentially the same as those described for any dictatorship anywhere.

Specifically, their governments are unresponsive to their demands for equitable distribution of community resources, financial accountability, fair elections, guarantees of due process. These individuals are natives, bona fide American citizens, who live on America's Indian reservations.

America is on record as being opposed to governments that do not offer civil rights guarantees and rule without the consent of the governed. If America is willing to support others worldwide in their quest for freedom and improved living conditions, she must be encouraged to oppose the situation that natives endure on reservations.

Because of media coverage, Americans know in depth what instigated the recent revolts in the Middle East, but they are lamentably uninformed as to the specifics of life for the average tribal member and as to Indian affairs in general. It is unfortunate that Americans do not know how closely the native situation on reservations here resembles the conditions that inspired revolutions elsewhere.

"The average American citizen is ignorant of Indian History"[19].

The following is a list of some of the facts that often surprise many non-natives.

12

-The majority of Native Americans do not live on reservations.[20]
-There are more non-Indians living on reservations than there are natives.[21]
-There is much disagreement as to the validity of the concept of tribal sovereignty. There are many who believe, as did Bill Lawrence, that it is the primary means by which tribal officials are empowered to deny civil rights to their members.[22]
-A considerable number of tribal governments do not have constitutions that limit the powers of officials, provide for an independent judiciary, or checks and balances on governmental authority; hence, tribal officials have enormous power.[23] Without the Constitutional protections enjoyed by other U.S. citizens, reservation natives are subject to the whims of their tribal officials.
-Native American rights to information concerning their own governments are often curtailed. Tribal newspapers are financially dependent on tribal governments. "This means tribal ... editors tend to stay away from news that calls [activities of] tribal leaders into question."[24] Tribal members do not have access to open meetings, and financial records. Without information, it is impossible to hold officials accountable.
-Although reservations are infamous for inescapable poverty and high unemployment rates among members, tribal leaders have access to billions of dollars.[25]
-As the rule of law is the foundation for successful economic development, the usual remedies, such as outside investments and non-tribal jobs, are ineffective and often unavailable on reservations.[26]
-The Indian Civil Rights Act of 1968 (ICRA) does not protect natives from their tribal governments. The Supreme Court ruled that tribal members must seek redress for wrongs from tribal courts.[27]
-Indian casinos are a mixed blessing. Increased crime and infrastructure costs associated with the presence of a casino, plus the rise in number and degree of social problems (domestic violence, addiction, job loss, theft to cover gambling debts, etc.) can create a reverse cost-to-benefit ratio.[28] Additionally, casino revenues allow

unaccountable tribal officials, many of whom hold office by illegal means, to misappropriate the cash and convert it to personal use. Casino monies are used as well to purchase influence with outside officials.[29] This practice assures the status quo doesn't change; Native American casino-related contributions purchase loyalty from ranking outside officials who rarely meet with ordinary tribal members. They get their information regarding reservation affairs exclusively from tribal leaders.

-Native Americans experience disproportionate rates of illness, disease, disability, poverty and unemployment. Such conditions contribute to dysfunctional communities and limit a people's ability to resist.[30]

The above examples are illustrative of that which is most obvious. A decidedly more serious gap in information is the fact that Americans frequently know nothing about federal Indian policy and its contribution to the status quo. There is also little knowledge of native values and traditions; nor does the general public know the complete truth of what was imposed on indigenous peoples and how the long-term effects have manifested in native communities. That is something Americans should not be allowed to escape knowing.[31]

The 24/7 news has contributed to the problem, particularly the broadcast sector, creating "crisis" in order to affect ratings. Rather than fulfilling the role of objectively informing the audience, much of the media have become alarmist gossip-mongers. Americans have therefore become increasingly inured to what they experience as "news," and discouraged about a possibility for making positive change.

Additionally, mainstream media is disinclined to cover issues that involve natives, hence, their problems are not made public. Tim Giago, well-known native journalist, reports "…many [off-reservation] newspapers have simply ignored the people of the Indian reservations."[32]

Other journalists have expressed the notion that, "Mainstream newspapers, like history books, [and] … mainstream

14

outlets should ... strive for better news coverage of indigenous issues."[33]

Without substantive mainstream coverage, ignorance of native life is widespread; hence, there is no outside scrutiny of tribal affairs on reservations.

Lastly, and probably because the total Native American population is small, the number of native journalists is small; "one-half of one percent of all newsroom employees are native."[34] The 2009 *Diversity Survey of the American Society of Newspaper Editors*, states that there are "only 293 Native Americans among the more than 47,000 employees in America's newsrooms."[35] The 2012 survey: Employees by Minority Group indicates that 132 Native Americans are included (.33) in the total numbers.

There is an irony that almost imperceptibly governs discourse on the subject. That is the vaguely distressing realization that America, although viewing herself as a champion of human and civil rights, has a history of being a villain when it comes to the subject of Native Americans. Our nation cannot be proud of words like dispossession, subjugation, and extermination in connection with securing the land for use by the immigrants who eventually peopled this continent.[36]

Hays, in his collection of editorials dealing with the "Indian Problem," states "... the *Times* expressed grave concern about calls for a war of extermination [against the natives]."[37]

From the early 19th century on, "... instead of spreading democracy, we [America] exported the ideology of white supremacy... Although European nations professed to be shocked by our actions on the western frontier, before long they were emulating us. Britain exterminated the Tasmanian aborigines; Germany pursued total war against the Herrero of Namibia. *Most western nations have to face this fact [emphasis added]*."[38] The treatment of indigenous peoples of Canada and Australia mimic the U.S. story as well.

Americans, in general, may intuit that problems in Indian country are so deeply entrenched, and have existed for such a very long time, that they defy solution. These complexities lead to a sense of powerlessness and apathy, tinged perhaps with feelings of latent shame that manifest in neglect and "looking the other way." The obstacles to reform are many and have perennially been formidable.[39]

Compounding this problem is the fact that outside officials rarely speak directly to tribal members, relying instead on information provided by tribal leaders. Lawrence stressed that true solutions must begin with substantive information collection and meetings between outside policy-makers and the people.

When tribal officers control all revenues, employment, housing, and access to services, can there be any doubt that the level of authority is absolute? On too many reservations elected officials control all aspects of tribal life, including tribal justice, law enforcement, election outcomes, etc. Those in power have much to give and even more to withhold. Many tribal members are held hostage politically and economically by their leaders.

Tribal leaders "bear responsibility for having created an atmosphere of fear by refusing to face the hard choice of free speech and hiding behind the smokescreen of Sovereignty, tradition and cultural values. Sovereignty is only as good as those who reign, and too often it has twisted the meaning ... into a heavy-handed city boss style of government well hidden in its isolation from public scrutiny."[40]

Despite Lawrence's success at exposing graft, mismanagement, dishonesty, violations of civil rights, and other wrongs, little has changed.[41] Many Native citizens remain afraid to speak out against tribal authorities who control all the benefits.

But change is still a possibility, and the rise and efficacy of the Internet contributes to the possibility of a solution.

The desire for democratic processes is on the rise in the world as evidenced by political demonstrations against tyrannical governments.

The collective presence of the Middle Eastern protestors in the streets, defying authority, calling for reform, and the perceived validity of their cause, has caught the world's attention and sympathy.

Americans expect their citizens to be self-sufficient and respect those who defend themselves against wrong. It's not uncommon to hear people assert that America's natives are to be blame for their circumstances.

Unfortunately, Native Americans could not join together in a powerful, unified protest to gain national attention for several reasons: The total reservation population is relatively small. Native populations are "too minute to register on established government tracking systems."[42] The 2010 U.S. Census figure for the total Native American population is 2.9 million.[43] According to past Census figures, approximately 40 percent of the total number live on reservations, that is about one million natives.[44] That number does not generate a powerful concern in a country with a total population of more than 300 million.

Individual tribes are separated geographically and many are located in remote parts of the country. Although they share many of the same conditions and problems, each of the more than 500 federally recognized tribes has its own culture, customs, beliefs and traditions. Additionally, there is usually not a single tribal leader to rally under, or an individual oppressive leader as a focus to rally against.

If these circumstances were not sufficient to inhibit a collective demonstration, consider the fact that many reservation natives, after years of neglect, dependency and commodities-based diets, are impaired with ill health. Diabetes, heart disease, addiction, depression are all conditions that natives endure disproportionately, and limit ability to participate fully in life.[45]

Many Americans realize reservation life has been deplorable for generations. There is a conception, however, that the problems are so complicated and entrenched that remedies are impossible.

Reform is increasingly possible, however, and probably inevitable. It appears the information revolution will contribute to solutions. Within a relatively few years, electronic media has become an antidote to secrecy and oppression. In regard to the 2011 Arab uprisings, the media declared the Internet saved the revolution.

Despite attempts by their governments to shut them down, the Arabs kept themselves in the center of the lens by sustained action. They were aided by cell phones, cameras, instantaneous Internet communications and access to social media. Pictures and messages kept the protestors informed about their chances of success and gave the outside world the truth about what was happening. This pattern has been successful and will no doubt continue.

In 2010, a *New York Times* commentator announced, "It is increasingly difficult to hide public protest, an act of repression or a violation of human rights. Mobile phones and Internet have given the citizens a critical means of expression … For oppressed peoples of the world, the Internet promises power beyond their wildest hopes."[46]

"Indians are organized in cyberspace, with thousands of websites."[47]

Inadequacies in access were remedied by a $1.5 billion award from the Obama administration to build infrastructure and broadband capability on reservations.[48] The pledge of continued support was repeated in the President's Proclamation for Native American Heritage Week, 2014.[49]

Electronic media could be the means by which natives on reservations can bypass their censors and, despite geographic isolation, communicate with each other and with the outside. It will be possible to expose the facts of reservation life and tribal governance without fear of reprisal. The stories will no doubt attract attention and raise concerns in the outside world.

As the Internet and social networks played a part in the success of the Arab Spring revolt, the same elements are potentially available to natives for use in finding solutions for their problems.

"... if you want to free a society, just give them Internet access."[50]

Social media can remove the barriers of isolation and geography. It is effective in creating awareness of what is happening, good or bad, on every reservation. The technology allows for the exchange of ideas and information from diverse sources without fear of retaliation. It can be used to compel the attention of outside policy-makers, and the general American public as to the plight of natives on many reservations.

Once the protestors have created an audience and made their situation known, reform-minded people, working in the American way, can join in. With increased numbers comes strength to resist and to demand change. This capability adds a new dimension and potentiality to tribal life and politics. The secrecy and ignorance, which allowed the situation to remain unchanged for so long, will have been overcome. Information motivates and sustains reform.

An obstacle, however, remains. This new source of abundant, interactive information, once implemented, will have no meaning for Americans who have little orientation regarding native affairs. Unlike the Arab and other Middle Eastern revolutions, native protests won't have immediate media commentary providing the background of the troubles, explaining the circumstances, and telling of the misery of life on some reservations as a component.

Press/ON's editorials, original source material, provide information heretofore not available to the American public. They also provide context and insight, and will substantiate the information that emerges from electronic media. The weight of the 21-year run of editorials creates credibility and impact.

Robert G. Hays in *A Race at Bay,* The *New York Times Editorials on "The Indian Problem,"* states, "... there was never a point ... in which the *Times* failed to serve as an important source of information and opinion for a significant segment of the public and a forum for the discussion of important questions... Treatment of the Native Americans, in the eyes of the *Times* became a matter of national honor."[51]

Lawrence's editorials, his purpose and his attitude, are surprisingly similar to those of the *Times* that were written during the time frame 1860-1900.

Nothing has changed – but could.

Hays reports in the preface to *A Race at Bay,* "... as I sat in a hearing conducted by the Senate Committee on Indian Affairs... I was hearing, restated in a ... committee room in the National Capitol ... virtually the same elements I had just read in a *Times* editorial published in 1891!

"If I have learned anything... it is the simple fact that many of the problems faced by Native Americans today already were widely recognized in the 1800s. We seem to continue through repeated cycles in which issues remain the same and problems rarely are fully resolved."[52]

The present generation of Americans has not had reason to be made aware of the "Indian Problem." That does not mean there is no problem.

Press/ON was, at the least, a veritable encyclopedia of information about native life and reservation politics. An abundance of information, it documented wrong-doing that almost always went (and still remains) unpunished. It was a lengthy record of abuses of power at many levels and of malevolent neglect by Congress of the needs of approximately a million people whose pleas for justice have not yet been heeded.

1. William J. "Bill" Lawrence, "A Warrior's Creed: Today is a good day to die." *The Native American Press/Ojibwe News,* September 1, 2009. Final editorial, 4.

2. See Annotated Bibliography of Relevant Articles from Current Publications, dated 2012-2018, that indicate conditions on reservations remain dismal.

3. Bill Lawrence, "Tribal Sovereign Immunity is the Single Biggest Factor Contributing to Corruption on American Indian Reservations," Presentation, American Indian Law and Policy Symposium (Norman: University of Oklahoma, March 21, 1998).

4. *Broken Promises*: Evaluating the Native American Health Care System," United States Commission on Civil Rights, (Washington, D.C., July 2, 2004). 37.

5. Ibid. 38.

6. Ibid. 20. See also National Relief Charities, Native American Reservation Facts, www.nrcprograms.org.

7. Joseph P. Kalt, "The Role of Constitutions in Native Nation Building. For many, judicial function of dispute resolution and law enforcement remain constitutionally under the control of the tribal council." In Miriam Jorgenson, ed., *Rebuilding Native Nations: Strategies for Governance and Development* (Tucson: University of Arizona Press, 2007), 91.

Ibid. 96, "Who or what prevents those who have the power of [tribal] government from turning that power to the service of their own interests at the expense of the community as a whole."

8. Raymond Beaulieu, "Housing Overpays Tribal Per Diem," *The Ojibwe News,* May 24, 1988, 1.

9. *Press/ON* is an abbreviation of the paper's full title: *The Native American Press/Ojibwe News*. It was initially dedicated solely to issues of concern to the Ojibwe people of northern Minnesota as *The Ojibwe News.* Later, Lawrence extended coverage and distribution to the other native populations of Minnesota as *The Native American*

Press. The two names were eventually combined. Various abbreviations were used over the life of the paper: the *News, The Press* and *NAPON.*

10. "David Cypress pleads guilty to falsifying taxes," ICTMN staff, *Indian Country Today,* April 14, 2012. For other examples see Annotated Bibliography of Relevant Articles in Current Publications, attached.

11. "Tex Hall no longer in chairman race amid scandal." *Shale News, BPS.* October 13, 2014.

12. Deborah Sontag and Brent McDonald, "In North Dakota, a Tale of Oil, Corruption and Death." The *New York Times,* December 28, 2014.

13. Lauren Donovan, "Council members call for investigation of former tribal chairman." *Bismarck Tribune,* August 19, 2015.

14. Robert G. Hays, *A Race at Bay, New York Times Editorials on "The Indian Problem," 1860-1900* (Carbondale and Edwardsville: Southern Illinois University Press, 1997), xxiv.

15. Steve Russell, *Sequoyah Rising. Problems in Post-Colonial Tribal Governments,* (Durham, SC: Carolina Academic Press, 2010), 80.

16. Notably, Egypt during the 2011 uprising.

17. Steve Russell, *Sequoyah.* 51.

18. Bill Lawrence, "Bringing the Bill of Rights to Indian Country." *The Native American Press/Ojibwe News,* May 5, 1998, 4.

19. Steve Russell, *Sequoyah.* 51.

20. "Twenty-two percent of American Indians . . . live on reservations. . . Sixty percent live in metropolitan areas. . ." The Office of Minority Health, U.S. Health and Human Services. American Indian/Alaska Native Profile. Other sources indicate the figure is forty percent to sixty percent on reservation. http://www.infoplease.com. Last modified December 12, 2014.

21. Facts about American Indians Today ". . . a high percentage of the land [on Indian reservations] is owned and occupied by non-Indians." www.infoplease.com. Accessed July 4, 2012.

"[The] Allotment [Act] caused 90 million acres of Indian land to be removed from Indian ownership and control. . . Large percentages of reservation land were now held by non-Indians." Indian Land Tenure Foundation. *www.iltf.org/resources/land-tenure-history/allotment*. Accessed July 4, 2012.

22. Judge R. A. "Jim" Randall, "[Tribal] Sovereignty is a phrase we have mouthed for over 200 years, but this country [America] has never, at any time, treated Indian tribes with any of the courtesy or respect accorded a true sovereign state or nation, such as Canada, Mexico, Great Britain, etc. None of the normal attributes of a true sovereign nation . . . has ever been gifted to, or attributed to, Indian Tribes.

"Real sovereignty includes, without limits, the right to seal one's own borders, declare war, make peace, coin one's own currency. . ." State of Minnesota Court of Appeals, Dissent-*Cohen v. Little. Six, Inc., d/b/a Mystic Lake Casino*. No.C6-95-928 (MN Ct. App. December 18, 1995).

Steve Russell, *Sequoyah*, "Everyone hates sovereign immunity of tribal governments even more because it is misunderstood . . . and because tribes have handled it less well than states." 52.

Numerous other articles in publications dealing with native issues actively support the validity of the concept.

23. Kalt, *Rebuilding Native Nations, "*. . . most tribal governments . . . are organizationally weak, with few separations of powers, few checks and balances, and unwieldy administrative structures," 65.

24. Jodi Rave, "Challenges Natives and Non-Native Journalists Confront." *Nieman Report* (Fall 2005), 59.

25. Gale Courey Toesing. "Gaming appears to be recession-proof." Indian casino income in billions: 2007–$26.1, 2008-$26.7, 2009-$26.5. Additionally, several billion in non-gaming revenue accrues annually. In 2009 it amounted to an additional $3.2 billion. *Indian Country Today,* April 4, 2011.

Vincent Shilling. "President Obama's Fiscal Year 2015 budget request of $11.9 billion translates into an additional $33.6 million for Indian initiatives. . ." "Modest proposals," *Indian Country Today,* March 16, 14.

National Indian Gaming Commission, Gaming Revenue Reports. Growth in Indian Gaming 2013, $28 billion.

"Severe Health, Education and Economic Troubles Still Bedevil the Reservations, Despite the Casino Riches of a Minority." The *New York Times,* Opinion, "The Long Trail to Apology." June 28, 2004.

26. Russell, "Economic development requires stable and reasonable democratic institutions," 70.

Ibid. "It is easy to understand that governmental corruption drives away capital investment," 84.

Kalt, *Rebuilding Native Nations,* "The evidence is overwhelming that a society's system of government is the make-or-break key to economic wellbeing . . ." 80.

William J. Lawrence "There is no denying that the lack of civil rights, the lack of legitimate courts, and the lack of governmental accountability is the single biggest reason there is so little economic activity on America's reservations." Testimony before the Senate Indian Affairs Committee," Field hearing, Seattle, Washington, April 7, 1998.

27. "The outcome was that the decision strengthened tribal self-determination, but an Indian with a complaint against a tribal government had little opportunity for relief. Few tribal court decisions were subsequently appealed." The Indian Civil Rights Act. Oxford Companion to the U.S. Supreme Court: *Santa Clara Pueblo v. Martinez.* Accessed April 21, 2012. Available at http://www.answers.com/topic/santaclarapueblovmartinez.

William B. Allen, Commissioner. Statement: "The government of the United States . . . has failed to provide for Indians living on reservations guarantees of those fundamental rights it is obligated to secure for all United States citizens under the laws. . . Enforcement of ICRA by tribal governments . . . has been uneven . . . often lacking altogether. Among the explanations for . . . the failures are a number of individual and systemic factors. Claims of sovereign immunity. Woeful lack of funding of tribal courts. The [failure] to use statutory means to enforce the ICRA. General allegations of illegal searches and seizures. Widespread denial of the right to counsel. Ex parte hearings. Restrictions of right to a jury trial. Violations of freedom of the press. Violations of due process and equal protections of the law." "The Indian Civil Rights Act," United States Commission on Civil Rights. June 1991. . ."

28. Earl L. Grinols. "Gambling fails a cost-benefit test: Conservatively estimated, costs to benefits exceed $3:$1 . . . 64

percent [of costs] are publicly borne and 39 percent are tax-supported public costs."
"Gambling Economics: Summary Facts." Independent research, not funded by gambling or anti-gambling organizations. Available at

http://www.texaspolicy.com, Accessed July 5, 2012.

Fergus M. Bordewich, "The Least Transparent Industry in America.
. . a murky world of tribal 'gaming,' which in less than 20 years has
exploded from a handful of basement bingo operations to a $19
billion industry [in 2009, casino revenue totaled $29.7 billion]."
Bordewich, citing Harvard economists Joseph Kalt and Jonathan
Taylor's 2005 study, acknowledges that some good has come to
tribes from the gaming phenomenon. He points out that in spite of
"the gains made in recent years, many Native Americans still live in
appalling poverty." He asserts "Tribal gambling may be the least
transparent industry in the United States. Constitutional protections
reach only feebly onto Indian land, where tribal governments enjoy
a degree of secrecy that would never be tolerated in any other
American community. Gigantic sums disappear from public view as
soon as they leave tribal gaming tables. This money is shielded from
outside regulation by the principal of Tribal Sovereignty. . ."
The *Wall Street Journal*. January 5, 2006.

See also: Kerri Toloczko, "As Native American Casinos Proliferate,
The Social Costs of the Gambling Boom Are Ignored," *Forbes*
Magazine, September 25, 2013.

ABC News. "Casinos Not Paying Off for Indians." August 31, no
date. abcnews.go.com/US/, accessed September 29, 2016

29. ABC News, Ibid. ". . . tribes have powerful friends. Nationally,
between 1990 and 2004, tribal political contributions to federal
candidates alone have ballooned from less than $2000 to more than
$7 million." Open Secrets.

Center for Responsive Government. Indian PAC contributions to
political campaigns in 2010 amounted to $9.08 million. [2017
update: National Indian Gaming Commission reports almost $30
billion for 2015.] The breakdown of contributions is 71 percent to

Democrats and 29 percent to Republicans. The total native on-reservation population is approximately one million people. In the editor's view, this number is disproportionally large given that it comes from the approximately 225 tribes that operate gaming casinos and represents approximately half the native population. http://www.opensecrets.org/industries/totals. Accessed June 6, 2012.

30. "Today, Native Americans continue to experience significant rates of disease, mental health disorders, cardiovascular disease, pneumonia, influenza, and injuries. Specifically, Native Americans are 775 percent more likely to die from alcoholism, 650 percent more likely to die from tuberculosis, 420 percent more likely to die from diabetes, 280 percent more likely to die from accidents, and 52 percent more likely to die from pneumonia or influenza than the rest of the United Sates, including white and minority populations." *Broken Promises*, 26. United States Commission on Civil Rights. Accessed June 4, 2012.

31. Ibid. "When you dispossess people of their land, their labor, their culture, their language, their traditions and their religion, you set into motion powerful forces that impact in a very negative and adverse way. This dispossession has led to a significant damage in health, in educational levels, and in social wellbeing."

32. Tim Giago, "Freedom of the Press in Indian Country." *Nieman Reports.* (Fall 2005), 59:3 13.

33. Rave. "Challenges . . ." 7.

34. Ibid. 8.

35. Sharon M. Murphy. (2010) "Journalism in Indian Country: Story Telling That Makes Sense." Howard Journal of Communications 21:4 (2010): 332.

36. Hayes. A January 1860 New York Times editorial "noted that

what the white settlers [of California] really wanted was 'the Indians exterminated.'"

See also: Hugh Reilly, "The *St. Cloud Democrat* editorials promoted genocide and encouraged paying bounties for scalps." *Bound to have Blood: Frontier Newspapers and the Plains Indian Wars.* Lincoln: University of Nebraska Press, 2011. 130.

37. Hays, 6.

38. James W. Loewes, *Lies My Teacher Told Me.* (New York: The New Press, 1995). 118. Also, Vincent Shilling. "Native History We Are Never Taught." *Indian Country Today.* January 17, 2018.

39. "The tendency of American Society to respond foremost to visible problems results in Native Americans being overlooked and . . . forgotten." United States Commission on Civil Rights, *A Quiet Crisis,* Washington, D.C. July 2003). 8.

40. Louise Mengelkoch. "Sovereignty and secrecy." *The Native American Press/Ojibwe News,* March 27, 2005, 1.

41. See: Annotated Bibliography of Relevant Articles in Current Publications 2012-2018, establishing that the conditions Lawrence observed and reported on are still prevalent.

42. *A Quiet Crisis.* United States Commission on Civil Rights, 8.

43. American Indian/Alaska Native Population. U.S. Census 2010,

44. *A Quiet Crisis.* United States Commission on Civil Rights, 8.

45. Ibid. "Poor health inhibits the economic, educational, and social development of Native Americans. . ." 8.

46. Bernard Boucher, "The Battle for the Internet," The *New York Times,* May 13, 2010.

47. Catherine C. Robbins. *All Indians Do Not Live in Teepees (or Casinos),* (Lincoln: University of Nebraska Press, 2010), page 224.

48. "Achieving a Better Future for Tribal Nations: Promoting Sustainable Economic Development in Indian Country," United States White House, White House Tribal Nations Conference Report December 2011, 2.

49. Barack Obama, "A Proclamation. National Native American Heritage Month, 2014, *Indian Country Today,* November 2, 2014.

50. Wael Ghonin. Interviewed by Ivan Watson on CNN. February 9, 2011. Reported on the Lede. *newyorktimes.com.*

51. Hays, 16, 17.

52. Hays, xx.

Chapter II. The Publisher and *Press/ON.*[1]
"...newspapers are expected to stand for something."[2]

In 1996, after several years of investigation, indictments and trials, three tribal officials of a Minnesota band of Ojibwe were convicted and sentenced to federal prison. The chair of a second band of Chippewa and two tribal council members were also indicted and served time in federal prison. Felony charges against these six elected officials, collectively, included: theft of tribal and federal funds, bid rigging, mail fraud, conspiracy and election violation of the Indian Civil Rights Act. These convictions are believed to be the first ever of Indian white-collar crimes under the Indian Civil Rights Act (ICRA).[3]

"A common denominator in the downfall of these once influential Minnesotans? A soft-spoken man named Bill Lawrence, the most tenacious newspaper publisher in the state. [He] publishes *The Native American Press...* [The] little paper, probably unknown by most non-Indians in Minnesota, was uncovering dirt on the likes of [the convicted officials] well before federal authorities began digging. In fact, it probably was headlines in *The Native American Press* that encouraged them to dig."[4&5]

Lawrence, and a group of activists from the Red Lake Reservation, started the paper in 1988 in order to combat an autocratic tribal chairman. Publication continued through September 1, 2009. Employed at Honeywell Inc., Minneapolis at the paper's onset, Lawrence's early role was as financial backer. He personally staked the $10,000 startup. Over the next few years he assumed primary responsibility for the paper's operation, content and philosophy.

His investigations, his relentless efforts to expose wrongdoing and his acute awareness of the problems facing reservation tribal residents, convinced him that unless something changed for the better, and soon, American Indian reservations would simply implode. Given the 19th century attitude of America's

31

immigrant societies that the "only good Indian was a dead Indian," the synchronicity is disquieting.

Lawrence believed this danger was coetaneously caused by flawed federal Indian policy as well as the propensity of tribal leaders to blatantly indulge in the "politics of spoils," the results of which cause great distress to on-reservation tribal members.[6] These topics were discussed frequently throughout the life of the newspaper. In an editorial dated June 6, 2003, Lawrence said, "The federal government ... left the Indian people saddled with unaccountable tribal governments... Most tribes do not give their members audited financial statements of tribal funds or casino revenues, which may represent thousands of dollars per tribal member. It is literally impossible for tribal members to find out where all the money is going."[7] Lawrence asserted that "one of the biggest needs in Indian Country is a free press."[8]

He said the *Ojibwe News* was "born out of the frustrations of the Native American community in dealing with the secrecy, rights abuses and unaccountability of tribal government."[9]

In an attempt to curtail his activities, tribal opposition sent a letter to his advertisers. In it the newspaper was denounced as "very offensive to most Indian people as it constantly degrades our people and attempts to destroy elected tribal government... [It] promotes racism, hatred and fuels the fires of bigotry..."

The letter ended with a veiled threat: "We hope you might reconsider advertising with this form of YELLOW JOURNALISM ... Dollars spent with this type of negative publication will not bring more money to your business."[10]

Lawrence's firm response, "We believe elected officials have a duty to act honestly and provide full disclosure... We believe that our people deserve better government than they are getting... And we want to be the ones who will bring them the good news when it starts to happen."[11]

Of his involvement in tribal politics, U.S. Attorney Thomas Hettelfinger said, "A true journalist. He was a friend to tribal government when he thought tribal government was working well. He was not a friend when he didn't think it was working well."[12]

The publisher felt it was his job to make public the abuses of tribal power. He fully believed that, upon learning of the deplorable conditions natives endure on reservations, there would be indignant outcry from right-minded individuals demanding positive change.

As an enrolled member of the Red Lake Band of Chippewa, knowledgeable of their traditions, values and sorrows, Lawrence attracted insider knowledge from all the Minnesota bands. Members "of the community frequently [brought in] evidence of corruption, including documents, photos from casino surveillance cameras, personal stories, false billing statements, and on and on."[13] They kept *Press/ON* well supplied with source material that supported sensational stories.

The numerous informants acted in great secrecy, "because if they are caught, it is all-over. They could lose not only their jobs, but it could be their housing, their kids' education... It's a whole different society."[14]

Lawrence hated "to see people abused... For those who keep their mouths shut about tribal leaders enriching themselves, there are jobs, health care, and other benefits. Those who speak out against corruption will be labeled dissenters and lose jobs and benefits."[15]

Ojibwe members saw Lawrence as a hero and the paper as their outlet for grievances. He validated their concerns by publishing their stories and protected his sources. They also counted on him for assistance with family, employment or legal matters because he was often able to solve their problems.

They believed, as he did, that exposure of tribal governmental misdeeds would improve their condition. They loved that Lawrence dared to tell about the unlawful acts of tribal officials. In addition to demanding comprehensive reform of tribal governments, open meetings and disclosure of financial information, *Press/ON* exposed corruption and mismanagement in tribal operations, election fraud, and civil rights violations.

Lawrence stated, "We report the news uncensored ... just as we receive it. As a result we have been accepted as the voice of the Anishinabe (Ojibwe) people."[16]

Tribal officials did not share their members' views about Lawrence and the newspaper. As a *Star Tribune* reporter noted, "The Indian establishment, which includes large numbers of white bureaucrats, lawyers and business people who are profiting from the status quo in Indian affairs, loathe Lawrence."[17]

Press/ON's criticism of their deeds was the first time their actions were publically laid out for all to see and, to throw the heat elsewhere, they dubbed him "anti-Indian."

In reply to the accusations, he wrote: "*The Native American Press* is not an anti-Indian paper. It's an *anti-corruption newspaper*. And if some of those engaged in criminal activities for self-gain at the expense of the people happen to be Indian, we will write about them."[18]

Tribal leaders smeared his reputation, saying he spewed half-truths and falsehoods. They declared him an enemy of the reservation, claiming "The views of the paper are very damaging to our people."[19] They denigrated the publisher and the paper as they stuffed hefty campaign contributions into the pockets of political candidates.[20]

This maneuver not only cast doubt on Lawrence's credibility; it bought influence and loyalty with non-native officials to maintain the status quo and avoid outside scrutiny of tribal affairs.

Susan Barberi, in a *Minnesota Magazine* interview reported: "Needless to say, he [got] no advertising from casinos." To which Lawrence quipped, "At least we can't be bought."[21]

In retaliation for his exposés, tribal officials banned the sale of the paper in tribal stores and seized and destroyed it from other sales venues. They blacklisted him with local businesses and "harassed and intimidated advertisers and retail outlets."[22]

The headline for the second issue of the paper, May 24, 1988, announced: "*Ojibwe News* pulled from Tribal Store shelves.*"*

Those who suffered from his reportage disliked him. On the other hand, despite all attempts by tribal officials to limit circulation, tribal members faithfully supported the paper and sought it out each week throughout the years.

By contrast to *Press/ON's* content the local newspapers, perhaps influenced by their ad revenues, favored their bottom lines over coverage of issues important to native peoples. The many, full-page, tribal casino ads were at stake.

Louise Mengelkoch, former Chair of the Mass Communications Department at Bemidji State University declared: "Bill Lawrence is a hero, but where is the mainstream media? They should be sending reporters to cover reservation politics...

"Tom Robertson, news director for KCRB ... Minnesota Public Radio ... thinks Indian politics needs to be taken more seriously by the mainstream media... He thinks it is easy to dismiss Indian politics because it is so 'tumultuous' and often 'mind-blowing.' However, he adds, the structure of their governments allows it to continue, and mainstream media either don't cover it at all or dismiss it as 'just Indian politics,' instead of realizing ordinary reservation residents have no voice."[23]

The reality of the paper's financial potential was obvious from the first year's experience. In a feature article in *City Pages*, Lawrence acknowledged that the sustainability of the paper was "something of a minor miracle ... 'It's been a struggle. Up and down,' he said with a shrug."[24]

Lawrence was proud of the fact that he "never asked for or received funding from any form of government, foundation or other entity. We are self-supporting, thoroughly independent."[25] He continued, "This publication is probably the only independent, privately-owned Native American newspaper in North America and could not have been in existence ... without the unequivocal support of the people."[26]

In an article published in the *Columbia Journalism Review,* Professor Mengelkoch commented: "Truly independent reservation media are almost nonexistent, except for a few persistent souls like Bill Lawrence, owner of *The Native American Press/Ojibwe News.* "... He has been waging a free-speech battle with all eleven tribes in Minnesota for seventeen years..."[27]

Most native-owned newspapers are controlled by tribal leaders who also control access to jobs, healthcare, housing, and other benefits. Not surprisingly, they do not allow for criticism of governmental affairs. "The watchdog function is critical to good government, whether the institution is Congress, a state legislature, a city government, a federal agency or a tribal council. But very few reservations have a press that fills that role."[28]

Like other free press operators, Lawrence's physical wellbeing was frequently threatened. In view of the level of violence that exists and is tolerated on reservations, there can be no doubt that he was always at risk of harm. Shots pierced the newspaper office windows; he was followed while entering or leaving the reservations; occupied cars parked outside his home at night. Yet Lawrence never sidestepped a confrontation whether in print or in person.

"Lawrence looking good..."

From playing Legion ball at an early age to running three Twin Cities Marathons after turning 60, Lawrence was a superior athlete.[29] He is honored with membership in both the Bemidji High School and the Bemidji State University Athletic Halls of Fame. In high school he lettered in football, baseball and basketball. Consistently named as an all-tournament player, he led several

36

championship teams in multiple tournaments.[30] Lawrence won a scholarship to the University of Minnesota in football and baseball.[31]

The Detroit Tigers farm team drew him away from his university studies for a year. He was a starting pitcher on the 1958 Valdosta Tigers championship team.[32]

After his professional baseball tour, he returned to college and obtained a B.S. degree with a double major in business accounting and finance from Bemidji State University.

Upon graduating, he enlisted in the Marine Corps Officers Training Program. Lieutenant Lawrence saw combat as a platoon leader in Viet Nam. After 16 years of service in the Marine Corp Reserves, he retired with the rank of Captain.

Lawrence credits his athletic training with molding his character. The years of team play, plus the observation skills he learned on the pitching mound, waiting for the right moment to throw a touchdown pass, or for a shot on the basketball court, taught him mindfulness, developed calm and patience under pressure. The years of practice and discipline paid off. When under attack he was thoughtful and applied intellectual analysis to his response instead of knee-jerk rancor.

Upon completion of active duty, he earned his juris doctorate from the University of North Dakota. While in law school he was also employed as the Economic Development Officer for the Red Lake Band in Northern Minnesota.

Noted author and fellow Ojibwe, Gerald Vizenor describes Bill in his first job at Red Lake: "Lawrence developed an impressive and ambitious five-year economic and industrial development plan for the reservation, ranging from private enterprise to a tribally-owned liquor store, a golf course, airport, motel, bulk oil distributorship, and water and power companies..."[33]

"The economic philosophy behind his five-year plan was to establish *oshki anishinabe* [Ojibwe] owned services on the reservation, creating an economic system independent of the federal government.... He is motivated to reduce the dependency the people have on ... federal funds, and to eliminate the control of jobs by tribal officials."[34]

Lawrence "is committed to improving the quality of life and the government on the reservation. He is a reformer and idealist who will not easily tire of demanding responsibility and fairness in government and law enforcement on the reservation."[35]

As a qualifier for his opinions, Lawrence often referred to his more than 40 years of involvement in native issues. Prior to his 21 years as owner/publisher of *The Native American Press/Ojibwe News,* he served as Director of Adult Indian Education for the State of Minnesota; as Bureau of Indian Affairs Superintendent for the Colorado River Indian Tribes and, in addition to having held the Economic Development officer position with the Red Lake Band of Minnesota, he was Business Manager for the Mojave Tribe in California. When he started the paper in 1988 he was a senior contract negotiator for Honeywell, Inc., in Minneapolis, a position he held for eight years.

Because of his quietude, the level of his intellectual achievement sometimes escaped his casual acquaintances. He was a lifelong learner, a fervent reader of biographies, histories and court proceedings. A friend described the scope of his knowledge as encyclopedic.

A self-described newshound,[36] Lawrence spent innumerable hours every week watching newscasts and reading newspapers. He sought out information on all subjects dealing with Native Americans everywhere as preparation for his articles and editorials.

He cultivated a wide circle of contacts that furnished him with stories and leads about the latest episodes of tribal government mischief and misdeeds.

Although discredited with many politicians whose favor had been purchased by tribal leaders, he worked closely with law enforcement and justice officials. United States Attorney David

Lillehaug, who successfully indicted and prosecuted tribal officials from two northern Minnesota reservations, said: "Bill Lawrence and *The Native American Press* performed a valuable service in identifying corruption in Indian Country... Some of his stories provided leads for federal law enforcement... When he was right, he was really right." He was, "a force for transparency in tribal government."[37]

In an article in *Minnesota Magazine,* Lillehaug described his first meeting with Lawrence. "I had no idea who he was, but he came to visit me and very much drew my attention to the issues of public corruption on the reservations... He said that the people on the reservations needed [my] help. It wasn't a plea. It was a statement of values. [I] 'cross examined' Lawrence to find out what sort of ax he was grinding.

"It became clear to me that he was not in the journalism business for the money, that this was a huge sacrifice on his part, and that he was very intelligent and probably could succeed in profit-making enterprises if he chose to, but that *The Native American Press/Ojibwe News* was clearly a labor of love."[38]

Throughout his adult life Lawrence was dedicated to improving the lives of reservation natives. Like many Americans, he believed a person "should be able to look at a wrong condition with the knowledge that we can change it."[39] It was his dream that *Press/ON* would be the mechanism that facilitated needed change.

He spent numberless hours obtaining and studying tribal documents. As accountant and lawyer, he was a uniquely qualified journalist. Upon publication of his analysis, he received a shower of protestations and renewed threats and epithets.

A fellow journalist said, "Lawrence's views have not made him popular among tribal leaders. He has been sued. He has been threatened. 'All in all' [Lawrence joked] 'I must be doing something right.'"[40]

      *   *   *

Press/ON provided "Native American news from the federal, state and reservation perspectives. Topics of interest include[d] articles on culture, education, health, the environment, and employment opportunities."[41] The paper focused mainly on the Minnesota tribes, but stories from the Associated Press (AP) and sources such as *Indian Country Today, News from Indian Country,* and *indianz.com,* provided discussion of events on reservations elsewhere that mirrored activities on the local reservations.

The paper's value rested in large part on Lawrence's skillful selection and republication of relevant articles from national sources (the AP) that reinforced his observations and articles on local issues.

Seemingly quiet by nature,[42] Lawrence's piercing editorials condemned and scolded.[43] He challenged the policies and activities of the federal government and tribal officials; he encouraged the people to demand better treatment. He planted new ideas and suggested workable solutions to long-established problems.

The editorials were the heart and soul of the newspaper. They protested the many wrongs in the lives of natives which included: substandard living conditions, health issues, drug related crime and violence, as well as corrupt tribal governments, civil rights violations, inequity in access and distribution of tribal assets, as well as the failure of the federal government to fulfill its fiduciary and guardianship responsibilities. It was Lawrence's contention that these conditions simply begged for reformative measures.[44]

The publisher persistently demanded records under the Freedom of Information Act [FOIA]. Lawrence's request to the Alcohol and Gaming Division [AGED] of the Department of Public Safety for copies of the Red Lake casino audits precipitated a lawsuit against the state by several of the state's most prosperous Indian casinos.

To forestall the appearance of the State versus a native issue, Lawrence intervened, at his own expense, in the lawsuit.

Though the AGED had denied Lawrence's request, the Minnesota Attorney General supported his claim that the casino audits were public documents subject to Minnesota open records law.

Tribal leaders lamented the State's willingness to release their audit information as "an injustice that rivals any of a number of past broken promises to sovereign tribal nations."[45]

The State ultimately prevailed in the case, but it turned out to be a hollow victory. The audits, when finally delivered by the casinos, had all pertinent data redacted.

After an unsuccessful appeal by the tribal casinos, the information was again delivered to the state, but in defiance of the court order, with all relevant information again blacked out. The tribes were never compelled to reveal their audit information.

The resources of the Alcohol and Gambling Division of the State Department of Public Safety were simply inadequate to deliver oversight and enforce compliance. Funding for the division, and its three full-time employees, for many years amounted to $150,000 per year since the gaming compacts were signed in 1988-89. The cost is shared equally by the participating tribes.

This manipulation of the state system may well be evidence of how tribal political contributions work in favor of the tribal establishment.[46]

Lawrence received the 2003 Freedom of Information Award given by the Society of Professional Journalists, St. Paul, "for aggressive defense of the public's right to know and consistent support of the First Amendment." The award was given in part for his involvement and reportage of this case.

As publisher, Lawrence was frequently criticized for publishing unsigned letters and news articles based solely on stories from the people. He was unperturbed by these judgments. He knew the people and assessed the credibility of the sender and the subject matter before he published. He understood very clearly that tribal members who dared to disclose governmental misdeeds would be punished severely. If he'd insisted on publishing names, the secrets would never be disclosed, and the activities of tribal officers would never be revealed.

In answer to this criticism the publisher wrote, "We're pretty liberal with what we publish about what people are saying about tribal administrations and politicians. We play that role. We are kind of the conscience of the community...

"We publish it all and the people can decide on their own."[47]

The role of the media has changed so dramatically since the birth of *Press/ON* and the advent of the 24/7 news, that the contemporary "talking heads" of cable news would no doubt find Lawrence's methods acceptable.

Long before a cable news entity declared "we report, you decide," it was Lawrence's policy to print as much information as accurately as possible and let his readers decide for themselves who/what was truthful.

Lynne Gray "... President of Native American Television, Inc., ... describes Lawrence as 'courageous' and 'brave' though 'she ... takes issue with him over use of unsubstantiated, undocumented, or poorly sourced reports... She recognizes [however] that his sources would likely be targets of violence if they were discovered leaking information to the paper. He has good reason to protect people,' she says."[48]

Eric Sevareid, revered television anchorman of years past, under attack for his commentaries, expressed the following classic sentiment that has relevance to the need for freedom of the press as well as the criticism leveled at Mr. Lawrence and *The Native American Press/Ojibwe News.*

"In October 1970 ... Vice President Spiro Agnew, in an attempt to intimidate the press, [criticized] commentators like Howard K. Smith and Eric Sevareid... ."[49]

To which Sevareid replied, "... at the risk of sounding a bit stuffy, we might say two things. One, that nobody in this business expects for a moment that the full truth of anything will be contained in any one account or commentary, but that through free reporting and discussion ... the truth will emerge. And second, that the central point about the free press is not that it be accurate, though it must try to be, not that it even be fair, though it must try to be that, but that it be free. And that means, in the first instance, freedom from any and all attempts by any power of government to coerce it or intimidate it in any way."[50]

Given the newspaper's meager resources over its long history, it is not surprising that accuracy sometimes suffered and the truth occasionally was skewed.

A substantive story about Lawrence, published in *City Pages,* gives this example: "'He just prints untruths about things, speculation, and all that" [said the tribal chairman of a northern Minnesota] reservation which is often the focus of Lawrence's harshest critiques. "There are so many things he's twisted; it just doesn't do justice to name a few. It is just a slam on his people.'" Pressed for an example, the chairman complains about a factual error in a story *The Native American Press* wrote about his heart by-pass surgery. "Yes,' [he] says, 'I had surgery recently; *but* it was at the University of Minnesota, not at the Mayo Clinic.'"[51]

Although it was rarely used, *Press/ON* consistently invited rebuttals or objections to its articles or editorials.

Another error that slipped by was a staff reporter's assertion that the paper's coverage of criminal activity that resulted in federal prosecutions had been rewarded with a Pulitzer Prize in investigative reporting.

Unfortunately, that was not true.

Press/ON was nominated in two categories for the 1997 Pulitzer by Robert A. Fairbanks, J.D., LL.M., president of the Native American College Preparatory Center in Norman, Oklahoma. In his cover letter, Fairbanks said, "Bill Lawrence ... started *The Native American Press/Ojibwe News* as an independent, self-supporting venture ... for the purpose of exposing corruption in tribal government, promoting tribal accountability, and supporting civil rights and constitutional protections, which many people are surprised to learn do not currently exist on reservations."[52]

Not unexpectedly, *Press/ON* was not the winner. The 1997 prize for Explanatory Journalism was awarded to the *Philadelphia Inquirer;* the *Times-Picayune*, of New Orleans, was recognized for Public Service by a newspaper. Nonetheless, *The Native American Press* of northern Minnesota, with its circulation of 12,000, counted the nomination among its recognitions.

The life expectancy of a free press in Indian country is usually short. Tribal governments are effective in cutting the supply line of supporting advertisers and controlling access to information from tribal members by their use of the spoils system. *The Native American Press/Ojibwe News,* owned, managed and distributed by a man of excellent qualification and demonstrated courage, is an exception.

As publisher, Lawrence proved that it is possible, and necessary, to maintain an independent free press in Indian country. He wagered a good part of his life, his financial and personal well-being, and his safety to do so. The industry regarded him as a hero because of his efforts.

Although tribal officials persistently assaulted the paper and made serious inroads against his reputation, the fact remains they were never able to silence or totally discredit him.

As a salute to the final issue the Minneapolis *Star Tribune* paid homage to Lawrence and to *Press/ON*. "For 21 years he celebrated regular peoples' accomplishments while becoming one of the nation's most ferocious tribal watch-dogs. Lawrence exposed financial irregularities in tribal government, and in the 1990s, his work helped put several tribal leaders behind bars on corruption charges...

"Lawrence's work is not only a reminder of the value of a free press, but also that important, meaningful journalism can be done far from the power centers of Washington, D.C., or New York City--and without the benefit of a big media byline. Lawrence inspired and nurtured several generations of Minnesota journalists. While they cannot replace his unique voice, they owe it to him to continue the crusade."[53]

It happens that praise is often withheld until the final compliment, but Lawrence had the benefit of seeing this article. Other sanguine articles described his character and his accomplishments after his death.[54] What was said about him at the end had been applicable to him for most of his life.

Lawrence was knowledgeable and supportive of native culture, but he was in many ways a myth breaker. He spoke out against immersion or retreat into the past. As a contemporary put it, "Neither Bill or I believe we are victims. We really believe there is an active way to participate in change, and it is not by screaming and crying about 200 years of abuse. It is really about contemporary change. This is an unpopular thing to do."[55]

In general, he acknowledged that a large measure of native alienation was due to the destruction of their culture. However, he also believed that what natives mourned most, in contemporary times, was the loss of integrity on the part of tribal leaders who have strayed from the traditions of mutual care and equitable sharing of the tribe's resources.

Cherokee scholar Steve Russell shares Lawrence's belief: "The only way to win and keep the hearts of our people is to create a tribal structure that reins in the high handedness and self-seeking behaviors that infect tribal governments today."[56]

Lawrence was an active opponent of two widely held concepts: that of the "noble savage" and the convention of tribal sovereign immunity. He held that the "noble savage" was a denigrating myth, a mere flattery that was intended to manipulate.

He insisted "The greatest hoax the Federal Government has played on Indian people in the 20th Century is to make us citizens, but give us no rights." He was convinced that without "rational limitations on tribal sovereign immunity," tribal officials are led to believe "that once they are in office they are above the law and can do whatever they please."[57]

Lawrence estimated that just 2 percent of reservation natives benefitted from tribal sovereignty and only 5 percent benefited from their own casino revenues. And he was firm in the belief that mainstream politicians saw "more financial benefit in the form of campaign contributions from tribal casinos than do most Indian people."[58]

He unabashedly attacked the federal government for its many failures in resolving issues that affected the safety and comfort of native lives. "Many people in Congress know what is going on in tribal government and they know it is wrong and destructive to Indian people. But it is not politically expedient for them to go against the tribal establishment... Politicians care about maintaining the status quo and keeping tribal money circulating in their favor."[59]

As a scholar, a hall of fame athlete, a combat Marine officer, a highly placed government official, a spokesman, an advocate, and a journalist, Lawrence was in many ways a benefit to native populations, and he was a mentor and role model to his fellow Ojibwe.

He educated the people as to what was fair and why they were entitled to better treatment. Lawrence justified their concerns about tribal corruption by publishing the information they provided. He created expectations.

**"Bill challenged people; that made them smarter...
Others were taught lessons."[60]**

Ever an activist, Lawrence carried his message on behalf of native peoples to the Minnesota Supreme Court;[61] to the Senate Indian Affairs Field Hearings in Seattle;[62] and he was a frequent visitor to the Minnesota State Legislature, where he testified as well as personally distributed the newspaper and made himself available to provide insights and answer questions.[63]

He ran for public office several times, including twice for the Chairmanship of the Red Lake Band, and once for the Minnesota Legislature at the request of the Speaker of the House. He was elected to School Boards both in Bemidji, Minnesota and in Mojave Valley, California.

In 2007, the United States Commission on Civil Rights, "due to [his] knowledge of the issue" invited Lawrence to be a panelist at a briefing entitled "Discrimination Against Native Americans in Border Towns."[64] He used this opportunity to submit a lengthy assessment of why discrimination exists, and what could be done to eliminate it.

The Native American Press contained extensive details of Anishinabe culture such as traditional recipes and articles on wild rice harvesting. From details of Ojibwe beading to Ojibwe word puzzles, to coverage of protests by tribal members demanding reform of tribal government, he published material that met the needs and interests of the people.

Within *Press/ON's* pages readers found excerpts from Sioux histories, and the sometimes controversial essays of notable native writers such as Tim Giago, Maynard Swan and Francis Blake.

The paper often published full transcripts of court cases, legal documents and lengthy selections from new books of interest. As publisher, Lawrence was always willing to give the complete story for the benefit of the people.

He encouraged input in all forms. Letters to the editor, cartoons and rebuttals were favored features.

The published letters were frequently unsigned. Lawrence's position was: "I'm dealing with eleven governments that deny people basic rights, so I have to get in an advocacy role."[65]

Paul DeMain, CEO of *News from Indian Country,* said, "I think he presents an incomplete picture. But the paper serves as a watchdog ... It just happens the watchdog is a vicious one. People operate knowing that Bill Lawrence isn't afraid to write about and expose scandal."[66]

His response was always to this effect: "I've got to do it ... the message has got to get out."[67] "No one else gets the information. No one else will write the stories we write."[68]

Letters that condemned the paper were also welcome. A prominent member of the Red Lake Band scolded: "In the October 2001 Gaming Times report, I was reminded how *The Native American Press/Ojibwe News* is instrumental in starting rumors by ordering an investigation and an entire mid-year independent audit just to dispel the rumor at a cost of over $20,000... In an honest world, those individuals who started these rumors, along with the *Ojibwe News,* should be required to pay this $20,000 back to the tribe.... Someone has to speak out about the *Ojibwe News'* total lack of credibility when they write anything to sell papers... "[69]

In the letters to the editor the people were able to convey their distress without fear.

The political cartoons are irreverent as well as astute. Often unsophisticated in artistic quality, the drawings were exceptionally informative. The suggestive gesture of a simply drawn figure on a blank field often was unmistakable in identity, action or behavior. Others were finely drawn. Many were unsolicited and intended to deride, others to protest or expose wrong or questionable doings, and some simply for the amusement of readers.[70]

The letters and the cartoons are evidence of the hearty participation in the paper by the people; letters and cartoons were the only means available to them for free expression. From the tenth week of publication on, Lawrence stressed the paper "provided a forum"[71] for his readers to express their views.

The Minnesota Digital Library has preserved the entire newspaper collection, assuring the ideas, the concerns and the need for tribal governmental reform will not continue to be overlooked.[72] The editorials, articles and commentaries, together in one place, constitute an uninterrupted picture of native life and politics for more than two decades. The chronicle of abuses and duplicity are testimony to the failures of federal Indian policy. Their preservation will be a catalyst for further investigation and as a permanent record for scholars and reformers. Digitizing assures tribal leaders will never be able to silence him. Their misdeeds will not fade away. Lawrence will have the last word, after all.

A run that covered the events of daily life on reservations for the final decade of the twentieth century and the opening decade of the twenty-first century is a remarkable achievement. The independence of *The Native American Press/Ojibwe News* and its longevity testify to the lasting value of the paper that was affectionately known as "The Redskin rag."

1. *Press/ON* is a working abbreviation for *The Native American Press/Ojibwe News*. Various other abbreviations were used over the life of the paper; they included the *NEWS, the PRESS, and NAP/ON.*

The newspaper was initially dedicated to issues involving Ojibwe people and began life as the *Ojibwe News*. As it matured, Lawrence extended coverage and distribution to the Minnesota Sioux communities. For a time a special edition, *The Native*

American Press, was distributed in the Twin Cities. The two names were afterward combined into *The Native American Press/Ojibwe News.* (*Press/ON* was also appropriate to describe the publisher's attitude.)

2. Robert G. Hays, *A Race at Bay: New York Times Editorials on "The Indian Problem," 1860-1900.* (Carbondale: Southern Illinois University Press, 1997), xxiv.

3. ". . . the U.S. Attorney believes this is the first time any tribal official has been convicted under the ICRA, because the 1978 *Martinez* decision has resulted in protecting tribal governments from most civil rights claims." Bill Lawrence, "Tribal Sovereign Immunity is the Single Biggest Factor Contributing to Corruption on American Indian Reservations," presentation at the American Indian Law and Policy Symposium (Norman, University of Oklahoma, March 21, 1998).

4. Doug Grow, "The Mighty have fallen to Indian editor," Minneapolis: *Star Tribune*, Metro/State Section, May 17, 1996. B2.

5. "The . . . case almost died for lack of a prosecutor willing to take it, but our frequent stories in the newspaper [and my personal appeals to the U.S. Attorney] helped keep it alive," William J. Lawrence, presentation, American Indian Law & Policy Symposium, University of Oklahoma, March 21, 1998.

6. "A Politics of Spoils. When a tribal government's primary function has become employment and service delivery, and where most financial resources are controlled by tribal government, the control of that government becomes the key to gaining access to economic resources: jobs, money, service. This turns reservation politics into a politics of spoils, having less to do with where the nation is headed or how best to organize tribal operations than with which faction will control the goodies that government can hand out."

Stephen Cornell in Miriam Jorgenson, ed., *Rebuilding Native Nations: Strategies for Governance and Development,* (Tucson: University of Arizona Press, 2007), 66.

7. Bill Lawrence, "Do Indian reservations equal apartheid?" *The Native American Press/Ojibwe News*, June 6, 2003, 4.

8. Lawrence, presentation, March 21, 1998.

9. Bill Lawrence quoted in Doug Grow, May 17, 1996.

10. Lawrence, "Consider this. . ." *The Native American Press/Ojibwe News,* January 27, 1995, 4.

11. Ibid.

12. Tom Heffelfinger quoted in "Losing a voice for American Indians," Minneapolis, *Star Tribune*, October 3, 2009.

13. Lawrence, presentation, March 21, 1998.

14. Bill Lawrence, quoted in Susan Barberi, "An Enemy of his People," *Minnesota Magazine,* April 1999, 52.

15. Bill Lawrence quoted in Grow, May 17, 1996.

16. Bill Lawrence, Advertising solicitation letter, June 6, 1991, Author's file.

17. Doug Grow, "The Mighty have fallen to Indian editor," May 17, 1996.

18. Lawrence, "Consider this," January 27, 1995, 4.

19. Ibid.

20. Administrator, State Government Finance Committee, Minnesota House of Representatives, December 2, 2011. Minnesota Tribal PAC contributions: 2010 $1.18 million, the second largest contributor; the largest contributor to campaigns was Minnesota Education at $1.24 million.

Tribal PAC reports filed with the State of Minnesota Campaign Finance and Public Disclosure Board. April 2011. Statement available from editor.

Total Indian PAC contributions to political campaigns amounted in 2010 to $9.08 Million. Found at: www.opensecrets.org/industries/totals, accessed June 6, 2012.

State of Minnesota Campaign Finance Board. Total Lobbying Disbursements Reported by Lobbyists for Principals January through December 2016. 'Principals with Disbursements over $250,000:' $1,160,402 from 4 tribes. Other Disbursements Reported by Lobbyists January 1-December 31, 2016: $433,735. Combined total from Minnesota Tribes - $1,594,137.

21. Barberi, "An Enemy of his People," 52.

22. Lawrence, presentation, March 21, 1998.

23. Louise Mengelkoch, "Sovereignty and secrecy," *Native American Press/Ojibwe News*, March 17, 2005, 1.

24. Mike Mosedale, "No Reservations," *City Pages,* Minneapolis, MN, June 20, 2001, 8.

25. Lawrence, presentation, March 21, 1998.

David E. Wilkins, *The Navaho Political Experience.* 4th Edition, Rowman & Littlefield Publishers, Inc. Lanham, Maryland. 2013.

". . . most of the nearly 300 reservation publications serve largely as newsletters touting their tribal government's accomplishments. In other words, most tribal newspapers are organs or instrumentalities of the governing body of the tribe." p.173.

26. Lawrence, "Consider this. . ." 4.

27. Louise Mengelkoch, "Blind in Red Lake: How the Press made a bad thing worse." *Columbia Journalism Review 44 no.6.* (March/April 2006): 12.

28. Tom Dennis, "Our Opinion: Reservations need, deserve a free press," *Grand Forks Herald,* March 30, 2011.

29. Lawrence followed the example set by his two older brothers, Dick and Jim Lawrence, also Hall of Fame members. They were inspired by their father Joseph William "Lefty" Lawrence. In his obituary the senior Lawrence was described as a "well known ball player. . . a prominent [baseball] figure in both North and South Dakota [as well as] a member of the old Northern league. . ." Obituary, *Bemidji Pioneer.* June 14, 1944.

30. "Three to go. Lawrence . . . will be going into the state tourney with perhaps the best record any boy ever took to the meet." Cliff Morlan, *Bemidji Pioneer.* Scrap-book clipping. No specific date, late 1950s. Lawrence family.

31. "[Minnesota] Gopher Frosh Boast Top Quarterback Crop. The best group of potential quarterbacks . . . are among the 130 freshmen who reported for practice. . . Billy Lawrence, the Bemidji all-around athlete . . . has been moved to quarterback." Sid Hartman, Minneapolis: *Star Tribune,* Fall 1957. Scrap-book clipping. Lawrence family.

32. "Lawrence making good. . . the Detroit Tiger scout was quoted in Sid Hartman's Column to the effect that Billy Lawrence, the

Bemidji pitcher with Valdosta, Ga., is rated as one of the prize Detroit Tigers farm rookies. I am sure that Bill is making the grade. If hard work and dedication have anything to do with it, I'm sure Bill will come out all right." Minneapolis, *Star Tribune*, 1958. Scrap-book clipping. Lawrence family.

33. Gerald Vizenor, *The Everlasting Sky: Voices of the Anishinabe*, (St. Paul: Minnesota Historical Society Press, 2000), 84.

34. Ibid, 85.

35. Ibid, 101.

36. A few hours before he passed, Lawrence requested the daily newspaper.

37. David Lillihaug, quoted in Curt Brown, "Indian watchdog issues its final bark," Minneapolis, *Star Tribune,* September 29, 2009, B2.

38. David Lillihaug, quoted in Barberi, "An Enemy of his People," 172.

39. Ernest Holmes, *The Science of Mind,* (New York: Dodd, Meade & Co.), 1938, 53.

40. Barberi, "An Enemy of his People," 51.

41. Lawrence, "Consider this. . ." 4.

42 ". . . he seldom raised his voice, instead offering his complaints as if he was reading a grocery list," Mosedale, "No Reservations,"8.

43. ". . . sometimes inflammatory rhetoric," Ibid.

44. United States Commission on Civil Rights Report, *Broken Promises*, Washington, D.C., 2004, confirms the stated living

conditions, 37; statements support the assertion of the federal government's failure, 8.

The United States Commission on Civil Rights Report, *A Quiet Crisis,* Washington, D.C., 2003, confirms the crime and violence statements, 72.

45. Todd Nelson and David Hawley, "Judge due to block release of tribe's casino audits," *Pioneer Press,* Bemidji, MN, September 21, 2001.

46. "Gambling monitors could use a hand. The state has two agents assigned to the 18 casinos, and they are responsible for almost 19,500 slot machines and 392 blackjack tables. . . Mark Brunswick, Minneapolis, *Star Tribune,* February 12, 2004.
    See also: "Slots get little or no state review. The State's biggest casinos have gone years without inspections. . . Slot machines and blackjack tables at Minnesota's Indian casinos have gone four years without inspections. . . The Alcohol and Gambling Enforcement Division of the Minnesota Department of Public Safety has attributed the decline in inspections to budget constraints. . . just 35 of 15,150 slot machines at the state's seven largest Indian casinos were inspected. . ." Todd Kennedy, Minneapolis, *Star Tribune,* February 7, 2012.
    A Minnesota House committee administrator reported to the editor that state legislators steered away from addressing the issue of greater revenue for this purpose. Conversation with the editor. April 2011.

47. Barberi, "An Enemy of his People," 51.

48. Ibid, 173.

49. Raymond A. Schroth, "He was All of America Talking to Itself." *On Second Thought: The Sevareid Issue,* North Dakota Humanities Council, (Bismarck, ND), Autumn 10, 15.

50. Ibid.

51. Mosedale, "No Reservations," 10.

52. Robert A. Fairbanks, Letter to Pulitzer Committee, January 24, 1997, publisher's file.

53. "Losing a voice for American Indians," Minneapolis, *Star Tribune,* October 3, 2009, A10. Published prior to Lawrence's death.

54. Industry articles include:
    Curt Brown, "Indian watchdog dies, newspaper issues its final bark," Minneapolis, Star *Tribune,* Metro, September 29, 2009, A1. Published prior to Lawrence's death.
    Curt Brown, "Watchdog journalist Bill Lawrence issues final bark," Minneapolis, Star *Tribune,* March 5, 2010, 70.
    Chuck Haga, "Minnesota journalist Bill Lawrence dies," Grand Forks, ND, *Grand Forks Herald,* March 7, 2010.
    "Minnesota tribal watchdog dies at age 70." Minneapolis, *Star Tribune,* March 5, 2010.
    "Remembering 'Bill' Lawrence, of *The Native American Press/Ojibwe News,"* *Bemidji Pioneer,* Bemidji, Minnesota, March 18, 2010.

55. Lynn Gray quoted in Barberi, "An Enemy of his People," 3.

56. Russell, Steve. *Sequoyah Rising. Problems in Post-Colonial Tribal Governments*. (Durham, NC, Carolina Academic Press), 84.

57. Lawrence, presentation, March 21, 1998.

58. Ibid.

59. William J. Lawrence testimony, *The American Equal Justice Act,* hearing on S1691 before the Committee on Indian Affairs,

United States Senate, 105th Congress, April 7, 1998.

60. Frank Bibeau, Tribal Attorney at Leech Lake Reservation, MN. Correspondence with the editor, June 6, 2012.

61. William J. Lawrence, Affidavit, State of Minnesota in Supreme Court, In RE: Rules of Procedure for the Recognition of Tribal Court Orders and Judgments, July 10, 2002.

62. Lawrence, testimony, U.S. Senate Field Hearing, Seattle, Washington. April 7, 1998.

63. Bill Lawrence testimony, "Tribal casinos must share the wealth," the Minnesota Joint House/Senate Tax Committee. St. Paul, Minnesota. April 30, 1997.

64. Bill Lawrence. "Discrimination Against Native Americans in Border Towns." United States Commission on Civil Rights Commission Briefing: Washington, D.C. November 9, 2007.

65. Mosedale, Mike. Lawrence quoted:
"No Reservations," June 20, 2012, 14. The following material is quoted from actual letters from readers in the publisher's file.
     "My instincts tell me that Indian gaming could be a two-headed monster. . . it would be a crying shame if tribal leaders were to sell their people and the unique status of our reservations down the river because of a little greed and corruption. That would be real white of them, and of the rest of us, if we sit idly by and let it happen in front of our noses." *Ojibwe News,* July 31, 1991.
     "Your recent article about . . . Gaming operation . . . is not surprising. Your call for an INVESTIGATION is warranted. . .
     "Your articles can be a basis for criminal allegation and yet nothing is being done." *The Native American Press/Ojibwe News,* February 13, 2004.

66. Paul DeMain, quoted in Mosedale, "No Reservations," June 20,

2001, 14.

67. Lawrence, quoted in Barberi," An Enemy of his People, " April 1999, 173.

68. Lawrence, quoted in Mosedale, "No Reservations, " June 20, 2001, 14.

69. Bruce Graves, "Letter to the Editor." *The Native American Press/Ojibwe News*, November 9, 2001.

70. Handwritten letter from a reader, publisher's file, May 2, 2005. "Dear Bill, I was wondering if you could/would put this cartoon in your paper, it was on the bulletin board where I live and found out who put this there – and I asked him if I can have it – wow. I think it would be appropriate for your newspaper at this turmoil time on the Leech Lake Reservation."

71. Bill Lawrence, Letter to Advertisers, publisher's file, July 27, 1988.

72. The complete collection of *The Native American Press/Ojibwe News* has been digitized. It can be found at Minnesota Digital Newspaper Hub. (Minnesota State Historical Society.)

Chapter III. Introduction: The Editorials.

The time span of the more than 900 editorials that appeared in *The Native American Press/Ojibwe News,* 1988-2009, might suggest historic rather than current relevance. The collection is definitely valuable as history but that fact doesn't limit its current instructive value. In addition to articles regarding local politics and issues, *The Native American Press/Ojibwe News* routinely carried articles carefully selected from the Associated Press (AP) that mirrored current events on other reservations.

In general, Americans have vague notions that conditions for Natives on America's reservations are disheartening, but they are unfamiliar with the facts and the extent of the problems.

Publisher Bill Lawrence was one of the few independent journalists who dared to spotlight the downside of reservation life and conditions. At the heart of his work was his indignation that many reservation members, as U.S. citizens, live in third world conditions.

Press/ON* routinely delivered accounts of fraud, theft, mismanagement, and denial of basic civil rights. Most reservation officials, because of his unreserved scrutiny and commentary, regarded him as a gadfly, a constant irritation. They were unsuccessful in completely silencing and/or discrediting him. There were times however when they appeared to have won.

Editions of the paper were seized and destroyed. In an attempt to cut off the pulse of the paper, Lawrence was blacklisted with advertisers. Sales of the paper were prohibited in local stores. Reservation leaders persuaded public officials that he was an enemy of his people. He wrote; they retaliated. That the discrediting was not effective is supported by the longevity of the paper. Publication of *The Native American Press/Ojibwe News* continued, uninterrupted for over two decades.

As editor/publisher he was controversial but fair, freely offering ink and space to those who opposed his beliefs or felt aggrieved by what he had written.

The Native American Press/Ojibwe News collection is available through the Minnesota Historical Society's Digital Newspaper Hub.

*   *   *

Chosen with a desire to educate about reservation affairs and problems, the editorials frequently present information provided, in large part, by reservation members. The details furnish insights as to why the conditions have developed and what can be done to change them for the better. This is information not usually available to the general public.

Because there is little opportunity or occasion for mainstreamers to visit reservations, ignorance of the predicament of reservation native remains.

It is not well known, but there is an enormous amount of money available from casino revenues and federal allocation to improve conditions and to fulfill the original intent (rehabilitation of reservation circumstances and peoples) of the Indian Gaming Regulatory Act. To illustrate with just two articles: The National Gaming Commission report, "Gross Gaming Revenue Trending," Fiscal Year 2015 reports $29.9 billion revenue; and an October 2015 article in *Indian Country Today Media Network,* cites "$20 Billion [federal allocation]: Total U.S. Support for American Indians." This is a substantial amount to address the problems that exist for approximately one million reservation residents.

While Americans have a general impression that reservation social, economic and political conditions are dismal, few have a clear idea of the magnitude of the problems and no idea at all as to what causes the situation and what can be done to correct it.

Secrecy permits oppression and the politics of spoils. Getting the information to the outside for help in initiating corrective actions has heretofore been impossible.

Press/ON is an acronym for the newspaper.

Chapter IV. Introduction: Reservation Conditions.
"Reservation turmoil is symptomatic of deep problems."
August 03, 2002.

As stated earlier, little has changed for the better on America's reservations since the inaugural issue of *The Native American Press/Ojibwe News,* 1988-2009.

Reservation conditions of this decade remain unchanged, deplorable and interfere with an individual's ability to benefit from educational and employment opportunities. The on-going situation is supported by geographic isolation, oppression and dishonesty by tribal officials. Ignorance of these facts by the 'outside,' and inattention by federal authorities, allow the situation to be on-going.

Multiple, current newspaper and journal articles support these statements. The Native American Aid program describes living condition on the reservations as "comparable to third world." Other comments: "Job opportunities are virtually non-existent... At the end of each month, children and elders often go hungry." "Many homes lack central heat, running water, electricity and telephones." "If you thought these conditions didn't exist in America today, you are sadly mistaken." *

Years have passed since Bill Lawrence began recording his observations of tribal life. During that time, and for decades before and after, multiple billions of dollars have been available to tribes through government funding and to those tribes with gambling facilities. Yet conditions on reservations are still similar to the worst scenarios of third world countries. The question is why?

Native America has access to enormous amounts of money. The National Indian Gaming Association (NIGA) reports $30 billion in 2017 from casino gambling proceeds. President Barack Obama's federal budget request for American Indian tribes for 2017 was $21 billion.

The 2010 US Census states the American Indian population is 2.9 million. Various reports indicate that the reservation population represents only about 40% of that total number, roughly one million individuals.

How can it be that natives on America's reservations, presumably with access to generous billions a year, occupy the lowest possible positions statistically for health, employment, education, welfare, business, etc.?

Reservation conditions have been and remain chronically deplorable. When tribal officials control all revenues, employment, housing, and access to services, can there be any doubt as to the level of authority or outcome?

It is fairly common knowledge that reservation conditions are, and have chronically been, deplorable. What has not been revealed is the cause.

Lawrence asserted that conditions observable on reservations are the direct result of a flawed federal Indian policy that recognizes and supports the concept of tribal sovereignty. He insisted there is little or no effective federal oversight on reservations to prevent violations of civil rights and provide protections under the law.

Funding and spending decisions are at the discretion of tribal governmental officials. There has been no insistence from the federal government on protections of natives (who are bona fide citizens of the United States) from tribal law, no oversight or expectation that the checks and balances that protect the non-native population be guaranteed for Indian people living on reservations.

---

*Native American Aid (formerly National Relief Charities) A Program of Partnership with Native Americans." (2015) www.naaprograms.org.
See also Annotated Bibliography for similar articles.

Native leadership's lack of respect for the law sets a bad example.
November 18, 1994.

It certainly would be nice to sit here every week and write about the good and positive things that go on in the native community. Believe me, we do encourage and even solicit stories of this type from anyone. However, when you continue to read headlines in the majority media like, "What the doctors don't see," about an incident of wife beating and abuse which resulted in the death of an unborn child on the White Earth Reservation (Minneapolis *Star Tribune* 11-13-94, edition, headline front page); "Suspect charged in slaying," a story about a stabbing on the Red Lake Reservation which appeared in the *Bemidji Pioneer* on 11-16-94; "Casino robbery charges dropped," another article in the *Bemidji Pioneer* about an armed robbery at the Palace Casino on the Leech Lake Reservation on September 22, 1993; and the numerous stories about Skip Finn's rip-off of the Leech Lake people, it's hard to maintain a positive perspective.

In addition, we are all overwhelmed by the frequent reports and stories that appear in the media about corruption, various abuses and mismanagement in our tribal governments and Indian programs. With the report that we got yesterday of the HUD Inspector General's (I.G.) office starting an investigation into allegations of bid rigging, gifts, and misuse of funds at the Red Lake Reservation Housing office, that will make about half a dozen I.G. investigations going on in Minnesota Indian programs at this time.

Also there are many reports made to us about sexual harassment, misuse of funds, abuses of authority that never make it into the media--even this one. What this all seems to mean is that we have a somewhat general attitude in the native community of a loss of respect for our own people when one of us gets in a leadership or management position. It's a kind of get-what-you-can-get-while-you-got-the-chance attitude. I think that before we cast all the blame for our socioeconomic problems on others, we should take a good look at what our native leadership, or lack of it, is doing to us.

66

What kind of example do our so-called leaders set for us by ripping us off or abusing us every chance they get? And what kind of example are they setting by hiding from us behind the veil of sovereign immunity every time we challenge them for abusing our civil rights? If our so-called leaders don't respect or obey the law, why should the rest of us?

The talk around Leech Lake after the armed robbery back in September 1993 was, "so what if some of our tribal members got to the money before our tribal leaders did." That is why there is a lack of sentiment around the Leech Lake community to convict anyone for the robbery.

Unfortunately, until Congress decides to take enough interest in Indian people and enact legislation which will ensure civil right on our reservations, we will go on seeing more of the same.

Star Tribune Indian series misses the point.
November 7, 1997.

I read with interest the three-part "The Casino Payoff" series by Pat Doyle in the *Star Tribune* this past week, in which he discussed at length the impact of tribal gaming on unemployment, education and disparities between life at the Red Lake versus the Mystic Lake reservations. He points out the inequities of the Indian Gaming Regulatory Act, and the fact that there is nothing in the act requiring distribution of the benefits among all tribes and tribal members.

He points out that more money is spent promoting pow-wows than in tribal schools. He also mentions that tribal governments consistently do not report their casino earnings even to tribal members, and where the money is going largely remains a mystery.

I commend Doyle for his efforts and recognize the difficulty in pulling together information for such extensive articles. I must, however, take issue with several of the assertions made:

Inaccurate numbers: First, in nearly all cases, the "on or near reservation" population figures used in the articles were overstated by over 100%. This inaccuracy skews the entire premise of the articles, and presents a much greater unemployment outlook than really exists on reservations. Tribal governments are notorious for inflating their population figures, because the more poverty-ridden Indians they can claim to have, the more federal program dollars they are able to get. The Bureau of Indian Affairs gladly uses these inflated figures because, with lots of poor Indians on reservations, they can justify their continued existence as well.

Had the *Star Tribune* looked at these figures with a critical eye, they could have discovered this fact, and used other sources such as U.S. census figures, eligible voter lists, or even population figures available at the Minnesota Housing Finance Agency to extrapolate more accurate figures.

For example, according to the above named sources, there are approximately 3,200 Indians living on the Red Lake reservation, and 800

68

living near. Doyle's articles stated there are over 8,100. Accurate numbers and better research would have found that there really is not much of an available labor force on most reservations.

Most of those who are able, and willing, to work are already employed in various tribal, state or federal government jobs on the reservations, e.g. in schools, casinos, and Indian Health clinics and hospitals. There have been multiple training programs over the past 30 years on reservations, starting with the federal Office of Economic Opportunity programs of the 1960's. Some unemployed tribal members have been trained up to six times over the years, but still aren't working.

It's hard to imagine why any of the 3,200 people living on the Red Lake reservation should be unemployed or in poverty when they have a $50 million annual economy, much of it federal money. Had the *Star Tribune* interviewed people other than tribal government officials, they would have learned that many tribal council members hold multiple tribal positions. Some are receiving up to five separate pay checks. Their family members are also given plum positions, resulting in an inordinate number of the highest paying jobs on reservations being controlled by a few families in power.

Most tribally-operated casinos are staffed with tribal council officers and their family members, friends and political supporters.

Little Opportunity: As *Press/ON* reported … in a feature story about a family, who returned to the Mille Lacs reservation to be part of what they thought would be a new age in tribal life, they, and many others, found that politics, nepotism, favoritism, abuses and mismanagement predominate.

The wife, a trained and experienced computer specialist, had earned three times the income that she was given at Grand Casino for the same type of computer work. For two years at one of the most lucrative tribal casinos in the nation, she, a Mille Lacs Band member, was denied training, had to pay for certification programs herself, was denied promotions she was well qualified for, and had to train non-Indians who were given advancements over her.

In frustration, she quit. Within months she got a computer job off the reservation, and is again making three times her casino salary.

In the real world, outside of the unaccountable, dark world of tribal casinos, she had received promotions, on-going training, and increased pay and responsibilities--everything she wasn't allowed on the Mille Lacs reservation. Her husband didn't fare any better with the tribe.

There are 60,000 Indians living in Minnesota, and only 20% live on or near reservations. Most of us who live off the reservation aren't willing to go back because we know all about the abuses, dysfunction, and lack of basic rights and protections resulting from sovereignty, sovereign immunity, and lack of accountability on reservations.

School Failure: Regarding education, the *Star Tribune* again missed the key issue. What kind of education are the kids getting for the money spent, and where is the money going? In Bemidji the budget is $6,900 per student. The state-wide average is $6,200.

The four reservation schools Doyle discussed in his article receive an average of over $14,000 per student from the federal government alone. Tribal governments claim they add even more money to their already overflowing education pot. If that's true, where does the money end up; what do they have to show for it? How much of the federal money that tribes receive for education actually goes to education? In just one example, the Bureau of Indian Affairs gives the Fond du Lac tribal government nearly $17,000 per student per year for education, yet teachers tell us they have virtually no books or supplies.

Why? Where is the money going? Despite the rhetoric, many tribal officials view federal education dollars as tribal revenue first, and job opportunity second. Educating kids is a distant third. By almost any measure, whether test scores, graduation rates or attendance, reservation schools, especially for the higher grades, do not pass muster.

On my reservation, for example, only about 10% of the students can pass the basic requirements for reading and math, compared with a state-wide average of about 70%. That's a 90% failure rate for

Indian kids. Many reservation high schools function more as "drop-in" centers, where attendance is sporadic at best.

Fortunately, tribal schools are not the only opportunity where Indian kids can get an education. Education is a state responsibility, and all the reservations are, thankfully, covered by state school districts where Indian kids can get a decent education.

It all comes back to **Accountability**: Doyle mentions, just in passing, that tribes do not account for their funds, whether federal or casino dollars. Only recently has the National Indian Gaming Commission required standards for tribal casino audited accounts, but still they are not available for any tribal member or other members of the public to review. The result is a lot of secrecy, unaccountability and financial darkness on reservations.

I would bet that if the cities of St. Paul and Minneapolis, or any small town in the state, had millions of dollars of unaccounted for federal and casino dollars, the *Star Tribune* would not simply accept, "trust us, we're putting it to good use" as an answer to questions of accountability.

But because it's Indian people and tribal governments, the *Star Tribune* sets aside hard-hitting journalistic scrutiny, perhaps because they are afraid of the repercussions. They know that anyone who questions, let alone challenges, tribal governments gets labelled a "racist."

Additionally, I'm sure they'd rather not face an advertising boycott from tribal casinos, as many others news services including this newspaper, have.

"Where is all the money going?" would be a good topic for a three-part *Star Tribune* expose. Because obviously millions of dollars are going somewhere and benefiting someone and, as Doyle points out, in most cases it's not going to the rank and file tribal members. Many of our former "leaders" are at this moment in federal prisons for stealing from their tribes, and sadly, many more probably should be.

Star Tribune series on sovereignty incomplete and misleading.
July 28, 1995.

The recent three-part series in the Minneapolis *Star Tribune* on tribal sovereignty, written by Pat Doyle, was informative, and perhaps timely, but really didn't break any new ground. It was kind of the *Trib's* version of how several minuscule tribal communities have benefited from, or even exploited, the Indian gaming act and, for whatever reason, have now chosen to protect their interests behind tribal sovereignty.

Some of us in Indian country are wondering why the *Star Tribune* did not include coverage of some northern Minnesota casinos that are losing money because of mismanagement. Is that not newsworthy enough for the *Star Tribune*?

Obviously, no one likes to see anybody abused, mistreated, not dealt with fairly, or not have an opportunity to seek redress of their grievances because, supposedly, that is the American way. But with the exception of the adjacent property owner at Shakopee, nearly all the others with complaints were gamblers and workers who entered the reservations on a voluntary basis.

This is unfortunate. And we believe that tribal governments should live up to their responsibilities as employers and business owners. But due to sovereign immunity, there is currently no way to force them to do so short of boycotting them, and/or pressuring Congress to change the law.

With Congress presently considering amendments to the Indian Gaming Act, there is a distinct possibility that change could happen in the very near future. But for the time being, if you work or play on the rez, you do it subject to their laws, like it or not...

It was disappointing to read the *Trib's* three-part series and not find anything about the issues surrounding the lack of civil rights of tribal members in dealing with their tribal governments, and the lack of accountability of gaming funds. Hardly a week goes by that a story or letter to the editor isn't carried in this publication about one of these two issues. Gaming has made these issues the biggest on the reservation, so it is hard to understand why the *Star Tribune* chose not to include them in the series.

In addition, it was disappointing that the series didn't include any comments on the issues by the Minnesota Congressional delegation. After all they are the ones who will be voting on changing the law and all but one will be seeking our votes next year.

Reservation turmoil is symptomatic of deeper problems.
August 30, 2002.

In last week's edition, *Press/ON* carried a story titled "Crow Creek Sioux debate federal takeover," in which members of the Crow Creek band sought to turn their tribe back over to the BIA because of excessive tribal indebtedness of $31 million. "We're in the hole so deep ... receivership is an option because we have no other way open to us," one community leader is quoted as saying.

This follows a story we published a couple of weeks ago, "Turtle Mountain tribe again facing turmoil," in which tribal officials face charges from embezzlement to witness tampering.

Standing Rock members are also suing their tribal government for misuse and failure to account for funds, and it's only been a year or so since tribal members on the Pine Ridge and Crow reservations took over their tribal governments.

Minnesota's three largest reservations, Red Lake, White Earth, and Leech Lake, have all gone through or are currently going through fairly tumultuous times, having been on the roller-coaster ride of gambling's rags-to-riches illusion, and now find themselves a combined $175 million in debt (Red Lake about $58 million, Leech Lake around $75 million, and White Earth an estimated $42 million).

There are also increasing rumblings at Mille Lacs, with concerned tribal membership asking, "Where has all the money gone?" Fortunately, on these reservations, the recent elections have given tribal governments time to deal with the problems. On all four reservations, there are either significant numbers of new tribal council members, or new officers in key positions on the tribal councils have recently been elected.

But, I don't think that tribal members are going to allow their representatives to sit back and not do anything. They were elected with a mandate from tribal members to address the problems, and although I think they will try to do so, tribal members are pressing for quick and effective action.

In order for the new council members to effectively deal with the indebtedness and the other problems tearing apart the social fabric on these reservations, they are going to need a lot of community support and perseverance in overcoming the forces of the status quo. To permanently overcome these problems, it will either take significant changes in the tribal systems through constitutional reforms, or Congressional legislation enacting a new and effective Indian Civil Rights Act.

The preferable course of action is for the tribal governments to take the initiative and enact constitutional reforms, and do it voluntarily. However, if that doesn't happen, then Congress must act. Any newly-enacted Indian Civil Rights Act must contain an inalienable Bill of Rights and create a legally-viable and effective forum guaranteeing enforcement of these fundamental civil rights.

There has to be a separation of powers, there have to be independent courts, and there have to be open and accountable tribal governments with full participation by the members of the tribes. If both the tribes and Congress abdicate their responsibility, then it will be up to the courts to protect the rights and interests of the First Americans.

Unless either the tribes or the federal government take action, nothing substantial is going to change. We have seen the same kinds of problems happening time and again, all over the country, on reservation after reservation. It's time for a thoughtful, serious, and effective remedy.

In passing the Indian Gaming Regulatory Act in 1988, the Congress and administration felt that bringing gambling to the reservations, with its potential for creating jobs and quick revenue, would be a panacea for dealing with the problems that have become entrenched in Indian country over the past century and a half. But, after 12 years of casino operation in Indian country, including in Minnesota, we have seen a lot of money change hands, and a handful of people getting very rich, but far too few of the beneficiaries have been Indian people. In addition, we don't even see any semblance of a non-gambling economy being developed on these reservations.

Indian gambling monopolies are not going to last forever, and unless a significant percentage of gambling revenues are invested in other profitable economic development, in 20 years the economic situation on reservations will be far worse than it is now. In fact, we have seen significant rises in crime rates, particularly violent crime, as well as worsening problems of alcohol and chemical abuse, and not a whole lot of improvement in education. Despite initial improvements in employment rates, on some reservations unemployment is beginning to regress to the catastrophic levels of persistent poverty which beset reservations before gambling.

A year ago, we began filling *Press/ON* with news, commentaries, and letters to the editor about the chaos and turmoil at Red Lake, mainly because of credible allegations about financial mismanagement. In the last three or four months, this newspaper's been filled up with much the same kind of articles and letters about the financial mismanagement and turmoil at Leech Lake. News coverage and reader commentary at White Earth has recently been high, but according to what we've been told, the silence is not because there are no problems, but rather because the situation has not yet reached the "boiling point."

Due to the problems currently affecting the United States economy, Indians on other reservations will probably soon find themselves embroiled in the same kinds of controversy. One of the biggest problems has been Congress's turning a "blind eye" to the serious problems confronting Indian country.

In my opinion, the social and other problems on Indian reservations are worse now than they were when [our Senator] took office 12 years ago. I think that [his] laissez-faire support of the tribal establishment, and refusal to do something about the problems festering on Indian reservations, should become a campaign issue. Posturing about human rights abuses overseas, while steadfastly ignoring the problems confronting his own constituents on Indian reservations at home, is blatant hypocrisy. We need to return what's left of Indian sovereignty back to the people.

Law & order lacking on the Rez.
August 22, 2003.

Two news stories this week remind us once more of the incredibly high incidence of violent crime on our Indian reservations. In both accounts, alcohol and/or drug use appear to have been the major contributing cause. Twenty-year-old Roger Grabow, Jr., of Mille Lacs, was found guilty in the beating death of Melvin Eagle, Jr., age 45.

According to a *Mille Lacs Messenger* story, Grabow admitted that he and two others "kicked, stomped and beat Eagle at the home of Eagle's girlfriend." The viciousness of the beating is frightening in its detail. According to the newspaper account, Eagle was unconscious, unable to defend himself as a result of an initial blow to his face. "Eagle was found with boot prints on his forehead, puncture wounds in the back of his head, multiple bruises to his abdomen and groin, 17 fractures to 16 ribs, lacerations to his liver and spleen, and a cigarette filter lodged in his throat."

When Grabow and the others left the girlfriend's home around 6 a.m., Eagle was still alive. However, help was not summoned until 9 a.m. According to testimony by an assistant county coroner, had Eagle received medical treatment within a half hour of the assault, he may have survived. During interrogation by police, Grabow confirmed that he and the others were drunk.

In another unrelated case reported in the *Star Tribune*, a 17 year old was sentenced to 35 years in prison for participating in the murder of a 21-year-old. A 21-year-old female accomplice was sentenced to 30 years in prison. A third participant, also 21- years-old, who testified against the others, received a one-year sentence and 40 years on probation.

Another unspeakable example of violence, a young man was beaten with a baseball bat and left unconscious in a swamp. The next morning hunters found him. He died the following day in a Twin Cities hospital. The beating occurred after a group of young people had been drinking heavily. Use of a prescription drug, Vicodin, was also involved. Cass County Minnesota District Judge John Smith, in sentencing remarked, "I don't know when in our community and county we will overcome the damage [done by] alcohol and drugs... don't know what it will take for people to realize what a menace [it is] to society."

What senseless, needless tragedy—all these young lives shattered or destroyed because of the influence of alcohol and drugs. Substance abuse is a pervasive and dangerous condition on all our reservations and in our other communities as well. That substance abuse is the contributing cause is apparent in that these murders are mostly Indians killing Indians. The murders do not seem to be racially motivated. The problem is systemic, affecting not just the reservations but also the entire region.

The violence extends into the Twin Cities regularly as well as into other communities. The brutality, the increased frequency, the use of alcohol are all matters of concern for us. Our youth seem to have turned completely away from traditional values and principals.

Hopelessness is present in so many of the perpetrators. Lack of morale in the communities works against constructive action to remedy the situation. There doesn't seem to be any overall plan to deal with these increased numbers of violent crimes. There have been perhaps as many as a dozen such murders committed within the last two years. These numbers are astounding for the relatively small population that has experienced these crimes. *Press/ON* has, nearly every week, reported on such incidents.

State, federal and tribal governments are all involved in the prosecution of these cases, yet no one entity has displayed an interest in really studying the situation and providing direction for the resolution of the problem. The situation has been going on far too long and is getting worse by the day.

There is a continual lack of respect for law and order, a continual lack of respect for each other. These awful events seem to be happening much more frequently than they did in the past. It is a problem of monumental proportion. It is clear that a solution will not appear without concerted effort from all fronts. It is clear that an innovative approach is necessary before we can experience relief from this series of tragic events. It is clear that the time has come to organize a special task force, perhaps under the combined leadership of the U.S. Attorney's Office, the Governor's Office and Tribal leadership, to examine the situation and take immediate action to bring about a cessation of such wasteful, destructive crimes.

Violence and fear in the native communities.
October 31, 2003.

The recent violence of two armed assaults on a local reservation, as reported in a Federal Bureau of Investigation (FBI) press release, is shocking. The assaults are extraordinarily vicious.

The FBI press release, combined with the recently released information detailing Indian and crime statistics, shows the magnitude of the ongoing problem of violent crime in Indian country. We have seen that crime statistics throughout the country seem to be on the decline, yet continue to increase in native communities.

There has been a lot of dissatisfaction in the communities about the slow movement of justice. The people have been waiting for action that will stop the drug trafficking, and address the violent crimes that have gone unpunished.

The emphasis recently in our country has been to devote money and resources to homeland security and to fight the war on terrorism. We question this expenditure while our Indian people, on midland American reservations, live in fear of violent crime that is associated with drug traffickers.

We see joint cooperation between the various law enforcement entities. We know the Multi-Government Drug Task Force is investigating the drug operations network, the whole incidence of drug traffic, and successfully apprehending drug pushers where ever they reside. We think the community is anticipating that we will see some results from these efforts in the near future.

The native community is no doubt appreciative to see charges filed against the alleged perpetrators, but several are still at large. The community needs to become involved; those with information about drug pushers and drug-related incidents need to come forward.

It is especially disturbing according to the FBI press release that the alleged perpetrators are all individuals in their 20s; the two youngest being 22 and 20 years old respectively. All are, already at such young ages, using aliases, some using several aliases.

The multiple charges against these individuals are terribly serious; they include robbery, burglary, assault with a dangerous weapon, and assault resulting in serious bodily harm.

The account of the assault is frightening in its viciousness: "Two adult victims were... bound with duct tape and violently assaulted, [allegedly with baseball bats], and [they] were threatened with death." The lives of two young children and a teenager were also threatened.

It is horrifying to know there are individuals breaking into the people's homes, robbing and beating their victims.

There have been indictments and arrests, but the people are still afraid.

Imagine hearing a knock on your door in the night. You open the door and weapons-bearing persons burst in. It seems there is a more concerted effort being made to apprehend individuals who are involved in these terror tactics. We recognize and applaud the work of the Drug Task Force and the enhanced cooperation of law enforcement services.

Success for law enforcement and the safety of the people requires a joint effort and total commitment by all parties in order that the communities are safe places to live.

Almost any reservation town—U.SA.
November 25, 2005.

I'm recreating a sight I saw recently on a series of road trips. I see multiple, small houses, sometimes clustered, resembling a neighborhood, and sometimes sitting at the outer limits of the gathering as if they wanted greater privacy. The houses are identical in shape and size, but their colors vary from the dun of weathered wood to garish lavender, electric blue and cloudy pink.

Both front and back yards, and the commonly shared areas are cluttered with refuse--appliances, crippled sofas, kitchen chairs, garbage containers overflowing with trash, plastic bags waving in the wind, and soda bottles scattered about. The rest of the litter is pretty much unidentifiable as to the specifics, but it is still clearly garbage. There are numerous vehicles parked or just scattered about--some clearly dead, some dying, some new, and many in between.

There's the occasional horse and often you can see a dog. These animals are lonely looking creatures with beaten-down expressions.

There is little activity in the small community. Few people are afoot, the streets and yards are usually empty; doors and windows remain shut even in hot weather. The only buildings that seem well cared for are the law enforcement, health services, governmental buildings, and, maybe, a school.

A cemetery, well decorated with wreaths and flowers, is the only cheerful-looking place in the area.

In the immediate vicinity of this community there are more abandoned cars, homes and trailer-houses. They stand, listing to one side, in mute testimony to harsh use, with broken windows and doors agape. Teepee frames stand like long-lost vacant thoughts of another time.

A sad-looking convenience store with gas pumps and no paved surfaces waits for the infrequent customer. Everywhere you

82

look there is litter; it lays about the parking lot and adorns the roadsides.

As I drive along, I also ponder what I didn't see in that small community. There were no tidy yards, no trees, no shrubs, plants or flowers. There wasn't a garden anywhere. There were no fenced yards for kids and dogs. If there was playground equipment, it was dilapidated. No house had a deck, lawn furniture or a BBQ. I didn't see tricycles or bikes, fire hydrants, paved streets, ballparks, or any evidence of residents' or municipal care.

There was no business or industry. The community was set in a geographically remote area, devoid of natural resources that could be used to the advantage of the inhabitants.

Environment affects people. The residents of this very unappealing, run-down community, situated in an isolated place must be very sad people indeed.

Who are these poor souls; where is this community? The answer may surprise and will, hopefully, challenge you. They are folks who live in at least 10 different Indian reservation towns. What I described above is a true picture for the Wind River Reservation in Wyoming; for the Pine Ridge and Rosebud reservations in South Dakota; Fort Peck, Lame Deer, Rocky Boy, Crow Agency and the Salish-Kootenai in Montana; Fort Belknap and New Town in North Dakota.

The Leech Lake and Red Lake reservations in Minnesota, although similar in detail, appear almost prosperous because of their appealing lakes and woods.

I asked what it meant. What has caused this awful way of life to evolve? Why have the inhabitants of these communities fallen so low as to accept these conditions as a way of life? What should/could be done about it?

One idea that keeps coming back to me is the suspicion that land ownership is one of the contributing factors to the conditions I saw in so many places. Holding all lands as tribally owned, rather than by individuals, doesn't generate any sense of ownership. Most people are not interested in investing in or making improvements to property they can never hope to own independently.

This situation inhibits personal initiative, economic development and property appreciation.

Another thought is always 'more money needed.' And most people would accept that. I know, however, from my years of working with Indian tribes and reservation governance, that tribal communities get lots of money, both federal and state. Their own casinos pump out millions a year as well. The money never seems to produce the desired outcome, nor does it seem to be equitably or intelligently used.

There may be a third factor--psychological and physical impairment of the inhabitants.

Argument is ongoing as to which is the dominant deciding factor in human development--heredity or environment. While neither one has been declared the strongest determinant of character, there is acknowledgement that both factors influence how a person turns out.

Stories abound of people who have overcome the effects of their early environment and become successful. But there are many more stories about people who have succumbed to the devastating effects of their surroundings and remained immersed in the deepest poverty.

I wonder how any one of us, who live in comfort, would react if we found ourselves imprisoned in such a forsaken village as I have described. Wire fences or concrete walls would not be necessary to keep you captive. You would be imprisoned by poverty, by isolation, by depression, by despair.

Eventually, all thoughts of escape would disappear as every morning you got up and looked out on that terrible landscape. You would remember how little excitement is available there, how little opportunity there is for bettering yourself or improving your community.

It's overwhelming. There are no jobs, school doesn't offer much. You probably couldn't hold a job or benefit from school anyway because your health is poor. You are weak in body from poor nutrition, no exercise, debilitating habits and lifestyle choices, addictions.

You are weak in spirit because of the unrelenting presence of extreme poverty. Violence, crime, gang activity and drug and alcohol abuse further destroys spirit and community.

The money rolls into the tribal headquarters but you receive almost no benefit from it. Tribal officials manipulate the system to use the money for the benefit of themselves, their families and their friends. The needs of the people are ignored or addressed superficially. Services exist, but not in sufficiency to meet human needs. Those holding political power exploit the resources intended for services to enrich themselves.

Education is a failure for many, many reasons. Indian schools, located as they often are in remote locations and subject to the vagaries of tribal politics, are not appealing places for most teachers. Truancy is rampant and goes unaddressed. Add to that the fact that the students may be underfed, live in overcrowded homes, may be affected with chronic despair and often with disease.

Tribes have lost at least two generations of youth in part to the failure of the educational system.

Additionally, I suspect the incidence of fetal alcohol syndrome (FAS) is a major contributing factor to the failure of education for native youth and to the awful state of affairs one sees on all these reservations. It is a factor that has not received enough attention, whether from a fear of offending people or from a reluctance to actually own and acknowledge the extent of the problem.

Alcohol use by Native Americans has been a problem since the earliest encounters with Europeans. I've read stories about how alcohol, because of tribal custom, was shared equally with all members of the band including the elderly, the children, and even the babies. This early and deliberate exposure to alcohol is probably the beginning of native children being born with fetal alcohol syndrome. The problem is now endemic in many bands and tribes.

A devastating pattern evolves--unimpaired adults deliver FAS children, who in turn produce more impaired offspring until finally there is a substantial number of the community who are affected. An Indian Health Services employee told me that FAS is four generations deep on some reservations. This information is corroborated by a local pediatrician.

FAS is a condition that is not easy to identify. A person may have the syndrome and appear to be completely like every other person in the community. However, this individual may experience subtle, but serious, differences. S/he may be unable to assimilate knowledge or interact positively with family members, peers or the society as a whole. An affected individual may erupt in sudden bursts of uncontrollable rage and/or be resistant to all forms of authority. Those affected often reside in reservation communities and their condition goes undiagnosed and/or unacknowledged.

As the incidence of individuals with FAS increases, the incidence of violence on the reservations also increases. I think the high number of violent outbursts and savage beatings, sometimes involving stomping, stabbing or assaulting victims with baseball bats, are all related to the high number of mostly undiagnosed cases of FAS.

This is a very serious issue. It warrants study to find out how many tribal members are affected, what preventive and remedial programs and follow-up services might be instituted to ameliorate the situation.

86

The ultimate solution to all this despair may be the elimination of the reservation system. This suggestion is worthy of consideration.

From the beginning, the reservation system and the Bureau of Indian Affairs guardianship were imposed on unwilling subjects. It was poorly intentioned and basically immoral. When given the best spin, reservations were initially intended to be temporary. There was no intention of confining native peoples to reservations for the indefinite future. Rather, the plan was to acculturate the tribes and mesh native individuals with the rest of American society. After all, this was a nation built by many ethnically diverse groups. Native peoples would melt into Americans as other groups had done.

The feds have attempted reparations by appropriating enormous amounts of money to the tribes. These measures have done little to make amends or rebuild native communities.

Over the past 20 or more years we have repeatedly seen tribal leaders take office on promises of making needed change. But those promises never seem to be realized. It's clear the system cannot change itself.

Intermarriage is seriously diminishing blood quantum. The majority of tribal members have moved away from reservations. Most of those individuals "have made good on the outside." Those natives who remain on the reservation fall into two categories-- those who hold or benefit from tribal political office, and the majority who do not.

Under these circumstances, the current system is impotent and irrelevant. Isn't it time we thought of some other way?

Reservation drug traffic attracts coverage in the *New York Times*.
February 24, 2006.

In what is now becoming common practice, successful drug criminals from the "outside" world are joining forces with tribal members in transporting drugs in and out of reservations. Much of the commodity is used within the native community. Some of it is carried to metropolitan areas for sale

Mexican nationals are marrying Indian women and moving onto Indian reservations in order to have a safe haven within which to operate their drug rings. A combination of confusing legal jurisdictions and tribal sovereign immunity issues provides a favorable environment for illicit gangs and drug operations.

This information comes from two lengthy articles by Sarah Kershaw that appeared February 20, 2006 in the *New York Times*. One story was devoted to an innovative Mohawk drug operative who obtained his sales stock from robbing other drug dealers.

The other article discussed drug-related activities on the Red Lake, Minnesota, reservation. Kershaw tells about a criminal investigator who was fired by the Red Lake Tribal Chairman.

The investigator charged that individuals within the Red Lake Police Department hampered his efforts to expose drug dealers. He told the *New York Times* reporter that he worked his leads at night to avoid detection by tribal police. He changed cars frequently to avoid being noticed. His partner said, "We quit using our own people" because "tribal police dispatchers would 'narc us out.'"

The Tribal Chairman refuted the allegations.

It's pretty big stuff when a *New York Times* reporter is paid to devote months to the investigation of events that occur in our isolated region where only 5,000 to 6,000 people live, and a minority population at that.

The Minneapolis *Star Tribune*, picked up the *Times* articles. In the February 20 article titled, "Does Red Lake protect drug traffickers?" staff writers recounted the investigator's allegation that the Chairman wanted him to back down in investigations of the Chairman's family, relatives, and political associates in regard to the 2005 school shooting at the Red Lake high school.

The Chairman asserted he fired the investigator because he had portrayed himself as a Federal Bureau of Investigation officer (FBI).

The criminal investigator was the tribal representative on a multi-unit drug enforcement task force. The FBI, the state, three local area Indian bands, and the county were all part of the coalition. As members of a federal/state/local/tribal task force, each member is cross deputized to be able to act appropriately under any jurisdictional circumstance. The investigator was therefore authorized to say that he was working with the feds.

So the real reason for firing the investigator is still undetermined. Since he was denied any kind of appeal, the real reason for his firing will never be known.

The Tribal Chairman subsequently withdrew the Band from the law enforcement agreement, saying the arrangement "threatened the Band's sovereignty."

In a subsequent *Star Tribune* article, the Chairman called the investigator's remarks "ludicrous," and said the statement was the act of a disgruntled employee trying to influence upcoming tribal elections. The Chairman is seeking another term.

He further asserted that it was lack of funding and not "official interference" that hinders progress in the battle against drugs.

As an academic exercise, I looked back at the 2005 budget figures. The Red Lake Band received between $65 and $70 million in federal and state funds, and about $10 million in other funds. Dividing these dollars by the Red Lake population gives a per capita amount of $14,000-$16,000 annually. That's a considerable amount, and is substantially higher than the annual per capita income of $9500 for individuals living in the Red Lake communities. It seems to me that is a huge amount available to meet the needs of a community that size.

The Tribal Chairman receives about $120,000 including benefits per year. Others on his immediate staff receive salaries ranging from $65,000-$110,000 each year. Given these salary figures, it seems more like a management issue than a matter of resources.

Some time ago we published information from a study done by two university economists that indicated that violent crime increases 10 to 12 percent wherever a casino opens. Since casinos attract crime, it also seems logical that some of the income from the tribal casinos ought to be redirected to law enforcement efforts. However, casino revenues are not public knowledge.

U.S. Attorney Tom Hefflefinger said in a February *Star Tribune* article that drug activity at the Red Lake Reservation has not been prosecuted because the band does not participate in the drug enforcement task force. He said the federal task force work on the White Earth and the Leech Lake reservations has led to a series of arrests and prosecutions of drug criminals.

It is widely known that drug traffic exists on the reservations. What was perhaps unknown is the extent of the problem.

The attention focused on Indian drug trafficking by a major media organ drives home the enormity of the problem. The attention from the outside drums in the realization that we have world-class crime on our own small, hometown reservations.

Because of the issue of tribal sovereign immunity, we find ourselves powerless to do anything about it. The Red Lake Chairman uses tribal sovereignty as an excuse to stay out of a federal drug enforcement task force that has been shown to have significant success in drug-related prosecutions on other reservations.

In January 2006, yet another major national newspaper, "The *Wall Street Journal,* published a column by Fergus Bordewich, in which he discusses tribal sovereign immunity. "Tribal Sovereignty has seemed like a cure-all for the genuine wounds of the past."

He continues, "Many Indians treat the scrutiny [of tribal government or businesses] as an attack on Tribal Sovereignty, and racist, virtually by definition. Tribal ideologues claim an absolute right to self-government without 'interference' from state or federal governments, or any other outside institutions, such as the independent press. This vision of Sovereignty serves the self-interest of tribal officials and predators ... much more than it does the welfare of rank-and-file tribal members, who are the most vulnerable victims of closed-door government and official corruption."

Jurisdictional problems created by tribal sovereignty, combined with spotty federal and state interest or involvement in reservation crime, have led us to this place. The dominant culture has heretofore not cared and, in fact, tacitly approved of Indians killing Indians, or blacks victimizing blacks, so long as they did not stray across the line and threaten the dominant culture.

Our reservations are now in the grasp of a problem that is growing and killing like a large cancer. The growth is accompanied by a paralyzing, deeply felt chill of fear that sweeps through us. National attention creates the realization that the problem is of a much greater and more dangerous scope than we ever realized.

Our homelands are occupied and controlled by professional criminals and drug warlords. They are protected by a system that was intended to protect us. Just as a cancer cell turns from a functional, beneficial cell to an aberrant, out-of-control cell that destroys life, the concept of tribal sovereignty has mutated; it now threatens that which we regard as essential to human freedoms.

Radical elimination of drug trafficking and its entourage of crime, violence and death is the only possible course of action.

In order to accomplish that goal, the use of tribal sovereignty as a defense of illegal and/or unethical behavior by tribal officials must be eliminated. To do anything less assures the continued growth of the cancer that has been destroying the health of Indian communities everywhere.

About four years ago, a Red Lake school official told me that close to 75 percent of all Red Lake individuals were involved with drugs, either selling or using. If one counted family involvement, the figure goes even higher. Sadly, I learned from this source that drug sale and use had trickled down even into the elementary school. We are now reaping the result of that drug contamination.

That Indian peoples have long been victims in this country is shameful. The only thing worse is to see Indian people victimizing other Indians.

NOTE: Early in 2011, a national news source reported that jihadists were working with Mexican drug organizations in order to finance terrorist activities. When it is reported in the *New York Times* that Mexican nationals are moving into the safe havens of Indian reservations, the possibility of greater calamity in the form of terrorists joining them is undoubted.

Legal, social, personal costs of Reservation drug cases are inestimable.
July 1, 2008.

In today's lead story, "In Federal court, a harsh light is cast on ... [reservation] crack trade ...," Mike Mosedale gives a description of the final resolution of cases against 33 reservation residents on drug charges. A prominent member of the band described the story as "devastating." That is probably as apt a description of the situation as is possible.

The article tells how a 12-member jury found ... [an individual] guilty of two counts of drug-conspiracy. On one of the counts he faces a potential sentence of ten years to life in prison. He had earlier pled to a lesser charge to avoid standing trial, however when he refused to disclose his supplier, a U.S. District Court Judge ordered that he stand trial and face the consequences.

The tale of the prosecutions is one of intrigue, double-cross, wiretaps, and the misdeeds of many. The proceedings of the trial revealed that another of the defendants acted simultaneously as both an informant for the Federal Bureau of Investigation (FBI) while he was also proceeding, unrepentant and uninterrupted, in his lucrative business of drug dealing. The informant, unlike many of the others, did not use drugs. He unapologetically stated he was in the business simply for the money.

Mosedale's article points out that all the while, between the time of arrest and the pleadings, the defendants were at large, presumably also doing drug business as usual. They will remain at large until sentencing takes place sometime later this year.

Mosedale described the community's reaction to the arrests and convictions as ranging from "relief, sadness, sympathy and fear." One individual pointed out that virtually every family [on the reservation] has at least one member affiliated, involved or affected by the drug trade. Another pointed out that "[crack] has just taken over" the community.

Others despair over the "inability of the tribe to address it [the drug problem], and lastly, and most disturbingly, another comment was

"Even after this, we see dealers that haven't been touched. The trafficking still goes on."

What does this mean to individual band members and to the Indian community? What is the cost to individuals, to Indian communities, to the greater community?

First of all, it is probably incalculable in its dimension, in its effect, and in dollar amounts. The best anyone can do is to guesstimate. One of the most obvious costs is that of investigating and prosecuting the accused. Then there is the cost of incarceration. The bill for maintaining an individual prisoner is higher than the average yearly income of the majority of citizens in this area.

On the other side of the issue is the cost of the defense for these individuals. Every one of those accused of drug trafficking at the reservation received the benefit of a court appointed attorney. Bless this nation that believes that everyone is entitled to a hearing, the opportunity to face one's accuser, and to a fair and speedy trial where s/he is judged by a jury of peers. This is a wonderful precept.

But ... it is costly. Taxpayer dollars fund it all. I was not able to get an idea of what an actual day in a federal trial would cost. The Judiciary in the state of Minnesota has a $300 million annual budget, and they are operating at a deficit. This at least gives a slight indication of how much money is involved. On top of that, law enforcement costs are an entirely separate matter.

But that's just the money. What is the cost in human capitol? How do you measure the cost of unspeakable suffering, addiction, impairment, loss of autonomy, loss of personal dignity and the loss of a future to an individual?

What is the cost to a community and to the greater society? These too are incalculable. They would include such things as the welfare system, food stamps, housing assistance; the human service expenditures, like foster care placements, rehabilitation programs and facilities, unemployed and unemployable persons, medical expenses, increased crime, domestic violence, high law enforcement costs, prosecution and defense costs, and ultimately the costs of keeping a huge number of persons in prison? Those are just a smattering of the concrete costs.

They do not include the intangibles, like the debilitation of a family due to drug addictions, things like incest, domestic violence, child abuse, neglect and assault, elder abuse, decline in personal health, loss of human values, etc., etc.

It does not include the loss of potential in our children, who cannot thrive in school. Rampant low achievement is evident in high truancy rates, low-test scores and low graduation rates for reservation schools.

What kind of environment does a drug-ridden community project? What do you see on a drive through the reservation? You see shabby houses in poor repair; unkempt, cluttered yards; very few businesses; empty streets and playgrounds. You see government provided red brick buildings for schools that are largely unattended, and a hospital that mostly just hands out prescription drugs. For serious health issues, patients must go to the area hospital for treatment.

These are signs of the high cost of a drug-ridden society. Upon entering a local reservation, a person's first sight is a welcome sign. The sign claims that the Reservation preserves sovereignty, traditions and heritage. It appears to be weathered and, where the other half of a centennial banner should be, there is an open hole. This sign tells it all; it is symbolic of actual conditions at the reservation--important pieces are missing, poor conditions are evident, meaningless rhetoric is prominent.

The Tribal Chairman should be ashamed of that sign. Any leader worth anything would realize how eloquently that object speaks of the deplorable conditions that exist there. But that is the least of the things he should be ashamed of.

That brings us around to another cost associated with the drug traffic on Indian Reservations. The evidence surfaces from time to time that there's something really rotten going on there. An article in the *New York Times* a few years ago pointed heavy fingers of shame at what was going on with drug traffic on the Reservation. How the network was so large as to include affiliations with Mexican drug lords; how Mexican nationals were eager to marry tribal members in order to have a safe drug haven on the Reservation.

The *Times* article suggested that tribal police were protecting the drug traffickers. It turns out that two tribal police were included in the recent round of drug arrests and convictions. The mother of two of the defendants is a police commissioner.

That entire exposé led to nothing. The Chairman denied it. The whole matter blew over. However, these recent drug related convictions have reopened the subject. Furthermore, attention flows logically to a renewed interest in those earlier charges made by the *New York Times*.

Reason also suggests that the reservation environment is friendly to drug trafficking because elected officials protect and profit from it. This leads to another recognition--the general corruption that permeates Indian Reservations, both here and elsewhere in the U.S.

A "politics of spoils" exists wherever leaders survive based on what goodies they can distribute. These leaders remain in office because of the ongoing support of the people who receive the jobs, the favors, the "plums" that are available for being on good terms with the leader.

A headline story this morning on national television expressed outrage at the discovery of extensive vote buying in elections in one of our southern states. Yet on Indian reservations that is a common practice. It is not regarded as a tainted practice but simply accepted as matter-of-fact activity, business as usual. In fact, to the Council's shame, there is not a prohibition against vote buying on many reservations. Had there been, several chairs would not be holding office.

Another story in this issue even makes the statement that if a candidate cannot buy votes, s/he has no chance of being elected. The implication is that people only take the trouble to vote if they can collect a few dollars for it. Is there any question as to why people have given up hope when their votes, their civil rights, their jobs, their housing, even their health care are determined, not by formal eligibility standards, but by who knows who, as well as WHAT one knows about WHO one knows.

Indian communities are disabled. This fact is evidenced by the deteriorating physical conditions visible to even a casual observer. These physical signs parallel the breakdown of values that can be seen in the increased incidence of societal and domestic crime, child abuse and neglect, the violation of civil rights, and the growth of the drug trade and the accompanying harms.

There is a similar breakdown due to drug use that renders the individual incapable of normal productive activity. The recent 30-plus drug related convictions are only a drop in the bucket. I suspect that the arrests would not be sufficient to curtail the drug trade. Reservation residents have expressed the same sentiment. It's clear that drug traffic goes on. Thirty cases have been resolved but the situation has not been remedied.

In the final analysis, who pays the most for the disgraceful drug situation? It's clear the general public foots the bill for the investigation, prosecution, defense and incarceration after a successful drug bust.

It's obvious there are other significant expenses that result from drug traffic. The community in general is suffering. But the most deplorable aspect of this entire business is the fact that the children pay the greatest cost associated with the drug trade. It is their lives that are ruined. It is their little bodies that are defiled either through violence or neglect. It is their brains that are scrambled with drugs, or damaged before they were born by their mothers' consumption of alcohol. It is their lot in life to be raised by drug-crazed adults. It is their future that is sold for the short-lived pleasure of a drug hit. It is the children who lose any chance for a wholesome life and an education that will prepare them to be self-sufficient, productive, positive adults. This situation seems hopeless.

On the plus side, there were 33 arrests, and convictions. Guilty individuals will do time in jail. But the drug trade will continue unabated. The costs in human collateral and societal ills will continue to rise.

If the American public ever tunes in on the situation, gets a clear picture of what is going on, their commitment to continued support for the reservations will diminish. John and Jane Citizen will begin to question the federal government's budget of over $12 billion a year for Indian related issues. Citizens' discomfort at the high gas prices that in turn raise prices for everything else might prompt them to complain. Their complaints may even go as far as their representatives in Washington. If that happens, support for the American Indian will suffer, and the demise of the reservation system may become inevitable. From my point of view, I see little that supports its continuance.

Crime statistics don't tell the whole story.
September 15, 2008.

Here's just a smattering of quotes from headline stories that appeared in newspapers over the past several weeks. These are but a small sampling of many such articles that appear daily in papers all over the country:

"A Bureau of Indian Affairs police officer...was shot early this morning while responding to a domestic violence call on Standing Rock Sioux Indian Reservation, said United States Attorney Marty J. Jackley." (Source: *Rapid City Journal*. 9/16/08.)

"American Indians and Alaska Natives accounted for 1.3 percent of arrests in cities and urban areas in 2007, the FBI reported on Monday.

"Based on data from over 8,600 agencies, 108,271 Native Americans were arrested last year. That figure includes 16,400 juvenile arrests.

"Property crimes and liquor law violations represented nearly a quarter of all arrests among Native Americans. Drunk-driving arrests accounted for 8.5 percent.

"Compared to the general population, Native Americans are more likely to be arrested for liquor law violations, vagrancy, runaways and offenses against family and children." (Source: FBI Reports... *Indianz.Com*. 9-16-08.)

"Two [Reservation] men were sentenced yesterday in federal court...and both were ordered to register as sex offenders...
"...United States District Court Chief Judge Michael Davis sentenced D.W.C, 27, to 170 months in prison and 15 years of supervised release... According to C.'s plea agreement, he knowingly engaged in forcible sexual intercourse with a 14-year old girl within the boundaries of the Red Lake Indian Reservation...

"... U.S. District Court Judge David Doty sentenced B.D.S., 21, to 144 months in prison and lifetime supervised release on one count of abusive sexual contact with a minor... According to S.'s pleas agreement, he admitted that on March 19, 2007, he knowingly engaged in sexual conduct with a 9-year-old girl on the...Indian Reservation." (Source: United States Department of Justice, United States Attorney's Office - District of Minnesota, NEWS RELEASE. Friday, Sept. 12, 2008).

"Testimony began on Thursday in the first-degree murder trial of G.H., a Navajo student accused of killing a fellow Navajo student at University of Arizona. H. allegedly stabbed her roommate... more than 20 times. H. died in the early morning hours of September 5, 2007." (Source: "Navajo student on trial for murder in Arizona. *indianz.com*, September 12, 2008.)

"The Senate Indian Affairs Committee will hold an oversight hearing...to examine federal declinations to prosecute crimes in Indian Country... U.S. Attorneys have declined to prosecute 62 percent of crimes on reservations. The *Denver Post* reported that 58 percent of serious assaults, 76 percent of sex crimes involving adults and 72 percent of sex crimes involving children went unpunished from fiscal year 2004 through the first nine months of fiscal year 2007." (Source: "Senate hearing on Indian Country declination. *indianz.com*, September 15, 2008).

"Almost 12 percent of the deaths among American Indians and Alaska Natives are alcohol related, more than three times the percentage in the general population, a new federal report says. The report released Thursday by the federal Centers for Disease Control and Prevention found 11.7 percent of deaths among American Indians... between 2001 and 2005 were alcohol-related, compared with 3.3 percent for the U.S. as a whole. [A] CDC epidemiologist who works for the Indian Health Service, one of the study's authors, said it is the first national survey that measures American Indian deaths due to alcohol. 'It should be a *call to action* for federal, state, local and tribal governments,' he said." (Source: Mary Clare Jalonick, "Study: 12 percent of Indian deaths due to alcohol." Associated Press *Newsfinder,* August 28, 2008).

A "call to action!" Indeed. Does anyone out there in Indian country care? Does anyone DARE to surmise or speculate as to what is at the root of this litany of troubling articles? Is there anyone out there who asks the question, WHY do these things happen so routinely and HOW can these actions be reversed? WHAT can be done to slow this dangerous and tragic momentum?

Maybe this dysfunction is in part a phenomenon associated with a conquered people. Perhaps it is the most obvious and common response. But isn't it a shame we let ourselves continue to be subjugated, no longer by superior weapons or by greater numbers, but by alcohol.

Euro-white invaders introduced Native Americans to the substance, in part, to further their subjugation. By continuing to ignore the cause of our dysfunction, by continuing to be victimized, now by our own chemical dependence, we re-enact the policy of annihilation. The difference today is we are doing it to ourselves. It has not been thrust upon us from the outside.

We've been addressing the issue of Fetal Alcohol Syndrome (FAS) intermittently for almost two years now (see Appendix for list of titles and dates). I firmly believe this is the prime cause for each of the statistics reported in the above articles.

A fellow traveler along this road, Jody Crowe who is a 20-year veteran in Indian educational systems, kindly submitted for publication in *Press/ON* a wake-up-call article, originally written for an Idaho newspaper.

The article, "Are we asking the right question?" starts out with this: "If I were to tell you my dad passed away from lung cancer, what is the first question that comes to your mind? Did he smoke?

"Now, if I were to tell you a 15-year-old boy walked into an apartment in a small town in a mid-western state and gunned down another 15-year-old boy, what is the first question that comes to mind? I believe the question we should be asking is: Could this child have been exposed before he was born to alcohol?

"Are we asking the right question when violent abnormal behavior happens? Do we know the root cause of this violence? I believe we would be amazed if we knew the extent of violence and societal damage brought on by the disabilities associated with FAS."

Crowe informs his readers that FAS is not confined to Indian nations. It is a worldwide epidemic, and the numbers of affected individuals are growing.

My interest in the subject is pretty much confined to its effect on native peoples and the relationship between FAS and tribal chaos, corruption, violence and waste.

For a variety of reasons, the problems associated with FAS go unacknowledged. But that does not diminish the fact that FAS is the number one problem in Indian Country. Until this issue is addressed, until affected individuals are diagnosed, until proper intervention and services are prescribed, and until positive steps are taken to educate everyone about the effects of alcohol on the unborn, there will be no hope for a better future for Native Americans. As long as the cause remains hidden in silence, the problem will continue to occur.

I believe that the reason the subject goes unacknowledged has to do with the possibility of blame. Understandably, no one wants to admit responsibility for having harmed an unborn child. Yet it happens every day and the outcome shows up in the headlines and the trauma we read about in the newspapers. It's the explanation for family violence, sexual aberrations, failure of educational and human service programs, for wide-scale unemployment, in short, for much of the societal dysfunction at the tribal level.

We must not fall into the trap of avoidance of the problem in order to escape blame. What's been done cannot be undone. A healthy future demands that we back away from the guilt, learn from it, and resolve to change. We must earn forgiveness by facing the facts, assessing who has been harmed, and what we can do to prevent it happening again. In short, the code of silence must be eliminated. The right kinds of questions must be asked, and the obvious answers must unflinchingly be accepted.

The first step in that direction is acknowledgement of the problem. Acceptance of the situation is critical. As long as the subject is kept secret, as long as no one says anything about it out loud, it will continue to grow, fester and destroy native communities. As long as no one speaks about it, the problems of FAS will continue to be a major cause of despair and continue to be a source of tribal dysfunction and a drain on tribal coffers.

The costs of FAS to a society are huge. They manifest in large jail populations and the social and financial burdens that go with maintaining the penal and legal systems.

Treatment for the victims takes another huge toll. It's no wonder, given this scenario, that there never seems to be enough money to go around for other needs, such as health care, law enforcement, jails, facilities, services, youth and elder programs, etc.

It is a simple lesson: Alcohol kills brain cells. It is a chemical substance that does irreparable damage to a fetus. Cocaine, meth and crack are wicked and create much harm, but recovery is possible for drug babies.

Alcohol damage is irreversible, and is difficult to diagnosis. Years can go by before the damage appears in the form of unacceptable and/or uncontrollable behavior. By then it is usually too late for successful intervention*. By continuing to ignore this situation, tribes are perpetuating despair among their peoples. And, worse, they are re-soldering the chains of oppression.

* On a positive note, Researchers state that disability caused by exposure to alcohol before birth is not genetically transmittable. That means an individual with fetal damage will not pass the disability on to their offspring PROVIDED they refrain from using alcohol during the pregnancy. See: Bill Lawrence, "Some good news, recommendations regarding Fetal Alcohol Spectrum Disorder," *The Native American Press/Ojibwe News,* May 4, 2007, p.4.

See: Jody Allen Crowe, *The Fatal Link: The connection between School Shooters and the Brain Damage from Prenatal Exposure to Alcohol.* Denver, CO., Outskirts Press. 2009.

Manifest Destiny by Mark Boswell

The Ojibwe News October 26, 1988

Chapter V. Federal Indian Policy.

Declaration of Independence: "We hold these truths to be self-evident: *all men are created equal...* **The History of the present King of Great-Britain is [one] of repeated Injuries and Usurpations... He has excited domestic Insurrections amongst us, and has endeavored to bring on the inhabitants of our frontiers,** *the merciless Indian savages...*[1]

In 2009 President Barack Obama signed a Defense Appropriations Bill that included an Apology to Native Americans. The press was not allowed to be present at the signing. The apology is public law but there has been no official White House announcement or acknowledgement.

A *Wall Street Journal* article relates this information about the document: "Buried in the billions of dollars of spending on new weapons and other items in the 2010 Defense Appropriations Bill is a little noted expression of regret over how the United States had in the past used its power.

"The just approved language says, in part, that 'the United States, acting through Congress... recognizes that there have been years of official depredations, ill-conceived policies, and the breaking of covenants by the Federal Government regarding Indian tribes.

"The United States apologizes... to all Native Peoples for the many instances of violence, maltreatments, and neglect inflicted on Native Peoples by citizens of the United States [and that it is committed] to move toward a better future where all the people of this land will have reconciled as brothers and sisters, and harmonious stewards and protect the land together." [2]

The statement adds, however, that [the apology] "is not intended to support any lawsuit claims against the government (and there are plenty)."

A 2011 article, "The Quiet American Apology to Indians," in *Politics and Government,* describes a Native American reaction to the issuance of the apology. "The legacies of European conquest in the forms of United States policies such as the Dawes Act, Relocation, forced sterilization, assimilation ... forced attendance at government boarding schools ... to say nothing of outright extermination have made a lasting impact on Native peoples.

"So it stuck in our craws when last month President Obama failed, once again, to make the United States Apology to Native Americans public...

"The White House Tribal Nations Conference earlier this month would have been a great time to read this Apology before the public...

"But despite the Obama administration's work on Native issues, many in Indian country still say that a public apology is warranted and would go a long way toward healing our people and the Nation as a whole..." [3]

The questionable handling of the United States Apology to Native Peoples, and Federal Indian policy in general, has been, in Publisher Lawrence's opinion, a calamitous failure. From the beginning to the present, the Federal government has been out of step; it seems to have started out on the wrong foot in regard to Native Americans and never recovered an acceptable balance.

The evidence that supports this charge lies in the situations that are visible on many Native American reservations.

Federal Indian policy (FIP), despite ongoing comment from the fourth estate, remains remarkably impervious to suggestions for reform. Robert G. Hays, in his book, *A Race at Bay. New York Times Editorials on the "Indian problem," 1860-1900,* reports that from the mid to late 1800s, "... the *Times* saw [government policy] as misguided, inconsistent and deceitful.

"... the *Times* Editorial columns would hammer at the failures of Presidents and Congress alike to develop a rational and humane national policy toward the Indians and would attack with some vigor the corrupt public officials responsible for mismanaging the policies that did exist." [4]

Publisher Lawrence believed Federal Indian Policy was the foundation for the dysfunction in tribal government, society, families, and in all interactions. FIP has ranged from extermination, to assimilation, re-organization, termination, and finally to self-determination.

Major federal initiatives have included the 1887 Allotment Act [also known as the Dawes Act] which ostensibly would permit "individual ownership of private property ... [and encourage adoption of] habits, practices and interests of the American settler population. Furthermore, many thought that Indian people had too much land and they were eager to see Indian lands opened up for settlement [by non-Indians] as well as for railroads, mining, forestry and other industries." The unintended consequence in allowed non-native people to own land on reservations created the situation where, on many reservations, non-native people now outnumber natives. [5]

The Indian Reorganization Act (IRA) of 1934 prohibited further allotment of Indian land and returned surplus reservation lands to Indian ownership. Steve Russell, in *Sequoyah Rising, Problems in Post-Colonial Tribal Governance,* gives this explanation of the IRA: "The Indian Reorganization Act of 1934 was intended to return some self-government to the reservations, creating in most cases an elected board of directors called a tribal council to speak for what was in essence a corporate entity. Self-government under the IRA was government on colonial terms, with constitutions based not on tribal traditions [or on the U.S. Constitution] but on models 'thoughtfully' provided by the Bureau of Indian Affairs. Separation of powers, judicial review, and many other trappings of American democracy were absent... some traditional people were passionately in favor of forming IRA governments because, regardless of their structure, they would be peopled by Indians and would in that sense be a return to self-government. [6]

"... it's ratification by some tribes was procured by means that would not pass democratic muster today." [7]

Russell observed: "the Bureau of Indian Affairs employed trickery "in securing ratification of tribal constitutions under the Indian Reorganization Act, where they counted anyone who failed to cast a ballot as in favor!" [8]

The Indian Civil Rights Act (ICRA) of 1968 was expected to clarify that Native Americans should have the same rights and protections as every other American. Unfortunately, it was nullified by the action of the Supreme Court in the 1978 *Santa Clara Pueblo v. Martinez* case.

Justice Byron White, the lone dissenter on the bench, asserted that the declared purpose of the Indian Civil Rights Act was "to insure that the American Indian is afforded the broad constitutional rights secured to other Americans."

White continued, "The Court today, by denying a federal forum to Indians who allege that their rights under the ICRA have been denied by their tribes, substantially undermines the goal of the ICRA and in particular frustrates Title 1's purpose of 'protect[ing] individual Indians from arbitrary and unjust actions of tribal governments...' I believe that implicit within [the ICRA] Title 1's declaration of constitutional rights is the authorization for an individual Indian to bring a civil action in federal court against tribal officials ..."

The dissent continues "As the majority readily concedes, respondents, American Indians living on the Santa Clara reservation, are among the class for whose especial benefit this legislation was enacted. In spite of this recognition of legislative intent to provide these particular respondents with the guarantee of equal protection of the laws, the Court denies them access to the federal courts to enforce this right..." [9]

Finally, as another example of the Federal government's lack of perspicacity, the Indian Gaming Regulatory Act was passed into law with no requirement for accountability either to the federal or to state governments. Lawrence repeatedly railed against this situation and called the act "a license to steal."

One of Lawrence's goals was to bring Native Americans on reservations into the fold of America's stated democratic values. He was continually optimistic that the Bureau of Indian Affairs would be reformed, or better yet, disbanded. Many editorials, based on news stories of the times, describe limiting the power and reducing the funding and positions of that Bureau.

Multiple investigations initiated by various elements of the federal government have confirmed the situation on reservations is as described in numerous *Press/ON* editorials. A cursory review of the digital newspaper file revealed numerous references to governmental investigations into, to name a few topics, fraud, criminal activity, theft, mismanagement, election irregularities and mob influence. Editorials discussing investigations appeared in, at least, 1990, 1993, 1994, 1995, 1997, 1998, 2003, and 2004.

In 1998, in testimony before the United States Senate Select Committee on Indian Affairs, Lawrence quoted the following passage from a 1989 report by that committee:

"Since Congress has the ultimate responsibility for federal Indian policy, we in the Senate and House must accept the blame for failing to adequately oversee and reform Indian affairs." [10]

Although the investigative report admitted Congressional failings, no remedial action followed that investigation or any further investigations since. No corrective action occurred, therefore, there has been no reprieve for Natives from the misdeeds of their tribal officials. The 1989 report continued:

"Rather than becoming actively engaged in Indian issues, Congress has demonstrated an attitude of benign neglect...[By] allowing tribal officials to handle hundreds of millions in federal funds without stringent criminal laws or adequate enforcement, Congress has left the American Indian people vulnerable to corruption." [11]

The situation, although seemingly irreparable, can and must be addressed. In addition to basic reorganization of tribal governments to assure tribal members have access to the protections of the Constitution and the Bill of Rights, effective solutions can be as simple as tying federal grant funds to performance and accountability. As obvious and as sensible as this practice might be, shockingly, it is not in effect as the results of the many federal investigations have proved.

Additionally, federal and state governmental officials must begin the process of assessing exactly what is going on by speaking directly to tribal members and by-passing the "official" pronouncements of reservation councils.

It's vital that these and other reformative measures be activated. Time is running out. Tribal populations are in danger of morphing out of existence as unemployment, poverty, disease, addiction and reduction of blood quantum continue to shrink Native American population figures.

[1] The U.S. Declaration of Independence.

[2] John D. McKinnon, "U.S. Offers an Apology to Native Americans. The *Wall Street Journal*. December 22, 2009.

[3] Mary Ann Pember, "The Quiet Apology to Indians." *Politics and Government*. December 13, 2011.

[4] Robert G. Hayes, *A Race at Bay: New York Times Editorials on the "Indian Problem."* Southern Illinois Press: Carbondale, 1997, p.4.

[5] Indian Land Tenure Foundation. ww.ilt.org.

[6] Steve Russell. *Sequoyah Rising: Post-Colonial Tribal Governance.* Durham, N.C.: Academic Press. 2010, p.74.

[7] Ibid.

[8] Ibid.

[9] Justice Byron White, Dissent, "Indian Civil Rights Act of 1968."

[10] William J. Lawrence, "The American Equal Justice Act," Testimony. U.S. Senate S1691, Committee Hearing, Seattle, WN. April 7, 1998.

[11] Ibid.

White Earth people owe one to Earl Barlow and his crew.
March 12, 1993.

It is not every day that Native Americans, and in this case White Earth tribal members, have much good to say about the Bureau of Indian Affairs. But after reading through the decision of the Interior Board of Indian Affairs on their gaming management control, White Earth owes a pat on the back to Area Director Earl Barlow, his staff and the Minneapolis Field Solicitor...

Without their dedicated and combined efforts, the tribe would have been stuck with an unconscionable contract costing them millions of dollars.

It is hard to believe that the tribal government, under the auspices of the Chairman, would invest $11.7 million of their WELSA (White Earth Land Settlement Act) funds and borrow $5.5 million for a total investment of $17.3 million, and then turn around and give away such a sweetheart deal to Gaming World International (GWI).

Even based on GWI's alleged investment of $5 to $7.5 million in the casino and other facilities, there is no way one could justify a 60/40 split of net profits or a contract term of seven years.

It is hard to imagine a tribal government working harder *against* the interests of its people than the White Earth Tribal Council. The White Earth people should thank Barlow for having the guts to take a stand and for giving them a better deal.

Because of this type of activity, we believe that the Indian Gaming Act should be revisited, and that an aggressive set of regulatory rules be implemented to stop this abuse of our inherent rights. This action by the White Earth Tribal Council and Gaming World International smacks of the abuse that is occurring within the gaming industry.

Now is the time to demand accountability by all Indian organizations that are supposedly looking after the best interests of the Indian community.

Cuts in BIA and IHS long overdue.
January 28, 1994.

The recent announcement by the Clinton administration that it intends to downsize the federal bureaucracy by eliminating 252,000 jobs beginning in 1995 has been met with mixed reviews in Indian country. The only reaction that we have seen in the media is several stories carried by *Indian Country Today* about the impact of the cuts on the Bureau of Indian Affairs (BIA) and Indian Health Service (IHS).

According to the stories, both agencies will be forced to accept reductions of 12% of their work forces over a four or five-year period. This translates into about 1600 positions at BIA and 770 at IHS. Although no one likes to see jobs cut in Indian country, most realize that with the increased level of these agencies contracting the delivery of their services with tribal governments, there is bound to be unneeded positions in those bureaucracies.

In view of the level of contracting, many of us wonder how either the BIA or IHS can justify their bloated, highly paid staff at the Area and Central office levels. Thinking of this situation makes me recall what the English are reported to have said of our GI's during the Second World War. "They are overpaid, over sexed and over here."

As far as the BIA and IHS are concerned it could be said, with a certain amount of authenticity, that "these agencies are over staffed, overpaid and, over-the-hill."

Audits, investigations and studies by the Office of Management and Budget, the Senate Committee on Indian Affairs, and other governmental entities, have confirmed that these two agencies are the most badly managed, bloated, and least effective in all the federal bureaucracy.

With nearly 75% of Native people now living off reservations, it is hard to justify the current staffing levels at both of these agencies. It would be far better to see some of the savings in dollars from the projected staff cuts go directly to tribal governments.

Truth of the matter is that many Native people would like to see the IHS replaced entirely by a plastic card entitling us to obtain our health care wherever we choose. Hopefully, the new Clinton health care program will give us that option.

It is interesting to note, and maybe a sign of the times, that the announcement of staff cuts at the BIA and IHS have been met with a disquieting silence from those who normally rush to their defense. About the only reaction that we have seen is the perfunctory call from the National Congress of American Indians calling for consultation. Perhaps, it is a sign that Native people are ready to dispense with the 150 years of the paternalism of these organizations.

Washington's "Noble Savage" mentality.
December 14, 1995
(Excerpt from original version)

I had occasion last week to talk with the Department of Justice official who heads the Indian desk... when our conversation reached the White Earth and Leech Lake indictments, ... the lack of accountability and denial of our civil rights by our tribal governments, the Justice Department's true colors came out.

In effect, the official said that he, and the Justice Department, were well aware of much of the tribal corruption in Minnesota but, because of the Clinton Administration's policy of not interfering with tribal sovereignty, the Department wouldn't do anything about the lack of accountability and civil rights violations on reservations.

So essentially this means there is no interest on the part of the Administration in bringing justice to the reservations. The only thing that the Department of Justice is concerned about is violations of *federal* law by tribal officials...

Any violations of tribal or, for that matter, state law by Tribal officials will continue to go unchallenged because there are no courts in which to bring action against the offending parties. This is because tribal leaders control the courts in which actions against them would have to be brought. And of course they are always free to hide behind sovereign immunity whenever they choose.

In pondering this situation, the term "Noble Savage" came to mind. It describes the mentality of the Clinton Administration and, apparently, many members of Congress in dealing with Indian tribal governments. The term "Noble Savage" is defined as follows:

"A mythic conception of people belonging to non-European cultures

116

as having innate natural simplicity and virtue uncorrupted by European civilization."

The Indian Gaming act was authorized without any requirements for local accountability, monitoring or enforcement; without providing us with an impartial forum to uphold our tribal and

U.S. Constitutional rights; without providing us with the means to insure fair tribal elections, the U.S. government has instead provided us with half democracies and with governments of men and not law.

The only rational explanation for this situation is that the federal bureaucracy and the politicians have been listening to our tribal politicos for too long.

Washington would be wise to start listening to the voices of the people. Then they will find out tribal politicians are as corrupt as their own, and that the "Noble Savage" mentality, as currently embraced, is simply another myth. It is time Washington faces up to the truth in Indian country.

Corruption, oppression--not reporting of it--jeopardize sovereignty.

October 11, 1996.

The Native American Press/Ojibwe News was established to provide an independent voice to the Anishinabe. It was designed to be both a vehicle to inform the native community and as an instrument for individual members of the community to express their views.

That prerogative obviously extends to those like the writer of the letter to the editor* (carried on this page) who, not only disagrees with our writing but also our thinking, as they relate to the issues of tribal sovereignty and gaming.

I don't have any trouble with the writer's disagreeing with what we write, but telling us how we should think is another thing.

I also don't have any problems with employees being loyal to their employers, because I know that a weekly tribal check buys a lot, but to advance specious arguments to justify lack of accountability and denial of civil rights, is also another thing.

It is unfortunate that the writer wasn't around to attend any of the Finn and Wadena trials* last spring to see, and hear, about some of the real abusers and exploiters of tribal sovereignty.

He would have found out just how few people really benefit from tribal sovereignty, at least from the current way it is practiced. If the writer was really interested in history, instead of trying to live in the past, he wouldn't have to go back 500 years to see just how the real owners of Spirit Lake were treated by the current inhabitants.

It is also unfortunate that the letter writer wasn't around to help demonstrate for accountability in gaming funds at the National Indian Gaming Association/Minnesota Indian Gaming Association meetings in Minneapolis several years ago. Nor have we ever seen him out demonstrating for civil rights at any reservation tribal headquarters or casinos.

Perhaps the writer's most spurious point is his calling Indian journalists the modern day Indian scouts. I realize that Freedom of the Press is a difficult concept for some to deal with, but to call us Indian scouts is pure folly.

The real, modern-day Indian scouts are the lawyers, CPAs, consultants, lobbyists, P.R. reps and, of course, tribal administrators who do the bidding for tribal officials so they can continue to deny accountability and rights to tribal members.

Reservation officers, like any other elected officials, will get their proper respect and support as soon as they deserve it. Fortunately for some tribal members, their officials have already earned their respect and support. It is unfortunate that some refuse to loosen their grip on the strings of power and join them.

*NOTE: See Letters Chapter X, "Writer critical of NAP..." dated October 11, 1996.

Federal Indian policy is problem not the solution.
June 1, 2007.

Senator Byron Dorgan (D-ND) and Senator John McCain (R-AZ) this week announced the passage in the Senate of S398, Amendments to the Indian Child Protection and Family Violence Prevention Act of 1990. The bill, according to Senator Dorgan's testimony, is "virtually identical to legislation which the Senate adopted last year..." The Senator continued, "The primary goals of that Act were to reduce the incidence of child abuse, and mandate the reporting and tracking of child abuse in Indian Country."

In addition to existing law, the bill authorizes "a study to identify impediments to the reduction of child abuse... as well as require[s] data collection and annual reporting to Congress concerning child abuse."

According to a press release issued by Senator Dorgan's office, the bill "will provide treatment programs" for victims, "background checks for employees who work with Indian children," as well as "training in suicide prevention and treatment for professional staff at Indian Child Resources and Family Service Centers." The bill will also "involve FBI and Attorneys General in ... tracking of data involving incidents of child abuse."

Since many victims of child abuse attempt or succeed in suicide, the bill includes a provision for assuring that trained behavioral health professionals, particularly those who have training in suicide prevention, be on staff at Indian Child Resources and Family Service Centers.

Late last month Amnesty International (AI) published a report: "Maze of Injustice: the failure to protect Indigenous women from sexual violence in the U.S.A." The press release announcing the report says, statistically more than one in three native (meaning American Indian and Alaska Native) women will be "raped in their lifetimes." This figure is 2.5 times more than the probability of this happening to U.S. women in general.

Because of the magnitude of the problem, AI asserts that this fact amounts to more than a criminal or social issue, and that it constitutes a human rights abuse. AI contends that government figures grossly underestimate the incidence "because many women are too fearful of inaction [on the part of law enforcement officials] to report their cases." The report indicates that jurisdictional issues "allow perpetrators to rape with impunity."

A support worker for Native American survivors of sexual violence is quoted in the report, "Before asking 'what happened,' police ask: 'Was it in our jurisdiction?'"

In Oklahoma, an employee reported: "When an emergency call comes in, the sheriff will say 'but this is Indian land.' Tribal police will show up and say the reverse. Then, they just bicker and don't do the job. Many times, this is what occurs." Law enforcement, according to AI, does not regard rape as a high priority assignment.

The mother of a victim, in seeking justice after an assault on her daughter, was told her only recourse was through the FBI, located 125 miles away. When she asked questions of an agent as to what they were doing to apprehend the suspect, she was told, "This case isn't on the top of our list."

Victims are often reluctant to report the assault because they know from the experiences of other women that the assault will often not be taken as a serious issue. An episode described in the report details how a 16-year-old female from Grand Forks, North Dakota, psychologically damaged by a sexual assault, stole a car. Her sentence for this offense was greater than that given to the person who raped her.

In addition, law enforcement personnel are frequently ignorant of how to handle evidence and rape kits are frequently and, it's suggested, conveniently, mishandled or lost making it impossible for a victim of sexual assault to prove her case.

Both the Senate Bill and the Amnesty International report are important. These documents point out the problems that exist and suggest solutions. The AI report contains especially explicit information, e.g.

giving reasons why native women are at risk, stating why victims/survivors of rape don't report the assault, why victims/survivors are denied justice, and why perpetrators are not apprehended and punished.

However, in my view, the recommendations presented in these two documents are inappropriate. The efforts are laudable, but have the right questions been asked? Are they proposing the right solutions? I think not. The suggested remedies in both documents call for action at the federal level.

With all due respect, how could anyone expect to turn to the federal government for a solution when the federal government is responsible for the situation in the first place?

In the case of the Senate bill, I believe mechanisms are already in place that do what this bill is proposing.

Both the Senate bill and the AI report call for more money from a number of different agencies: health services, education, training of relevant personnel, more money for law enforcement, for solving jurisdictional problems, for new positions, for support of tribal courts, etc.

The federal government allocates many billions annually [in 2015, $20 billion] to, at most, 600,000 enrolled tribal members living on reservations. Add to that, these same 'needy' people control a gaming industry that produces, roughly, many billion a year [$29.7 billion in 2010]. How much money is it going to take?

But is that the right question? Additionally, AI would like to see the federal government boost the authority of tribal governments. This is a gross error in judgment. The problem here lies with the on-going failure of Federal Indian policy. It began in the 1700s and the tragedies that have resulted for the Indian people, as a result of these policies, are still perfectly visible today.

The outward appearance has changed since earlier time, but the effects are manifest today in modern form, and are just as devastating..

Some of the attempts by the federal government to address the "Indian problem" have been the Indian Self-Determination and Indian Education Act, and the Indian Gaming Regulatory Act.

Indians have been managing their own governmental affairs, educational systems, health services, businesses and economic development programs for over thirty years now as a result of these acts, and the results have been astonishingly ineffectual.

Reservation Indians today are further removed from self-sufficiency than they were 200 years ago. It is probably true that many Indians want to be government Indians, i.e. those who are satisfied to live on the government dole, and that is unfortunate. Proportionally, I believe there are more such persons today than there were when I was a boy. Since the enactment of the Indian Self-Determination Act (ISDA), the state of affairs on reservations has grown exponentially worse.

Self-determination has allowed tribal governments to control the courts, the police force, economic development, jobs, services, policies and procedures. Yet there is no provision for separation of powers, no checks and balances against misuse of authority.

The Tribal Council holds all powers. In third world nations this form of government is called dictatorship. In America it is referred to as "tribal sovereignty."

The concept of tribal sovereignty is inherent in all these acts. Because of this myth, despite being citizens of the United States as well as tribal members, reservation residents are consistently denied the protections and guarantees of the U.S. Constitution. Traditional guarantees, protections and liberties apply to Native Americans only when they live off reservation.

Constitutional violations are prevalent on reservations; tribes are not required to uphold individual rights; tribal officials determine what rights the people will have. Sovereignty is the number-one cause of corruption and poverty on reservations.

Dominant society erroneously thinks that supporting tribal sovereign immunity is the right thing to do. Federal officials perform the ingratiating dance of publicly acknowledging "the right" of tribal sovereignty and, at the same time, continue the paternalistic practices that have undermined legitimate law and order.

Corrupt tribal officials pay themselves and their political favorites enormous salaries. There is a terrible disparity between the income of elected officials, and their appointees, who enjoy the privilege of high position and pay based on political favoritism or family connection. Tribal members, without political power, live at subsistence or poverty level.

The problems so visible on the reservations--governmental, social and familial dysfunction, poverty, alcohol and drug abuse, lack of adequate housing and employment, oppression, hopelessness and, in general, a lack of basic necessities to meet human needs--are traceable back to federal government policy and tribal sovereignty.[1]

The litany of problems translates into the perfect formula to turn people to crime, drugs and violence in protest of the perceived, and felt inequality. Drug use and traffic, along with their partners, crime and violence, are overwhelming Indian reservations everywhere.

The number of tribal individuals affected by fetal alcohol effects is incredibly high and continues to rise. There are now, at least, three or four generations of fetal impaired individuals living on reservations. This fact contributes significantly to the over-all dysfunction of Indian communities. Ironically, the people that are trying to address these issues are turning to the government for a solution when in fact that is the source, the fountainhead, of the problems.

The effects of these two Federal acts--the Indian Self-Determination and Indian Education Act, and the Indian Gaming Regulatory Act--have been disastrous.

Since the tribes have taken control of the education system, [i.e. The Indian Education act] over 30 years ago, the situation has deteriorated visibly each decade. School attendance, test scores and graduation rates are at all-time lows. A great number of those who do receive a high school diploma receive what is essentially a worthless piece of paper stating the student has completed an "alternative" program.

Illiteracy is on the increase, children are not prepared to earn a living and become responsible, productive members of society. This is unavoidable given the fact that the numbers of special education kids, including those with fetal alcohol effects (who unfortunately remain largely undiagnosed), have increased to the point where they constitute 50-80% of the school population.

At the same time, because of poor attendance, athletics and extracurricular activities are decreasing, leading to a decline in children's health. Obesity and diabetes are the result.

The Indian Gaming Act was intended to give Indian peoples the means to create jobs and improve living standards. Part of the rationale for approving the act was the concept that jobs would increase self-sufficiency and productivity. It would produce revenue that could be used to support needed programs and services and tribes would begin to pay their own way. But that has not happened.

Tribal gaming has improved life for an elite few. For the majority of tribal members, the situation has gotten progressively worse.

The presence of a casino has been demonstrated to be a magnet for criminal activity. Crime rates in neighborhoods where a casino has opened have grown at least by 10-12 percent. Revenue from tribal gaming should be available to offset these costs. Tribes should be capable of paying the costs associated with the crime and violence that comes in the wake of a casino opening. But that is far from actuality.

There is confusion about how much is owed to the Indians and what the burden of guilt should require in restitution.

Over the many years of its existence, BIA officials and employees have built an elaborate structure to deal with the various Indian problems as they arose. The Bureau runs on the basis of self-interest by civil servants whose careers have been sustained by "Indian problems."

In a close-to-home example of BIA behavior, over 600 lawful petitioners at Leech Lake, after being denied due process by their Tribal

125

Council, submitted their case to the BIA for an opinion. More than 18 months passed and the BIA had yet to answer. [See "Wrongful Termination suit: Another test of the rule of law at Leech Lake, *The Native American Press...* December 3, 2004.]

The Indian Health Service (IHS) is culpable as well. Both agencies use inflated numbers to justify their budgets and the number of jobs authorized to each. They include Indians who live near reservations as well as actual reservation residents. This practice creates a fiction as to the monetary need of the number of individuals eligible for services.

Although fewer than 600,000 Indians live on America's reservations, the BIA and IHS reported to Congress that they had service populations of 1.5 million and 1.6 million respectively for their fiscal-year budget justifications.

Our two starting points for this commentary, S398 and the Amnesty International report are correct in one fundamental way: Congress must be forced to do something. Unfortunately, the solution to the problems they expose does not lie in business-as-usual processes. The answer lies in radically changing present policy.

Many Indians, including myself, believe the reservation system is beyond salvage. Most Native Americans do not want to be wards of the government, aka government Indians. They have demonstrated this fact by going away to school and to decent jobs. The failed principles and policies of the feds are responsible in large part for the deplorable conditions that AI and the U.S. Senate are hoping to address. To turn to the federal government for solutions, however, is simply a ridiculous premise.

Timothy Williams wrote several articles in the *New York Times* in 2012, 2013, detailing on-going child abuse in North Dakota. Two examples: "Child abuse at Reservation is Topic for Three Lawmakers," February 15, 2013 and "Officials see Child Welfare Dangers on a North Dakota Indian Reservation." July 7, 2012.

Wikipedia.com "Among all ethnic groups…the American Indians have the … highest rate of infant mortality… Domestic violence, rape, child abuse and child neglect are reported to take place very often on the reservation…"

Strickland, Patrick. "Life on the Pine Ridge Native American Reservation… a quarter of children are born with fetal alcohol syndrome… Many Pine Ridge residents say that they have been forgotten by mainstream society, abandoned by politicians and neglected by state institutions."
Aljazeers.com.

The Justice System in Indian Country needs new strategies.
December 1, 2007.

"A nongovernmental study of the Indian Bureau undertaken at the request of the Secretary of the Interior ... examined the administration of Indian policy and its impact on Indian life. It described the poverty, disease, suffering, and discontent that pervaded the life of the overwhelming majority of Indians.

"It also criticized the inefficient, paternalistic administration of Indian policy that neither encouraged nor supported Indian self-sufficiency. Positive recommendations stressed the need for comprehensive educational programs designed to meet the problems of reservation life, for systematic economic planning and development, and for more efficient and better-paid personnel. Encouragement [for] ... strengthening of community life, elimination of confusion concerning law and order on the reservations and the settlement of outstanding legal claims were all advised."

"... a task force of Indian matters," within the Department of Justice (DOJ) "found that law enforcement on most reservations is in serious trouble."

This task force stated the following reasons for reservation crime: "a confusing jurisdictional structure, inadequate funding of tribal justice systems, inadequate training of tribal and federal police, and a lack of coordination between and within government law enforcement agencies responsible for reservation crimes."

Current quotes? No. The non-governmental report was the Meriam Report, published in 1928. The second quote is dated 1975.

The conditions mentioned in the Meriam Report of 1928 are unchanged for nearly 80 years since publication. Poverty, despair, unemployment, lack of adequate housing, lack of services, an educational system that is not working, all of this seems to be unchanged.

The 1928 description could just as aptly be a 2018 description of affairs on Indian reservations but for two additional details. Reservations today are also afflicted with huge alcohol/drug use and dependency rates, and the presence of Indian casinos has increased both the crime rate and the incidence of crime.

Not much has changed for the better since then. The federal government, for a variety of reasons, has created a mishmash of tribal governance. The core problems must be resolved before the symptomatic issues can begin to be solved.

Indians are citizens of the United States as well as tribal members. They are presumed to have the protections of the federal government passed on to them by their tribal governments. However, since tribal governments have been allowed to create fiefdoms on reservations, ordinary tribal members do not enjoy the protections and guarantees that they are entitled to as U.S. citizens.

Although several acts of Congress require it, tribal governments are not organized in the traditional three-branch system. Tribal councils act as policy-makers, administrators and judges. Tribal court judges are hired and sit 'at the pleasure' of the council. Obviously, with the councils having the power to run the courts, there is little expectation that justice will be the outcome.

Acts by the council are not reviewed by or subject to any other authority. The end result is dictatorship. With no accountability, there is no evidence for removal of corrupt officials.

There is voluminous evidence of graft and fraud in governmental building projects and economic development programs on local reservations. Activities like bid rigging, false billing, kickbacks, collusion between tribal officials and contractors, and unresolved discrepancies in federal reports on construction grants are the norm.

Voting irregularities and campaign law violations are rampant. Campaigning officials buy votes. This practice is not regarded as a problem. In a recent series of elections, a voter turned over a check signed by a candidate, given to him in exchange for his vote. Although this, and other incidents, were made public there was no legal action against the offenders.

An Election Board ordered a new election when evidence of wrongdoing surfaced. The incoming Chairman ignored the Board's decision and took office despite formal charges of campaign misconduct.

The majority of tribal members live a life of hopelessness. Their poverty contrasts vividly with the conspicuous income of their elected officials. They are denied the basic rights other Americans enjoy by virtue of citizenship. Housing and services are apportioned to secure political support. Employment is awarded on the basis of political expediency rather than on the basis of need or merit.

Tribal governments control all assets. Economic development is exclusively an in-house entity. Without the rule of law, no outside businesses will invest in a reservation site; hence, no new dollars and no new job possibilities outside the tribal enterprises.

Alcohol and drug use are the predictable refuge of people who live in these conditions. Drug trafficking is rampant and is responsible for most of the violence and the high crime rates.

Alcohol-related statistics are incredible. Eighty percent of all crimes involve alcohol. Native Americans have an alcoholism rate 627 times higher than the national average. If you are Native American, you are 770 times more likely to die of alcoholism than is anyone in any other culture.

Sad as the situation is, it is made worse by the fact that the incidence of Fetal Alcohol Syndrome, reputed to be four generations deep in some families, remains unacknowledged and unrelieved. Tribal, local and state school officials are in denial about the problem. Yet everyone seems to be aware of the increasing numbers of alternative schools and kids with serious behavioral issues.

In general, Indian kids have the lowest test scores and graduation rates. They have the highest dropout rates and truancy rates. All this despite the fact that many Indian school districts enjoy substantially higher than average per pupil payments.

Casinos were intended to provide economic opportunity in the form of jobs and new wealth. Because there has been a glaring lack of regulation and no consistent, systematic scrutiny, the presence of a casino allows for indiscriminate stealing. It's a common story that tribal officials walk into the vaults and walk out with fistfuls of money.

Financial audits are withheld from tribal members. No one knows how much money is being taken in or how much is legitimately spent.

Few Indian members hold jobs at Indian casinos. Almost no management-level jobs go to tribal members. Officials argue that native peoples do not want the jobs or do not perform satisfactorily.

Dollars from tribal casinos buy influence for tribal leaders from mainstream officials. Indian contributions to political campaigns add-up to astonishing amounts. These dollars buy political favor that enable tribes to avoid tighter regulation, oversight and scrutiny.

What can be done about this situation? The answer to this question has successfully evaded identification for a very long time.

Possibilities include: Field hearings, by both Congressional chambers, would be useful, especially if they took on the task of examining the leadership of every single tribal council that has a license to gamble or does business in any way with the federal government.

Great numbers of ordinary tribal members should be brought in at government expense to testify. Their anonymity assured, they would no doubt give ample evidence of the wrongdoing that goes on.

The federal government should continue to make grants but tie the requirements and the award of money to obtaining information that gives a clear picture of what is really going on. Create a mechanism (maybe a simple questionnaire available online) wherein members could tell what they know about tribal governance and what it contributes to the health (or detriment) of the general society.

Another option would be to require tribal governments to provide full disclose, by way of outside independent audits, of their true financial situation. Require that tribes master and use standard accounting and standard business practices. Enforce the Single Audit Act.

Require open meetings, open records, and proof that this is happening. Make unadvertised local visits a necessary part of the award process. Have reviewers talk with a substantial number of randomly selected, ordinary members. Find out about election and campaign practices. Ask about civil rights protections/violations.

All of this information should be included as substantiation of a tribe's fitness and eligibility to receive grants from the federal government. Do not make the award until the requested information is complete.

Do not make future awards if there is not perceivable progress toward improving the social climate on reservations. The U.S. government does not provide financial aid to countries where human rights violations occur. Aid to Indian tribes should also be made subject to the same rule.

The federal government has consistently looked the other way. It has refused to see what is happening to ordinary members on Indian reservations.

Minnesota Chippewa Tribe Swearing-in Ritual
By Wagosh minawa Migizi, Leech Lake Rez

Chapter VI: Introduction: Tribal Sovereignty.

The following paragraphs are from an editorial Publisher Lawrence wrote subsequent to his appearance before the United States Senate Committee on Indian Affairs field hearing in Seattle, Washington in April 1998. Lawrence appeared in support of Senator Slade Gorton's proposed American Equal Justice Act, S1691. [1, 2.]

"There is no rational basis on which to justify the present way tribal sovereign immunity is being utilized. It is not in the Constitution; it is not in any treaty; it is not in any law; it is merely a figment of the imagination of a few judges and politicians afflicted with the 'noble savage' mentality.

"Tribal sovereign immunity is killing the Indian people. Just look at the reservation homicide and suicide rates if you don't believe me. Tribal sovereign immunity is like giving tribal leaders 'a license to steal.' Why else do they have to conduct our financial affairs in secret and deny us access to our tribal financial statements?

"Indian tribal governments should be compelled to conduct our affairs within the law and insure themselves against negligence like any other government. This action would take care of most of the potential lawsuits that they claim they would face without sovereign immunity.

"Tribal sovereign immunity has created a culture of corruption, unaccountability and oppression on most Indian reservations. It causes despair and discord. It creates divisiveness and hostility among people and communities.

"Tribal sovereign immunity is destroying anything that yet remains of Indian culture and tradition. It has placed a small segment of the native community above the law, which results in a lack of respect for the law on most reservations. Tribal sovereign immunity causes favoritism, nepotism and mismanagement on most reservations. Tribal sovereign immunity takes away rights ... from Indian people that we're entitled to as U.S. citizens. Tribal sovereign immunity has caused living conditions on most reservations to deteriorate.

"Despite the present effort by the tribal establishment to maintain the status quo of tribal sovereign immunity, the effort to change it by Indian people and others is growing. The myth of tribal sovereign immunity is evident when you consider that Indian people do not even own their reservation lands, must serve in the military in time of war, pay federal income tax, conduct gambling operations according to federal law and state compacts, and are subject to the criminal laws of the U.S. and/or of their respective states.

"Corruption is so imbedded and pervasive in some Indian communities, and those in control have so much influence over the election and court functions, that only major legislation ... will eradicate it."

*   *   *

Minnesota Appellate Judge R.A. "Jim" Randall also testified at the 1998 Senate Indian Affairs Committee.[3] He shared Bill Lawrence's belief that tribal sovereign immunity was a damaging concept.

Judge Randall's testimony: "Under the pretense of 'sovereignty,' we deny Indians living on reservations the most basic right given all other Americans, the right to own land and the rights, privileges, and obligations of state constitutions and the federal constitution."

He addressed the concerns both of the Indian Community on the basic concept of sovereignty and also the issues that the unregulated practice of tribal sovereignty raises. His solution to the conundrum is conversion of tribal governments into municipalities. His testimony follows:

Testimony: Before the U.S. Senate Committee on Indian Affairs, Field Hearing, Seattle, Washington, March 11, 1998. (Excerpt.)

"I came here today ... to talk about why this presently held view of sovereignty with the inherent tribal immunity from suit has been turned on its head and deprives the people living within a reservation's boundaries, whether Indian or non-Indian, of the most precious rights possible, the benefits of State constitutions and the U.S. Constitution and the Bill of Rights.

"What is happening on reservations today has become a form of an autocratic collective. All of the power goes to the tribal council and the individual rights have been submerged.

"There is only a ... fragment of people still living within reservation boundaries. Once they leave a reservation, they are entitled to all the benefits of the state constitutions ... and the U.S. Constitution. Once they go back inside [the reservation], those rights disappear.

"Things that Indian tribes need to protect their right to develop as any other city, town or unit of local government are in place already under the State and Federal Constitutions, if you choose to use them. There is a limited form of immunity for cities, towns, counties and school districts. They are administered by the State Legislature in proper legislative forums...

"If you organized the reservations like all other cities and towns in the State [i.e. as municipalities], ... tribes would have this limited immunity, they would have a complete absence of taxation on municipal buildings." ... [and all other rights and responsibilities inherent in governmental entities].

"So the present form of government has been sufficient for all of us in this country, including all Indian people living off a reservation... You have to understand the following.

"On any piece of reservation or trust land, there is no guarantee the State constitution, the United States Constitution and its precious Bill of Rights ... control. There are no guarantees [as provided by the various acts of Congress] ... no freedom of the press and no freedom of speech...

"It is ironic that every time an American Indian sets one foot off the reservations, he is now guaranteed the benefits of that state

136

constitution of which he is a citizen, The United States Constitution and the Bill of rights..."

In regard to the validity of true sovereignty for Indian tribes, Randall said, "The very fact that Congress has the power to eliminate tribal immunity ... shows [Indians] are under the plenary power of Congress, as all of us are. They are not independent entities."

Judge Randall, in his concurrence in the *Granite Valley vs. Jackpot Junction* case, elaborated on the possibility of the Minnesota Legislature's transforming reservation entities into semi-sovereign municipalities. He asserted counties, towns, school districts, etc. are "semi-sovereign entities with some limited ... immunity from law suits" and, as semi-sovereign units of government have "carefully structured limited ... immunity to make certain discretionary decisions without fear of being sued."

He further believes that as semi-sovereign entities, tribes "should have a right to this [limited immunity], once their organizations, as law-abiding municipalities, subject to state law ... are in place." He states further, "This is the only way to give Indian people half a chance to make it in the 21st century.

"... the only true freedom for Indian people will be when the federal government and the federal courts require state legislatures and state courts to take over the regulation of Indian reservations, just like states regulate all towns and cities within their borders.

"State legislatures and state courts today are required to regulate the lives of the 98 percent of the citizens of America who do not live on Indian reservations."

If this reorganization should happen, he believes it would halt the exodus of natives from reservations to avoid the vagaries of tribal politics and the nepotism and non-accountability of tribal governments.

Judge Randall continues: "Tribal governments have to be allowed to organize under Minnesota laws pertaining to municipalities. Without that ability, reservation residents can never be guaranteed constitutional governments, fairly elected tribal officials, and a fair share of gaming proceeds."

The Concurrence continues, "the changeover, from unregulated reservations to Minnesota towns and municipalities, will cause no damage whatsoever to the right of tribal government to continue to make the decisions necessary to serve their residents."

Randall further states, "When they become municipalities, Indian reservations, like all Minnesota towns, will enjoy the same rights, privileges, and obligations as do every other governmental entity in this state. But for now they stand out as a glaring exception to the maxim that no person or entity is above the law."

1. William J. Lawrence, "Indian country needs the American Equal Justice Act, and fast." April 27, 1998. p.4

2. It is unfortunate but few people, who share the opinions of Lawrence and Randall about tribal sovereign immunity, have the means or the opportunity to travel to appear before a Congressional committee. This situation contrasts greatly with tribal and other governmental officials who appear in great numbers at such hearings, and are subsidized for their time and reimbursed for their travel expenses. Lawrence, Randall and others paid their own expenses.

3. Judge R. A. "Jim Randall, Concurrence State of Minnesota in Court of Appeals, Granite Valley Hotel vs. Jackpot Junction Bingo and Casino, Feb 11, 1997, p.10.

Tribes' abuse of sovereignty will kill the goose that laid the golden egg.
November 5, 1993.

Minneapolis *Star Tribune* columnist Jim Klobuchar is right on target in his column titled, "It's time casinos stop using 'tribal sovereignty' as a shield," which was published in the November 2, 1993, edition of the *Star Tribune* and reprinted, with permission, in this edition of *Press/ON*.

It is a well-settled point of Indian law that tribal governments possess certain attributes of sovereignty over their membership and reservation lands in conducting their governmental affairs. However, it becomes a legal no man's land when non-Indians and commercial ventures of tribal governments come into play. Since members of tribal government often appoint themselves to sit on boards of directors for their enterprises, and put on their corporation caps when conducting commercial enterprise business such as casinos, they make a mockery of their sovereign immunity. That is why their attempts to hide behind sovereignty in their commercial dealings are ridiculous.

In addition, it is just plain bad business. There is no surer and quicker way to scare away the public, both as workers and patrons, than hiding behind sovereignty when it comes to managing people, providing employee benefits, safe working conditions and liability insurance coverage for injuries and negligent acts of casino workers.

Besides, not being hospitable and protecting friends and guests from harm has never been the Indian way, or at least it wasn't until the advent of the reservation casino.

If this is what the highly paid attorneys, consultants, lobbyists, advertising agencies, public relations firms and others are telling them to do, it is just plain bad advice. There is no better way to kill the goose that laid the golden egg than to hide business responsibility behind the facade of tribal sovereignty.

139

It is time that tribal governments accept responsibility for their actions or inactions by taking ownership of the problems on their reservations instead of blaming someone else or hiding behind sovereignty. If they are to operate multi-million dollar businesses, then they ought to be held to the same standards as any other business operation. It is bad enough that some tribal governments have to hide their mismanagement and misuse of our funds from us behind the facade of sovereignty.

It is too bad that this state doesn't have a politician who will stand up and be counted when it comes to bringing the Bill of Rights to reservation Indians and making our tribal governments accountable to us, enrolled members of the various Minnesota Indian communities and tribes.

Red Lake Tribal Council releases 1994 tribal budget:

The Red Lake Tribal Council's publication of their 1994 tribal budget is a step in the right direction for accountability on the Reservation. Now all we need is for them to release audited financial statements for all tribal operations, including gambling and release their grip on the Red Lake Tribal Court.

Mystic Lake's CEO's conduct could prove to be the arrow that pierces the veil of tribal sovereign immunity.
April 21, 1995.

For about 20 years now tribal councils have been routinely hiding behind sovereignty in denying tribal members their civil rights...

Last week the Shakopee Mdewakanton Sioux community leadership hid behind it [*Cohen v. Little Six*] in denying an elder who fell off a chair at their Mystic Lake casino her day in court [Sylvia Cohen, age 84]. Now that same Sioux community is trying to use sovereignty to hide the brutal misconduct of a female employee by their former chairman and Mystic Lake CEO.

Just how far will the Congress, the courts and the public go in allowing the casinos and, in some cases, the tribes, to hide behind this myth of sovereignty. No one seriously questions that tribal governments, like the state and federal governments, enjoy certain immunities as governmental entities.

However, as far as tribal governments are concerned, these immunities are permitted to extend to nearly everything they do, including violating their own constitutions as well as the U.S. Constitution. This is so because Congress has abdicated responsibility by not amending the Indian Civil Rights Act of 1968 to give federal courts jurisdiction over civil rights violations on Indian reservations, or to require tribes to waive their immunity under the Indian Gaming Regulatory Act if they go into gaming.

This may sound anti-gaming ... but if gaming is to continue as an economic tool for the tribes, they must live up to the responsibilities of being good business people and neighbors.

In reality, this shouldn't be such a big deal because many tribes throughout the country are currently honoring their members' civil rights and living up to all their responsibilities in running their casinos. It is only the greedy, and those with much to hide in managing their casinos or denying their members their civil rights, that resist living up to their responsibilities.

It is doubtful that the Minnesota Court of Appeals will strike down the Shakopee Mdewakanton's exertion of the defense of sovereign immunity in the case involving the CEO. No matter how blatant the misuse of the defense of sovereign immunity, Minnesota courts have traditionally turned their backs.

The important thing about this case is that it focuses public attention on this issue when Congress is looking at amending the Indian Gaming Act. In addition, the plaintiff has indicated that she intends to pursue the suit all the way to the U. S. Supreme Court if necessary. With all this happening, it is likely that tribal sovereign immunity will undergo some badly needed changes.

It is time the Roman idea of imperium (dominion), Pope Gregory VII attempting to legislate from the Vatican, and the divine rule of 800 years of European monarchs be put to rest. We can do without the types who think they are our monarchs running our reservations.

Congress can't see forest of civil rights for trees of sovereign immunity.
August 22, 1997.

It's disturbing to read in the media that three very prominent U.S. Senators on the Indian Affairs Committee ... express extreme concern when tribal sovereign immunity is threatened, but apparently don't care that tribal governments continue to deny Indian people the basic protections and liberties guaranteed in the Bill of Rights.

The latest hubbub is in response to Senator Slade Gorton's amendment that tribes waive sovereign immunity if they accept federal money. (The American Equal Justice Act, S1691, April 1998). Apparently it's okay by the senators if our elected tribal officials steal our money, deny our rights, hold office illegally, subject our reservations to rampant corruption, discord and violence, and mismanage our resources to the point that many reservations are almost completely dysfunctional. These issues don't seem to be important enough to get noticed by the three good senators.

It is about time they, and other members of Congress, look beyond the propaganda that the Tribal Establishment hauls to Washington every time someone so much as looks cross-eyed at tribal governments.

It's time Congress looked behind the charade of "Potemkin Village," and saw how few Indian people are really benefiting from sovereign immunity. Currently tribal officials claim "sovereign immunity" whenever they are challenged.

If the senators bothered to look, they would see that 80% of Indian people don't, or won't, live on reservations because of the dismal conditions there, and nearly half of those currently living on reservations are not even Indian.

The knee-jerk reaction of the Indian Establishment that damage awards from lawsuits would bankrupt tribes is pure bunk. First of all, most lawsuits brought by tribal members against tribal governments are for "declaratory relief" only, trying to get recognition of basic civil rights, and are not for monetary relief at all.

143

Secondly tribes, like any other responsible business owners, can buy liability insurance to protect themselves from lawsuits resulting from injuries and accidents. In cases involving tribal wrong-doing and violations of the law, which liability insurance does not cover, tribes should be held responsible for their acts or omissions.

It is time for Congress to ask where all the federal dollars, in addition to the new "buffalo chips" [casino revenues], are going, and just who is really benefiting?

Tribal casinos are proving to be the savior of Indian people, but not in the way initially claimed. Because of the extreme abuses against workers and customers at tribal casinos, the longtime abuses by tribal governments against their own people are coming to light, for those who care to notice.

It is time for ACCOUNTABILITY in INDIAN COUNTRY, and Senator Gorton's amendment is a good place to start. The hearings next month on Gorton's amendment will undoubtedly bring out the Tribal Establishment with all of its money, all of its cronies, and all of its blather about tribal culture. It's only too bad they couldn't have seen the "forest for the trees" and done something voluntarily to limit ...sovereign immunity. For example by creating tribal courts that are separate from the authority of tribal councils, and allowing due process, before tribal sovereign immunity goes the way of other outdated concepts that have outlived their usefulness.

Unfortunately, Congress is no better than the tribes in not seeing the "forest for the trees," judging by their inaction on the issue and their relegating the matter to the courts.

Note: The U.S. Supreme Court may soon force Congress' hand. See Gavle, Cohen, Matsch, and many other pending cases for where the front lines of the tribal sovereignty issue really are.

Giving tribal sovereign immunity a run for its money,
April 24, 1998.

Tribal sovereign immunity is on its way out. You can feel it in the air--which means Indian people will start having more rights over their tribal governments.

Minnesota Public Radio (MPR) could only find three out-of-state tribal enrollees to speak in defense of tribal sovereign immunity in a recent broadcast. All of whom draw big salaries or contract fees from tribal governments, but none of them hold elected office. Why is it that to represent us?

They, along with their hired army ... led by public relations firms, are part of the "Tribal Establishment" that is standing in the way of Indian rights. They are the ones benefiting from tribal sovereign immunity, whereas the vast majority of Indian people get only fewer rights than they would otherwise have, and less accounting than they would otherwise get, that would show where all their money is going...

Tribal Sovereignty and the NCAI.

I can't help but laugh out loud at the goofy survey sponsored by the National Congress of American Indians (NCAI) recently. It's all very funny until I consider that the money could be better spent for the real needs of Indian people.

Here's the question, supposedly about tribal sovereignty, posed in the NCAI survey: "Should Native American tribal governments have the freedom to improve the social and economic conditions of their people as they see fit?"

Of course, most people (81%) would agree with that statement.

But NCAI then makes the leap that those 81% therefore support tribal sovereignty and, by implication, tribal sovereign immunity.

If only NCAI would tell their member tribal governments that if they would conduct their affairs within the law, live up to the terms of their contracts and agreements, and buy liability insurance, they wouldn't have to fear the coming tide of change that will strip away the anachronism of tribal sovereign immunity.

145

Maybe we should commission a survey too. One that would ask, "Should tribal governments be able to deny Indian and non-Indian American citizens their basic Constitutional protections?" and "Should tribal governments and businesses, such as casinos, be held to the same standards of responsibility for misconduct as other governments and businesses in this country?" That would get at the heart of the issue.

Just like Black Americans said in the 1960's, "We have had enough," Indian people today, along with non-Indian people who are aggrieved by the unjust policy of tribal sovereign immunity, will not rest until the abusiveness in tribal governments is stopped.

Tribal sovereign immunity begets unaccountability. Unaccountability begets corruption. And together unaccountability and corruption beget poverty, lack of respect for the rule of law, despair, discord, disunity, and violence.

Future bright for Indian people on reservations, only if tribal sovereign immunity limited.
January 7, 2000.

As we in Indian country enter the new millennium along with the rest of society, it is hard to imagine an event occurring in the next thousand years as momentous as the coming of the Europeans in the previous. Without getting into the pros and cons of the major event of the last millennium, suffice it to say, we are now better off because Europeans came here. With all the amenities of modern life, brought to us by the technologies of European culture, few of us would really want to go back to the over-idealized days when Indians were the only ones on this continent. It was no Garden of Eden, no Golden era.

One thing that appears to be carrying over from the old millennium to the new is politically correct white people telling us who our leaders and heroes should be. For example, the *Star Tribune* selected several Native Americans in their list of "Most Notable Minnesotans of the Last Century," many of whom had no business being on such a list. Some are criminal, violent, abusive, incompetent, or simply have not done anything noteworthy enough to cause them to make the cut.

The *Star Tribune* apparently just wanted to increase ethnic diversity on their list, which I consider a racist approach. The *St. Paul Pioneer* in its January 3 edition carried guest columns by Indian writer Tim Giago and the Mille Lacs Band of Ojibwe Chief Executive [see page 4 of this issue for excerpted versions of their columns.]

Giago's column, titled "Indians aren't eager to join a club that long excluded them," tries to explain why Indian people supposedly want to stay on reservations. He conveniently neglected to mention that over 80% of us, nationwide, have already left the reservations and, for good reason, don't ever intend to go back. Those circumstances are primarily the result of a lack of

147

accountability in tribal governments, abuse of power and no civil rights for individuals. Because sovereign immunity makes it nearly impossible to hold tribal officials accountable in a court of law, they become above the law. The result is corruption and abuse, which fosters crime, and a general disrespect for the law and for each other, which only intensifies all the social and cultural problems on reservations. While crime rates are in decline all over the country, they continue to soar on reservations.

Giago also didn't mention while he was touting how much Indian people are attached to the land, he sits in his nice, safe residence in Rapid City, South Dakota, enjoying the security and benefits of off-reservation life.

The Mille Lacs executive, in her column titled "Future bright for Indian youths despite lingering economic threats," also seems to get amnesia when it comes to current conditions at the reservation. The future can't be too bright for the youth at Mille Lacs when fully half of the children entering the reservation school system are affected with Fetal Alcohol Syndrome, that student test scores and drop-out rates are among the worst in the state. The reservation school did not graduate a single student last year. Youth gangs and violence are a rampant problem.

The persistent question of who really is in charge at Mille Lacs is big among tribal members and observers. If things were so good at Mille Lacs, why does the majority of tribal membership choose to live off the reservation?

To quote a saying of the most recent decade, the *Star Tribune* and *Pioneer Press* "just don't get it."

In my eleven and a half years publishing this newspapers, or "rag" as some of my detractors call it, I have changed my thinking of what needs to be done if reservations are to ever become good places to live. I used to think that by changing a few names on tribal councils we could bring some accountability and civil rights to reservations. Now I have come to the conclusion that changing the individuals in power makes no difference when the system itself remains the same.

New tribal council members quickly get accustomed to their unencumbered power, and the accompanying largess, and forget why they ever wanted accountability in tribal government. I have come to the conclusion that tribal sovereign immunity is the single biggest contributor to corruption, abuse and oppression of Indian people on America's Indian reservations.

Perhaps our May 7, 1999 "Quote of the Week" says it most eloquently. Czechoslovakian President Vaclav Havel said in a speech to the Parliament in Ottawa, Canada, on April 29, 1999: "Human rights rank above the rights of ... [government]. Human liberties constitute a higher value than ... sovereignty."

Incidentally President Havel lived most of his life in a country "where the principles of sovereignty and nonintervention were often invoked to shield a ... tyranny from outside criticism." Sounds like an American Indian reservation to me. May the next thousand years be better than the last.

State needs to develop clear policy for review of tribal court decisions.
March 16, 2001.

Twenty-nine years ago, I published an article in the *North Dakota Law Review* entitled "Tribal Injustice, the Red Lake Court of Indian Offenses." In that article, I detailed serious civil rights problems at the Red Lake Reservation, as well as other misuses of the tribal courts by the politically powerful on the reservation.

These problems, and other civil rights abuses, were investigated and confirmed by the United States Civil Rights Commission more than ten years ago. And nothing, or little, has been done. It is disturbing to have to report yet another incident of the Red Lake Tribal Court being misused by special interests on the Red Lake reservation.

It is more disturbing that the State Courts are accepting judgments and orders from the Red Lake Tribal Court without doing a critical analysis of the facts--particularly in ex parte proceedings.

As is detailed in the page one article, "Illegal Process: Red Lake Courts [and] State Legal System Fail Young Mother and Daughter," the young woman was denied custody of her daughter by the Red Lake tribal court after she had been awarded custody by a state court. She was then subjected to a tribal order which, in effect, barred her from Red Lake reservation.

It is even more disturbing that the whole judicial system not only failed the young mother, but actually worked against her, and rewarded those who had exploited tribal injustices for their own benefit.

Under current Minnesota law, state courts have the discretion to recognize orders of tribal courts and to enforce them. Minnesota state courts also have the discretion not to recognize an Indian tribal court decision. It is clear that in this case, the discretion of the State was abused.

It is time that definite policies be issued by the State of Minnesota Supreme Court promulgating minimum standards which tribal court decisions must meet in order to be recognized. In less than three years, *Press/ON* has reported at least six instances of nonmembers being

150

removed from the Red Lake reservation in conjunction with tribal court hearings, including people being removed right out of the courtroom by Red Lake law enforcement officers.

Without constitutionally structured separation of powers, the tribal courts are subject to abuse. The State of Minnesota should require that the burden be on tribal courts to prove that they afforded due process, and that they had jurisdiction. Something needs to be done to change the whole process of "recognizing" tribal court decisions.

The tribal courts are getting worse, instead of better. State of Minnesota Judges, County Attorneys and Public Defenders should be required to have training from lawyers and individuals familiar with both sides of the issue.

Financial chaos at Red Lake even worse than expected.

Press/ON has obtained Red Lake tribal council financial information, which we are currently in the process of reviewing. According to the documents that we have obtained, the tribal council overspent its fiscal year 2000 budget by $2,864,139. Most of the overspending was for unplanned development projects and salaries. They had to draw most of the money to cover the shortfall out of trust funds.

Now, they want us to accept the risk of their spending another $27 million dollars to expand the River Road Casino, including the water park. In addition, they want us to now go along with their spending another $8 million dollars for a new casino on the south boundary of the Red Lake reservation, when in fact the current casino is losing money. I think it's time for the Red Lake people to demand a full accounting of our financial condition.

Press/ON will be carrying more information regarding Red Lake financial information in the next several editions, as we are able to analyze and review these documents. I still haven't received any reply from the Red lake Tribal Council to review the closing documents for the $27 million loan for the River Road Casino.

Minnesota Indian gambling: an unregulated, unaccountable, monopoly, with nearly unlimited cash, hiding behind tribal sovereign immunity.
July 13, 2001.

The Minnesota Commissioner of Public Safety (DPS) expressed a remarkable philosophy in the Department's June 27 temporary classification request, when he asked the State Department of Administration to reclassify tribal gambling enterprise audits held by the state as "private" information. He writes that secrecy "shields the gaming operations 'from organized crime and other corrupting influences.'"

The truth of the matter is that stealing funds from casinos has been a longstanding problem, as *Press/ON* has reported throughout the ten years during which Indian gambling has been in existence.

Some of the thefts and embezzlements were prosecuted and some weren't. Political considerations played a major role in the declination to prosecute certain influential individuals. *Press/ON* has received dozens of phone calls about money being stolen out of casino vaults. The secrecy advocated by the Commissioner has not prevented the problems of theft and "corrupting influences" at Indian casinos.

In my estimation, secrecy breeds crime, mismanagement, corruption and political intrigues. Indian tribal governments operate within a cloak of secrecy that is very detrimental to Indian people. There are no open meeting laws and no data practices acts on the reservations.

Can it be that the Commissioner would like to have that same kind of unaccountable secrecy within State government if legally-mandated disclosure of information might affect "his" organization. If there is nothing to hide, why are the tribes, and for that matter DPS, afraid to reveal the financial status of tribal casinos?

Some tribal governments have claimed that they make their financial information available, but no tribal member in the state has had an opportunity to thoroughly review the financial statements that should be open, as a matter of right, under the tribal constitutions. If tribal governments deign to make gambling audits "available," it is done under circumstances in which it is impossible to make a full and proper review. In the instances that I have been told about, tribal officials bring in a big pile of documents, and give one hour to look at them.

The Red Lake Tribal Chairman recently proposed to the State that he make the casino audits "available" to the State DPS in this manner.

I have brought two lawsuits in the Red Lake Court of Indian Offenses in an attempt to obtain audited casino financial records from the Red Lake tribal government. With the tribal council in control of the Court of Indian Offenses, my efforts went nowhere. In each instance the tribal council abused "sovereign immunity" as a defense for their secrecy.

In his quest to cloak the operations of his Minnesota State agency with Indian secrecy, the Commissioner also writes, "release of the data to the public would have a detrimental effect on each tribe's willingness to provide audit information under the tribal-state compacts to Public Safety." It is questionable how much monitoring DPS has actually done since the compacts were negotiated in 1990-1991 and the Department was assigned the task of overseeing Indian gambling operations.

During the past ten years, how many investigations of tribal gambling operations under the compacts have been conducted by DPS? How many people have been charged with violations of the compacts by State, tribal, or the federal government? The Commissioner of Public Safety's notion that the State of Minnesota should wriggle out of complying with State law (the Data Practices Act), because the organizations that he is charged with monitoring might not be "willing" to comply with State laws (i.e. providing gambling audits to DPS), is really astonishing if you think about it.

How many highly placed law enforcement officials would even think of arguing that organizations that have demonstrated corruption and links with organized crime in the past, should be placated by State policies of secrecy, and that State laws should not be enforced because those organizations might not be "willing" to comply?

Based on the Ninth U.S. District Court of Appeals' *Siletz* decision in 1998, the arguments raised in the Commissioner's request for reclassification are pure folly (see "Official correspondence" article on page 1). It is evident that some DPS staff are confused about who they are working for and who is paying their checks: is it the taxpayers of the State of Minnesota, or the Indian tribal gambling interests?

Whether they like it or not, in order to monitor tribal gambling enterprises properly, there is bound to be an adversarial relationship between the Department of Public Safety and Indian casinos. DPS's role should be to monitor casinos and ensure compliance with the State-Tribal compacts.

How can they do that without obtaining audits and doing investigations? Financial audits and investigation reports can be effective tools in monitoring an industry laden with cash.

Indian gambling is a powerful monopoly with a lot of unaccountable cash. At the very minimum the Department should obtain casino audits regularly, and provide full information to the legislature and administration. If any honest and meaningful gambling policy is ever to be developed in this state, the agency should take a leadership role rather than pander to tribal governments and casino interests.

It appears that the DPS is adhering to a patty-cake policy in dealing with Indian tribes, and the Commissioner seems to be taking an attitude of, "Hear No Evil, See No Evil, and There Will Be No Evil." But we in the native community know different.

With ten years of gambling in the State of Minnesota, and tens of billions of dollars having passed through Indian casinos in the State, there is no significant improvement in social conditions on the reservations. Instead we have seen increased crime, and particularly disturbing increases in violent crime, low educational statistics, inadequate housing, high abuse and neglect, alcoholism and drug use, the rise of gangs, misuse of resources, increased welfare and unemployment, and many other social problems that persist on the reservations.

154

Rather than relying on casino and other business income to pay for social programs, Indian tribal governments show an increasing dependency on federal government funding. At one moment, Indian tribal governments are "sovereign," but at the next they are still "wards," with their hands out, begging from Uncle Sam and the State of Minnesota. They are refusing to exercise their own initiative and energies, or to fulfill their fundamental responsibilities to the people who they claim to "democratically represent."

Five years ago I made a request for information under the Data Practices Act to find out just how much regulating the State of Minnesota was doing "in this sea of cash that has been changing hands." My request was sent to the Director of the Gaming Enforcement Division of DPS.

In my August 23, 1996 editorial, I detailed my subsequent conversations with the Office of Gaming Enforcement. According to information furnished by that office, in 1996 there was a staff of three investigators, and one clerk, to do the background investigations on over 10,000 persons employed by tribal casinos in Minnesota. They were also responsible for testing more than 11,000 video machines at the 17 Indian casinos in the state.

In August 1996, only one casino had been inspected by DPS, with minor violations reported. It did not appear that either the National Indian Gaming Commission or the State of Minnesota had either sought or received copies of audits from any of the tribes.

As I wrote in 1996, since tribal councils are secretive with their tribal members, and the State is neglecting its legally mandated obligations to monitor the casinos, "just who is looking over the shoulders of some of our less than trustworthy tribal officials?"

Given what has happened in the past, it is my opinion that DPS would like to cover up just how poor a job they are really doing in monitoring tribal gambling in Minnesota.

With a decade of Indian gambling under our belts, we should have learned something. Unfortunately, the state agency charged with monitoring Indian casinos has developed an all-too-cozy relationship with the very organizations it is supposed to monitor.

LLRBC RESPONSES TO PETITION CHARGES

Chapter VII: Introduction: Tribal Corruption.

Publisher Lawrence often stated, "Unless and until we have some means of holding our tribal governments accountable to us, such as civil rights guarantees, we have nothing. This is why corruption grows and conditions continue to worsen on all of our reservations."

An anecdote delivered in August 2012[1] by *New York Times* columnist David Brooks: The setting is the Middle East. The participants are United States Military advisers and local personnel. The discussion centers on governmental corruption and its effects on a democratization process.

The question is asked: What actually is governmental corruption? An American advisor volunteered this example: When you, as a governmental official have an employment position to fill, and instead of going through proper channels, you give the job to a family member or a friend. That is, in our view, an example of corruption.

Then he asked that the local officer give an example. His reply was: Corruption is when you have an employment position to fill, and you go through regular channels, and you don't give it to your family member or close friend.

The story is both amusing and, for those imbued with Western democratic philosophy, enlightening. It illustrates a tribal versus a democratic approach to the practice of hiring.

As the story indicates, corruption has several facets. Simplistically, democratic cultures seek to avoid the possibility of malfeasance in governmental operations. Tribalism emphasizes and supports the practice of rewarding loyalty to a particular group.

Given the early circumstances that resulted in Native Americans being deprived of their usual ways of life and consigned to reservations, it is understandable why the second approach would be preferred action for reservation natives. Add to that the U.S. governments' (state and/or federal) practice of herding indigenous peoples on to reservations without regard to their true tribal affiliation. This process no doubt created antipathetic "in" groups that felt entitled to dictate to newcomers or those in the minority.

Over time the barriers between the groups fade but habit still reigns. One group on a reservation could dominate all other groups with the 'why' of the domination lost over the years.

Finally there is this: the possibility that tribal corruption is so ubiquitous and has persisted for so long that certain practices are accepted as convention and are not seen as corrupt.

There are parallels between Middle Eastern and American native beliefs, practices and conditions. Thomas L. Friedman, author of *Hot, Flat and Crowded,* lays out a scenario that could as likely apply to America's reservations: "The people conclude that their country is poor and their leaders ... are rich—not because the country has failed to promote education, innovation, rule of law and entrepreneurship, but only because someone is stealing the ... money and depriving them of their due. Often they are right. Someone is stealing. But people start to think that in order to become prosperous all they have to do is stop the stealing—not build a society ... on the foundations of better education, rule of law, innovation and entrepreneurship."

Despite the influx of multimillions of dollars from casino gambling, Native unemployment remains high, exceeding seventy percent in some places. As a consequence, abject poverty continues as a fact of reservation life.

Adding to this unfortunate situation, tribal assets are used to purchase influence with politicians at all levels with the intention that the status quo remain unchanged.

The traditional "fixes" for depressed economies are described by Friedman, "build a society ... on the foundations of better education, rule of law, innovation and entrepreneurship."

Without the rule of law as the foundation, there can be no innovation, investment or improvement in reservation economic, and social conditions. Tribal corruption will exist de facto until the elements of stable government such as equitable distribution of tribal resources and assets, civil rights protections, an independent judiciary, merit-based employment systems, open meetings and records become status quo.

[1] Note from a lecture, by David Brooks, attended by the editor at the annual writer's conference delivered in Ketchum, Idaho.

Candidate seeks presidential assistance.
April 18, 1990.

Dear Mr. President: I recently became a candidate for the Office of Chairman of the Tribal Council of the Red Lake band of Chippewa Indians in northern Minnesota. The Tribal Council is the governing body for the Red Lake Reservation.

My candidacy is the result of a Red Lake peoples' movement to end 95 years of dictatorship and to bring democracy to our reservation. We at Red Lake have decided that if we are to share in the blessings and bounty that is America, we must put an end to the most repressive, the most secretive, and the most unconstitutional government in America.

Mr. President, if we are to achieve democracy on the Red Lake Reservation, we will need your help. Please be assured that we recognize the many important demands on your time and that we do not frivolously seek your assistance. However, during the last six tribal elections, *covering 24 years*, tribal members have protested each election on the grounds of unfair practices on the part of the incumbent tribal government.

All protests are the result of the Red Lake Tribal Council's total control over the election process on the Red Lake Reservation. These protests have resulted in petitions to the Bureau of Indian Affairs, lawsuits in tribal and federal courts, and a reservation-wide riot in 1979.

Through our many protests of previous tribal elections, we have come to view the Bureau of Indian Affairs as part of the problem and have lost confidence in that organization.

Therefore, we urgently request that you direct the Secretary of the Interior to utilize the Department of the Interior's Rights Protection Office to monitor our next tribal election, which is scheduled for May 23, 1990. The monitoring of this election by an impartial third party is necessary if we are to have an open and fair election on the Red Lake Reservation.

The government-to-government agreement, called the Red Lake Tribal Constitution, guarantees to all Red Lake tribal members civil

161

rights protection by both the tribal government and the federal government. Obviously, the most basic of those rights is that of a fair and open election. These tenets have never been observed.

Furthermore, we also request that if the Secretary of the Interior, for any reason, is unable to certify the said election, that he then be directed to withhold or suspend all current and future contracts with the Red Lake Tribal Council until the election is conducted, and certified to have been held in a fair and impartial manner.

Most likely, if you direct our requested action, the incumbent government, and others, will cry "foul" on the grounds of interference with the internal affairs of the tribe and/or violation of the tribe's sovereignty.

We would respond, that regardless of what basis federal funds are made available to the Red Lake tribal government--contract, grant, or foreign aid--conditions are still attached. Obviously, the most paramount of those conditions is the observance of the peoples' civil/human rights by the recipient governments.

Certainly if the United States government can send observers or monitors to elections in Nicaragua and the Philippines, it should surely do no less in protecting the vote of Indian citizens on the Red Lake Reservation.

We believe that, in addition to the rights guaranteed to us by our tribal constitution, adequate terms and conditions must exist in all current federal grants and contracts between the Red Lake Tribe and the various agencies of the federal government, which gives the government the authority to take this action.

Mr. President, we realize this request for your assistance is highly unusual; however, we know of no other alternative if we are to see democracy come to the Red Lake Reservation. We are certain that Senators Rudy Boschwitz and David Durenberger, and our Congressman Arlan Stangeland, are aware of this situation on the Red Lake Reservation and would support this request.

In addition, Mr. President, tribal members from the White Earth Reservation in western Minnesota have also asked that I request your assistance in helping them bring a fair and open election to their reservation scheduled for June of this year. We would appreciate your response to these requests and would welcome the opportunity to meet with you or your representative to discuss these issues in more detail.

If you have any questions or would like additional information concerning this matter, please contact me, William J. Lawrence, at the *Ojibwe News*.

Mismanagement, fraud and improvident deals have cost Native community nearly $100 million.
May 26, 1995.

The 11 federally recognized Indian tribes and communities located in the state of Minnesota have been in the gambling business for an average of four years now. In that time, our tribal governments, through mismanagement, fraud, and improvident management contracts have succeeded in losing, misusing or giving away about $100 million of our money.

According to the intent of the Indian Gaming Regulatory Act of 1988, Indian gambling proceeds are earmarked for the benefit of Indian people, not for the benefit of a few tribal officials, management companies or a few per capitas [payments] to tribal members. With most tribal governments in Minnesota using gambling profits like a giant secret slush fund, it is no wonder tribal members are becoming more vocal, militant and demanding that something be done about this ridiculous situation. With Congress now in the process of amending the Indian Gaming Act it would seem that members of our congressional delegation would be interested in soliciting the views of those who the act is supposed to benefit, the Indian people themselves.

With a number of tribal officials now targets of a massive federal investigation into probable felony indictments for misuse of tribal funds, their input is hardly creditable. Unless accountability to tribal membership (like requiring tribal governments to furnish annual certified CPA audits to tribal members on demand) is built into the amendment, the Indian Gaming Act will never achieve its intended purpose of benefiting the Indian people.

Reservation boondoggle:

According to reports received at *Press/ON* this week, 25 tribal officials (council members and employees) flew to Washington, D.C. last Sunday. Calls to the Tribal Council office to ask the purpose of the trip, and the names of travelers, were not returned at press time. Estimated costs of the trip for all 25 travelers is $25,000- $30,000. By authorizing a trip like this one, the Council certainly doesn't show much concern for needy tribal members.

Everything the Tribal establishment doesn't want you to know about Tribal courts...

April 28, 2000.

Imagine going to court for a scheduled probate hearing, but before the hearing begins, being physically removed by armed police officers, escorted to the boundary of the reservation, and told if you ever come back you will be thrown in jail. This happened to a non-Indian acquaintance, in the Red Lake tribal court May 1998.

The Red Lake Tribal Chairman had issued a "Reservation Removal Order" against my friend, at the request of the children of her late husband. As a result, she was not only denied a hearing but also all of her personal possessions. Her appeal of the removal order to the Red Lake Tribal Council was never answered.

Imagine being thrown in jail for being 20 minutes late for a custody hearing when the other party didn't even show up. This happened to another non-Indian in the Red Lake tribal court last December when she was Director of Red Lake Children and Family Services. She was shortly thereafter fired from her job and ordered off the reservation because she was trying to protect the interests of a vulnerable child against the interests of a politically-connected reservation family.

Imagine 11 tribal court systems in this state doing these and dozens of other well-documented, egregious acts, and no one stopping them.

Imagine being eligible in every way to represent other tribal members in tribal court, and being the only tribal member at the time with a law degree, but denied the right to do so because the tribal council is afraid cases will be brought against them. This happened to me in 1994.

Imagine attempting to exercise my tribal constitutional rights on three occasions to get an accounting of the expenditures of tribal funds, only to have the political branch of the tribe use sovereign immunity to deny me that information.

This happened to me in 1984, 1992 and 1994 under three different Red Lake administrations. I wrote about similar abuses in a 1972 article published in the *University of North Dakota Law Review*. If anything has changed since then, it's been for the worse.

Imagine further that the tribal councils who control the courts also control the tribal law enforcement

The Minnesota American Indian Bar Association (MAIBA), and others in the tribal establishment, continue to think they can, and should, control what anyone in this state says about tribally-related matters. With no separation of powers, no checks and balances, and no means to hold tribal governments accountable, it can get awfully scary on Minnesota's Indian reservations.

Given that this is the way tribal courts operate, why would the tribal establishment and their sycophant, the Minnesota American Indian Bar Association, react so vehemently when Judge R.A. (Jim) Randall, Vincent Hill and myself were asked to appear on this week's panel to discuss tribal justice as part of the St. Paul City Attorney's Continuing Legal Education program?

Could it be that they don't want the truth to get out? Could it be that they are so caught up in the tribal money tree that they don't want anyone to upset their status quo? A status quo that I have been saying for years is literally killing Indian people.

MAIBA's pattern of throwing temper tantrums and pulling power plays to prohibit free speech, described in the cover article, "Panel on state, tribal, federal courts draws criticism," in this edition, only serves to reveal their true colors.

MAIBA, and others in the tribal establishment, continue to think they can control what anyone in this state says about tribally-related matters. Their intimidation tactics may work on the reservation, but off the reservation we DO have constitutional rights.

Red Lake's financing of Water Park Project made public in round-about way.
January 5, 2001.

It wasn't an accident that Miller & Schroeder Financial, Inc. of Minneapolis--and not the Red Lake Tribal Council---announced the closing of the $27 million in financing for the Water Park Project at the Band's River Road Casino, near Thief River Falls.

Why didn't the Red Lake Tribal Council announce that the financing had been secured? Why did they leave it up to the financial firm to let the public know, and not very effectively at that, by issuing a press release through PR Newswire whose distribution list does not include *The Native American Press/Ojibwe News?* The *Bemidji Pioneer* did not receive the story either, nor did other newspapers surrounding Red Lake. We discovered the story through a web search.

The project has created a lot of controversy on the Red Lake Reservation because of its cost, feasibility and the secrecy surrounding it. Construction actually started last May 10 with an $8 million loan from Miller & Schroeder.

Many tribal members consider the project far too ambitious because of the state of the local economy and because of competition from other area tribal casinos. Tribal members are also upset with the manner in which the Council waived the tribe's sovereign immunity and pledged the casino as security for the loan. Many members also strongly believe that a development of this magnitude should have been submitted to a referendum vote of the tribal membership.

In addition, the resignation of the Red Lake District Representative from the Red Lake Tribal Council has caused concern among tribal members. He is considered to be the Council's most knowledgeable member about the tribe's financial affairs and is considered one of the "Fab Four." Without him, the Fab Four, which also includes the Chairman ... the Treasurer, and the Little Rock District Representative, would lose its clout and ability to run things. Prior to his election to the Red Lake Tribal Council, the Red Lake Representative had been a longtime advocate for accountability and openness in tribal government. To see him go along with questionable projects, and now apparently, abandoning his leadership position altogether, is disconcerting. His absence from the past two council meetings creates even more doubt about the feasibility of the Water Project and other recent economic development projects.

It is time that steadier hands took back control of the Council and look at where the tribe is at financially. It also shouldn't be forgotten that the Chairman only won the 1998 election by 43 votes and the Treasurer by 36. Hardly a mandate for what they have been doing financially.

Buying the status quo is killing us.
October 25, 2002.

With elections for federal, state and local offices just a little more than a week away, it is important for our readers to know what's going on behind the scenes. The information about campaign contributions published in *Press/ON* over the past few weeks has not usually been publicly disclosed in Indian country. This week's issue includes additional information about tribal PAC contributions, and next week we plan on publishing a summary of the campaign finance reports slated to be released in the next few days.

Tribal members have not often had access to tribal financial information, and have had little or no information about which policies, agendas, and candidates are going to be supported with tribal money. In Indian country, these decisions have usually been decided behind closed doors.

I think that almost all of us have been "turned off" by the seamy financial underside of recent political campaigns. With widespread charges of financial improprieties, soft money, PAC money, voter registration and polling frauds, and the generally nonpublic nature of campaign financing, it seems that American democracy is rapidly eroding into public manipulation and slick marketing of political candidates instead of the genuine mandate of the people upon which democracy depends.

We understand that this is the way politics is played in this country and that Indian people have a right to play a role, like anybody else, in buying politicians. But spending tribal money to buy political influence should represent the interests of tribal members, and not just the personal interests of a few tribal politicians and their cronies.

Indian PAC money is usually spent either to maintain the status quo or to entrench the power of the tribal government, which is not in the best interests of the majority of Indian people. Drugs, crime, gangs, and the whole gamut of social problems have steadily worsened as high-stakes gambling income has increased the influence-buying capabilities of

170

tribal governments. Although the policies of "sovereignty" and "strong tribal government" promoted by perhaps well-intended politicians and policymakers might sound like an honorable remedy for past wrongs, the reality is that the state and federal government are actively imposing unaccountable, utterly unconstitutional governments on Indian people.

Once fostered by the United States, and well established on reservations, strong tribal governments tend to consolidate and amplify their own power. They have been consistently buying politicians who support ever-expanding "sovereignty" for "strong tribal governments." In fact, these allegedly "democratic" governments are resisting community mandates for the changes needed to deal with the runaway social problems on reservations, and to underwrite open and accountable government. Among the changes demanded by the Indian community are enforceable civil rights, accountability, and open government.

Tribal governments are using PAC money to buy Congress and, in many cases, also buying federal and state administrations. The only branch of government which has recently attempted to address the problems of tribal sovereignty is the courts. But now, the tribal governments are trying to buy congressional action to override the courts, to amend decisions like *Nevada v. Hicks* and *Atkinson v. Shirley*.

The real irony is that while Indian tribal governments are entrenching their own power and expanding the grasp of gambling and other vested interests, tribal members are the ones paying the price for campaign contributions, PACs, lobbyists, and other modes of political influence. And, as can be seen by visiting most Indian reservations, there is almost no benefit to the Indian communities.

In the last few elections over the past few years, despite what looks bad, we have seen signs of encouragement. In recent tribal elections, tribal officials at Red Lake, Leech Lake, Mille Lacs, White Earth, and elsewhere were thrown out of office through democratic action and community organization by the people, because tribal officers spent too much of their time and money playing professional Indian power

171

games with whites rather than staying at home working with their own people to improve conditions on the reservation.

We have seen far too many Indian politicians buying influence, playing the role of Indian at the people's expense. People think that tribes should be able to do the same thing as everybody else. They want to be both "sovereign" *and* "wards," but the real problem is that tribal governments have almost unlimited power over tribal members on the reservation. They do not have to comply with the U.S. Constitution, and tribal members are not protected by a Bill of Rights. None of the tribes in this state have seriously and effectively addressed these problems.

Worthiness of Minnesota Indian Economic Development Fund questioned.
March 12, 2004.

So Where Does all the Money go? MIGA's answer and "the rest of the story."

In the media spotlight this week is the showy demonstration at the State Capitol against House file 2135, the bill that would remove slot machines from Indian casinos if the tribes failed to come to the table to renegotiate gaming compacts. The nine tribes that make up the Minnesota Indian Gaming Association (MIGA) orchestrated the demonstration.

Also creating a splash is the grandiose print advertisement by MIGA distributed as a supplement to newspapers statewide. The piece was produced by and for the public relations benefit of the MIGA tribes. The print supplement articulates the Utopian dream that was envisioned when Indian gaming compacts were created in the 1990s.

What a glorious promise: gaming proceeds would revitalize the tribes, provide jobs, pull the tribes up from poverty, and greatly improve "quality of life."

AND what an absolutely effective revenge against the white man's outrages of the 19th century when Indians were subjugated, robbed of their lands, displaced, despoiled, etc. Now the tribes could strike a devastating blow to the heart of white Americans by taking away that which all Americans treasure most highly--their dollars. Indians could get rich AND kick their former tormentors in the butt. Yes, the vision was glorious. The reality of gaming, however, is an unexpected and dismaying tragedy.

Let's take a look at this multicolor, pricey, 8-page, advertising supplement with the objective of analyzing what is rhetoric versus what is truth; what is half-truth as opposed to the true picture.

Let's examine the six "Talking Points" of the MIGA supplement: Our response (1.) Rebuilding Reservation Communities. (2.) Creating jobs, changing lives. (3.) Getting healthy. (4.) Educating youth. (5.) Preserving Native Culture. (6.) Renewing a Tradition of sharing.

(1.) "On most reservations, conditions before gaming resembled those found in third world countries...   Tribes began the difficult and costly task of bringing their communities back to life after more than a century of poverty and neglect... Minnesota tribes have literally rebuilt their reservations from the ground up."

Our response: No question about it. Poverty and neglect are facts of life on Indian reservations——before gaming and, unfortunately, after gaming. Gambling has made some differences on the reservations. It has created two classes——the rich and those who still remain in poverty. The majority of tribal members remain poor while those "blessed" with leadership positions have been elevated to the upper class.

(2.) "Creating jobs, changing lives... Reservation communities faced the terrible consequences of long-term joblessness: poverty, despair, crime, alcohol and drug abuse, and domestic violence. Tribal gaming has changed the picture dramatically."

Response: We simply cannot argue with that. Several researchers have come to the same conclusion. Using an econometric cost-benefit analysis, economists found that "the costs of casinos are at least 1.9 times greater than the benefits." Further "Casinos create crime, rather than attracting it from elsewhere... casinos accounted for 10.3 percent of violent crime, and 7.7 percent of property crime in casino counties."

Casinos change lives. We agree, but not for the better. In regard to job creation, the MIGA supplement indicated that 78 percent of jobs were held by non-Indians. Is that a desired outcome? Other questions abound: What is the pay level of the majority of these jobs? What is the percentage of full-time versus part-time jobs? Do most positions offer full benefits? I dare to suggest the answers are not positive.

(3.) "Getting Healthy... tribes are building and renovating clinics on the reservations, developing partnerships with health care institutions…"

Response: I suspect the tribes are building medical facilities on reservations largely with federal dollars.

This is supposition because tribes have consistently suppressed the publication of audited financial statements. This kind of behavior leads one naturally to suspect the tribes don't want the public, including their own membership, to know how money is handled. Why?

(4.) "Educating Youth... education programs and services account for a substantial percentage of most tribal budgets."

Response: Why then does the federal government contribute many millions of dollars to tribal schools? Per pupil payments on reservations are higher than off-reservation schools, as much as double the amount in some cases.

(5.) "Preserving Native Culture... Indian people believe tradition is a powerful force for healing past wounds and leading tribal communities to spiritual and physical health."

Response: Does Indian tradition support the idea that only a few members of the tribe are entitled to the majority of benefits that accrue to the tribe? Does tradition support a tribe's failure to acknowledge legitimate members' rights to share in the benefits?

Response: The Mdewakanton Sioux tribe, the most prosperous and smallest tribe in the State, has systematically excluded legitimate tribal members from enjoying the fruits of casino gambling. The issue is currently under litigation.

(6.) "Renewing a Tradition of Sharing... Because the emphasis in Indian culture was on community rather than on the individual, all resources were shared for the common benefit."

Response: This one is the point that strikes me as most preposterous. Have the nine MIGA tribes (who represent 40% of the on-reservation Indian population) seen fit to share their largess in any substantial way with the other two tribes (who represent the majority of Minnesota Indians on reservations)?

The answer is no. They have consistently opposed the expansion of gambling into the metro area by other Minnesota tribes, thus denying them the opportunity to capitalize on the gambling bonanza.

The MIGA tribes refer to their charitable contributions. I question their generosity. I suspect the actual ratio of contributions to net revenue is miniscule. Indian greed, as demonstrated by the MIGA supplement, is not much different from the greed of the white immigrants. MIGA tribes have shown themselves to be no fairer than, and absolutely as devastating as, the 19th century wave of white greed.

Tribal casinos have done more to destroy Indian values and culture than the whites were ever able to do. When the white man's answer to the Indian Problem was extermination in the 1800s, it was much less effective than what the tribes are doing to themselves. No one could have foreseen what effective means of destruction the casinos would turn out to be.

Researchers claim "casinos are making crime" both by providing a concentration of people with money that creates an "attractive nuisance" to criminal activity, but also by pointing out that "corruption is a statistical certainty" in the gambling industry, and that problems of corruption are exacerbated with respect to Indian casinos because of the jurisdictional ambiguities in which they are entangled.

Few would argue that crime, fueled both by the corruption and the disparity the new wealth has created among tribal members, is a fact of life on the reservations. The facts speak for themselves.

The MIGA piece touts the benefits that gaming has produced. Number 1, the "success" is limited to those tribes that have location. Number 2, if gaming was indeed the golden goose, laying golden eggs, why has the American taxpayer had to subsidize these same tribes to the tune of roughly $82 million in FY 2002. Why should we be giving out this kind of money to about 7000 people on nine reservations who, we estimate, produce a net profit of $750 million a year from their gaming operations? These same tribes have consistently refused to willingly provide financial disclosure of their enterprises.

The presence of casino gambling has the effect of an implosion on the tribes themselves. The negative forces exerted by gaming are capable of further destroying Indians' ability to create the world they articulate for themselves in their advertising supplement.

Note: References to research by economists in regard to gambling on reservations was taken from Clara Niiska's article entitled "Casinos, crime and community costs," first published by *Press/ON* January 25, 2002.

Niiska's source: Grinols, Earl L. "Gambling Economics: Summary Facts." www.texaspolicy.com November 17, 2004. This report substantiates the editorial material concerning the downside of gambling.

Also See: *Press/ON,* April 4, 2003 "Former Shakopee chairman ... threatens [Barbara] Buttes on letter questioning his eligibility for enrollment in the Shakopee Mdewakanton Community." This piece contains Ms. Buttes' letter to the former chairman, and his response. Page 4 and continuing.

Press/ON November 6. 2004, page 4 displays the text of LAWSUIT, In the U.S. Court of Federal Claims No. 03-2684 (Filed October 27, 2004). Sheldon Peters Wolfchild, et al Plaintiffs, v. United States, Defendant. Page 4,5.

The text of the Lawsuit tells the back story of the Mdewakanton enrollment dispute.

What do you know about corruption?
April 21, 2006.

"Corruption hurts everyone, and it harms the poor the most." "Corruption appears to be on the increase." "What is corruption? ... [it] is the abuse of entrusted power for private gain. It hurts everyone whose life, livelihood or happiness depends on the integrity of people in a position of authority." (The above quotes, and others that appear in this column, are from various documents found on the website of Transparency International.) Their "mission is to create change toward a world free of corruption..."

A local instance of open corruption would be the appointment by a tribal official, based on political favoritism, of a relative or friend to an employment position; or conversely, removing a qualified individual from a position and to make it available to a crony in repayment of a political favor.

Another blatant act of corruption is handing out money in exchange for a vote. Unlike less obvious acts, if it can be proven, the candidate buying votes is subject to prosecution. A further example would be where the majority of the people live at poverty level while their elected and appointed officials enjoy salaries of many, many multiples above what the average member receives in annual income.

Less visible examples of corruption would be: the denial of civil rights through the manipulation of decisions in a tribal court; not showing up for work on a regular basis; taking unnecessary trips at tribal expense. Other common practices that constitute corruption are failure to disclose financial information, conducting business during secret meetings, and allowing mismanagement of tribal resources for the benefit of the few and at the expense of the greater society.

"There is no culture, anywhere and at any time in history ... where [corruption] has been accepted by society... [where] the leaders are entitled ... to make decisions in their own favor and against the group interest. No such society would survive for long."

The reservations obviously continue to survive but they are certainly not prospering. And not one of them is surviving in anything like a healthy state. I have frequently stated that certain reservations are in danger of imploding, that is, of exploding into splinters from the inside out. Conditions on our reservations are such that it would be difficult to ascribe to them the slightest virtue of being positive, productive societies.

Legitimate governments are founded on the basis of shared beliefs, goals and aspirations. In such societies, power is bestowed based on the provision of benefits for the members. There is a concern for the well-being of all its members. Its institutions are created to benefit the majority of its members, not just those privileged to hold power. This situation is not in evidence on any of the Minnesota, and many other, reservations.

Instead we only see greater and more outrageous incidents of corruption. This fact taints the entire community. It demoralizes its citizens and destroys the future for its youth. Consider the situation at Leech Lake where the Tribal Council has systematically ignored the wishes of the majority of voters in their choice of a Secretary/Treasurer. By stripping authority from an elected officer, the Council has, in effect, disempowered the voters.

At Red Lake, tribal officials have burdened the membership with an enormous debt, which was largely engendered through circumvention of the Tribal Council. Nonetheless the obligation remains and is being repaid at the expense of needed services.

Members on every reservation complain that they are kept in the dark about financial matters. Audits are performed, but the information is not made public, even to members. Tribal business is too often conducted in closed meetings, the results of which are not ever made public.

The use of tribal funds, assets or resources for the benefit of insiders is corruption. Indulging in activities that enhance the situation, or fortunes, of insiders and excludes the ordinary members from the benefits, is corruption. It's everywhere and exists in many different forms;

"there is no 'quick fix'... for curbing corruption." Meaningful reform will require long-term, effective action by capable persons of integrity and dedication.

Transparency International gives many good ideas for controlling and/or reversing corrupt situations. Not all of them are applicable or appropriate to reservations, but here are a few I thought might be worth considering.

First, of course, is the prerequisite of "free and fair elections ... a lack of legitimacy almost inevitably breeds a climate in which corruption can blossom."

Your elected representatives on the tribal councils can be instrumental in corrective action. However, if they are allowed to exist as a "corrupt political elite," there is no hope of reform.

A qualified and honest tribal chairman ideally will develop an administrative plan, set priorities, make realistic assessments and lead the council in action that will result in prosperity for the members.

If the chairman is isolated by a corrupt tribal council coalition, the majority of the populace will suffer. And perhaps they will only have themselves to blame for this effect.

It's up to the citizens to elect honorable, qualified (through education and work experience) persons of integrity. It's up to the public to demand accountability from their elected policy makers. The duties of the citizen are: to know what is going on; to know your rights; to be willing to fight for your rights; to be willing to publicly, and lawfully, protest if what is going on is suspect or openly corrupt.

Coincident with a responsible citizenry, tribal officials, entrusted with authority bestowed upon them by the public [tribal members], must provide guarantees that citizens will not be subjected to punishment in any form for their protests. The people are entitled to speak out. Too often they remain silent out of fear of retaliation, job loss, etc. Only those who are not indebted to tribal regimes for their livelihood dare to speak. This situation must change.

180

In this country, it is widely held that a balance of governmental powers provides the best protections for the welfare of the society. Along with elected representatives [i.e., councils] and a separate executive [i.e., tribal chairman], a competent, independent and fair court system is essential. If the court can be manipulated by the other elected officials, it becomes "simply a tool in the hands of a powerful, and corrupt, elite."

Transparency International (TI) suggests some elements that we do not find in our tribal governments, but that I believe would be worth considering. For example, a position similar to a <u>controller,</u> or independent inspector general, could be created that would be responsible for the auditing (preferably by outside auditors) of all tribal financial affairs. This position would be the watchdog for all tribal agencies and departmental heads. Publication of tribal annual reports, including all financial information, would also be a responsibility for this position.

TI points out that this position should not be dependent on any current council. The position (and all other government positions) should be protected by an appropriate job description, remunerated on the basis of a published salary scale, and subject to published policies and procedures, including an appeals process. It would be the responsibility of this position to develop and adopt good financial management and standard business practices as important deterrents to corruption, and to make financial information available to every interested tribal member. Nearly every tribal financial audit I've reviewed over the past years has admonished that these elements are absent from the financial records they've examined.

Another position enlightened governments might consider adding is <u>Ombudsman</u>. TI describes this function: "receives and investigates complaints about maladministration [faulty or inappropriate administrative practices]. It gives individuals the opportunity to have decisions which affect them reviewed by an independent and expert body, without the expenses and delays of court proceedings. Independence from political interference, adequate resources, and accessibility, and high levels of public recognition are among the prerequisites for its effectiveness."

Perhaps these two duties could be combined into one office. Any additional expenditure that this entails would be more than recovered through the reforms that would be possible with the addition of these two services.

A tool that would assist in achieving the goal of reform would be the formulation and <u>adoption of a code of conduct or a code of ethical practices.</u> Implementing such a code would guide expectations of performance, behavior and decision making by public officials. It could also articulate procedures and consequences that might result for violations.

Such <u>codes</u> are widely recognized as contributing to high standards, high expectations and play a powerful role in fighting corruption. An ethics code would address areas like nepotism, cronyism, and policies governing procurement procedures. It could affirm that elected and appointed officials are expected to maintain high standards of integrity and avoid conflicts of interest. Many codes specify that officials must avoid all corrupt practices, such as bribery, perjury, inappropriate pecuniary gain, or theft, and must not benefit in any way from information, or privilege, their position may present. An effective code would prohibit elected or appointed officials from using the influence inherent in the position for financial gain, privilege or exceptions for themselves, their families, friends or business associates.

Public officials have power to make decisions and create situations that have an impact on many levels for tribal members, both on and off reservations. According to TI, "Codes of ethics or conduct can be important guides to making decisions on complicated ethical issues."

Codes, published and distributed to the community, help make residents aware that they are entitled to certain, well-defined standards of service and action by their officials. It's important that reservation residents are aware of the many ways their elected and appointed officials can affect their lives. The voters have given a sacred trust to those they put in office. It is simple decency that those elected reward the trust expressed in them by conducting themselves in honorable ways.

Public officials, particularly on reservations, enjoy unwarranted power. They have access to and the means by which to enrich themselves by misuse of the power given to them in trust by the people.

That, as you know by now, is the definition of corruption. Corruption damages the ability of a community to prosper in many ways. In terms of economic development, it frightens prospective investors away. It guarantees no new investments and is responsible for the lack of growth.

It allows those in power to misuse resources by building enterprises or facilities that are ill-advised and create unnecessary debt loads that are a drain on the communities. These projects often carry with them the opportunity for financial and other enhancements for the planners, but no benefits, tangible or otherwise, for the people.

The fight against corruption is a step toward restoring self-sufficiency, hope and better living environments. Reform will assure that our tribal governments are more accountable and display more integrity and fairness. A climate of corruption not only robs members of their resources, but of their hope; it creates an attitude of despair.

Effective reform requires: well-thought-out processes, by individuals who have demonstrated the moral, intellectual and experiential capacity to create, develop, implement and sustain meaningful change.

Illegitimacy in tribal governments is entrenched. It's strengthened by the fact that most of our tribal officials have not completed higher education. Their work experience has not been sufficient to prepare them to be effective, competent public servants. To successfully manage casinos and administer million-dollar budgets requires formal education and supervised apprenticeships. It's not an OJT situation.

Conditions on our reservations reflect these deficiencies in leadership. It's time we did something about it. Adoption of TI's well-thought-out ideas, by experts from around the world, would take us in a positive direction. There is no need for us to re-invent the wheel. We do need, however, to re-invent our communities.

Additionally, we need to grow a crop of new leaders. Our educational systems are failing our children. Family life is in a decline. Our future prospects are diminished as we lose our kids to ignorance, crime, drugs and violence. It seems the only hope is to change our ways and give our youth some role models to follow. It could be as simple as that. Reservation voters, you owe it to yourselves:

1. To elect people who acknowledge that corruption exists and will pledge themselves to fight against it.

2. To protest acts of corruption, and to report such acts to the media where the light of exposure will help eradicate them.

When this happens in sufficient measure, you can be sure you will feel better about your life and your community. And, your children will have a better future. Hope, ambition, and self-sufficiency will all again be visible on our reservations.

Pardon me, please, if you catch me grinning. I just love it when I find a well-articulated source that agrees with me. See below:

TI: "An independent and free media: Availability of information is a prerequisite for the creation of an informed public, empowered to participate meaningfully in public debates and to hold those who govern accountable. It is fundamental to democracy itself.... A free, independent, accountable and ethical media whose status is protected by the law and who is not subject to political or otherwise opportunistic leadership can assume an important watchdog function and act as an agent of awareness. Leadership can assume an important watchdog function and act as an agent of awareness."

**New Casino at Red Lake: A risky and ill-advised venture.
August 15, 2008.**

  A plan to develop a new casino at Red Lake is evolving quickly. The project is being moved forward based, somewhat, on recommendations and conclusions contained in a study "Recommended Gaming Development at Red Lake and Warroad Minnesota," performed by the GVA Marquette Advisors of Minneapolis, Seattle and Las Vegas. The November 2007 report is addressed to the CFO for Red Lake Gaming Enterprises (RLGE).

  As can be seen from the title, the report had a dual purpose: first to establish the feasibility of replacing the existing casino that is currently housed at the Humanities Center in Red Lake, and secondly to study the feasibility of expanding the casino at Warroad, Minnesota on its present site.

  The Tribal Council has evidently opted for the first consideration, although the second one seems to be the more logical and appears to make more sense economically. The advisory group, while acknowledging the Red Lake Casino only draws from locals, and also admitting a new casino would take revenue away from the tribe's River Road Casino at Thief River Falls, still recommended the construction of a new facility on Highway 89 at the southern edge of the reservation. It's a shame too.

  Their choice will further burden their own people and any profit will come at their expense. There are at least 10 reasons why the decision to build a new casino at Red Lake is wrong, will harm the people, and will cause more problems than anyone could imagine:

  1. It is detrimental to build a new casino that attracts, even according to outside observers, primarily Red Lake residents. Tribal leaders everywhere should have been giving their people this message at the beginning of the gaming era: "Do not gamble at the casino. It is designed to take money away from people. Avoid the temptation. Keep your money in your pocket."

If that had happened, the gambling process could have been the means for a lawful revenge against the historic losses American Indians experienced at the hands of European invaders.

2. The hired experts tell Red Lake leadership that a new casino will provide only a relatively small benefit, and they warn the competition for the gaming dollar is widespread and fierce. That doesn't appear to be a strong 'go ahead' to me.

3. The Marquette conclusion in regard to an increase in revenue is dependent on conditions I'm not sure the tribe is meeting now. Those conditions are: assure competent, professional marketing and management; use standard accounting practices and apply controls to protect the large amounts of cash from theft and/or diversion by insiders; keep the properties well maintained, attractive and up to date--keep on top of this aspect so other casinos do not surpass you in appearance, amenities, etc.

Their recommendation is based on economic conditions and financial information from 2006. That's a red flag. Today's economy is much less strong. Costs for everything are up noticeably, unemployment is up in many sectors, and revenues are down. There are decidedly fewer gamblers in today's market.

4. Speaking of financial considerations, the specific figures given in the study need to be fleshed out. Does the projected revenue increase reflect the costs of capitol? And what about the costs associated with infrastructure additions and improvements, things like new roads, sewer capability, waste management, etc.

5. Red Lake has a reputation that does not make it attractive to outsiders. News stories about drug busts, crime, violence, and inhospitality to outsiders make it uninviting, even ominous. The Chairman often describes it as a "closed reservation." It is clear Red Lake does not want people using their resources, particularly the lake itself. Unlike the Lake of the Woods at Warroad, Red Lake does not encourage visitors. Given the heavy competition, people are likely to choose a friendlier gaming site.

6. Law enforcement concerns are serious and growing in magnitude. Red Lake has opted out of cooperative agreements with neighboring law enforcement entities, making the reservation a refuge for wrong doers of all kinds. We've heard stories about individuals seeking refuge from pursuing police by simply stepping across the line on to the reservation. There are stories about police involvement in drug trafficking. Two Red Lake police officers were arrested recently and plea-bargained to avoid trial. They face sentencing in September. A community where the police are involved in criminal activity is not a place others want to visit.

If the new casino should ever be successful in drawing gamblers to the area, there will be increased demand for police personnel to counter the accompanying increase in crime as well as to manage increased traffic flow, problems and congestion. Will the small increase in gambling revenue that has been projected cover these new costs?

7. Infrastructure costs will increase. Waste management is already a problem at Red Lake. What plans are being considered to resolve this issue? It's been on-going for months now and the new casino's presence will do nothing but add to this problem. New roads are likely to be needed. There will be substantial increases in all utilities, e.g. heating, air conditioning, ventilation, lighting, water, electrical usage, etc. etc. Are these concerns factored in?

8. The plan to increase tribal debt to build another casino raises another concern—per capita payments for the members. In spite of the many years that Red Lake has had a gaming operation, there has never been a per capita established for the members. There has instead been ever-increasing expenses and repayment of debt that have prevented such a payment. Now, with these new plans, Tribal government is again making a choice that will put the tribe in big debt, and this new debt makes the possibility of a per capita payment nothing but remote.

9. Social costs associated with a new casino at Red Lake did not even get a nod of attention in the report. The advisors say they have considerable experience in the gaming industry, yet they make no

mention of the predictable downside that accompanies any new casino. Study after study, done by individuals who have no connection to the gaming industry, show there is an irrefutable increase in crime, addiction, domestic and community violence, abused and neglected children, job loss, and family upheaval when a new casino opens its doors.

The Red Lake Gaming audit indicates the Red Lake Casino produced $240,000 in profit for the Band in 2007. I suggest that amount did not go far to address the kinds of problems mentioned above. What is the budget for Child Protective Services, for members' Emergency Fund, or other human services? I bet the costs in service areas like these far surpass the modest amount of profit that the Red Lake casino contributed.

10. If the Band feels they can afford and are ready to improve its gaming operation, they would be wise to consider the expansion of the facility at Warroad. That would at least protect their own people from gambling addictions, and other related ills. The Marquette Advisors recommended improving and enlarging the facility at Warroad. They pointed out that it's currently marginal in terms of furnishings, lighting, amenities and customer appeal. Refurbishing under those conditions is certainly justifiable and supportable. Furthermore, this project would not compete so directly with the River Road casino in Thief River Falls, and it would not prey on tribal members who spend their meager incomes gambling at the Red Lake Casino.

Additionally, unlike Red Lake, Warroad is a tourist destination. Visitors in high numbers are attracted to the Lake of the Woods and return often to enjoy the area. Also unlike Red Lake, the Warroad casino draws mostly non-native customers. It has a more favorable geographic location and is supported by a strong community that offers other attractions, amenities and infrastructure.

The advisory group has not issued an all clear, full-speed-ahead recommendation. The report did not give promise of huge revenues and warned that success is dependent on beating out the heavy competition that exists in this market.

They did not address situations that may arise during the building phase that would add to the construction costs and to the debt. Red Lake's governing body has not demonstrated strong efforts to alleviate the problems the people on the reservation are facing. There have been no reports of improved conditions developed by the current council. Therefore, it gives me pause to consider, does this administration have what it takes to make this marginal deal go?

As usual with the governing group at Red Lake, we are left scratching our heads in wonder at their actions. How can a casino at Red Lake possibly be justified? Why did this study cost twice as much as the one the city of Bemidji, with a population of 14,000, ordered for a study of a proposed new events center?

Given the small proposed revenues that are possible, only if Red Lake can beat out the fierce existing competition, where's the benefit?

Politics played too big a role at the Band's Thief River Falls casino, and it appears that will be the case for the proposed casino as well. Is the hierarchy up there involved in all too familiar scams? The air surrounding these proposed transactions is beginning to smell like rotten walleye.

Consider the overpriced feasibility report by Marquette, who also studied the feasibility of building the casino at Thief River Falls several years ago.

Notice that a local Engineering and Consulting firm has already been involved in the new project, doing "pre-construction site preparation." Red Lake Builders is rumored to be the general contractor.

These principals were all involved in the construction of the Band's original Thief River casino operation and in the subsequent expansion project. Much concern surrounded that project: specifically, irregular bid lettings; multiple, unapproved expenditures for change orders; substantial, unexplained budget overrides; and a general lack of arm's length relationships among the principals involved in the process.

Add to that the firing of key personnel whose job it was to look for wrongdoing, and you have a scenario that casts a shadow of suspicion on any future project. When you look at the facts, small revenue dependent on being wrenched away from other casinos, and high costs (both social costs and actual cash outlay) and subsequent huge debt, how would any leader consider taking the step to build the new casino?

There must be something going on that is not above board. A new casino in Red Lake simply cannot be justified money wise; the return is too small. And in terms of human service costs, the proposed new project would be like trying to put out a fire by pouring kerosene on it. All that will happen is a huge explosion and more damage.

Also See:
"King recalled," *The Native American Press/Ojibwe News* March 15, 2002;
"King fails in attempt to revoke Recall Petition," *The Native American Press/Ojibwe News* December 14, 2001.
"King thwarted in attempt to derail Recall Petition," and "King ... resigns." *The Native American Press/Ojibwe News* January 11, 2002.
Also note:
Meuers, Michael. "Red Lake Capitol Construction ahead of schedule." *Indian Country Today.* September 20, 2014. And "New Red Lake Nation College Takes the Shape of an Eagle. *Indian Country Today.* March 28, 2015.

The two article describe another very large building project and includes comments by Red Lake Nation College President Dan King.

King was Tribal Treasurer but was recalled in March 2002. He had resigned his position but the tribe pursued the recall process against him because, according to the Tribal Constitution, if recalled, King could never again hold tribal office.

The following is a quote from an editorial published March 16, 2001.
Financial chaos at Red Lake even worse than expected.

Press/ON has obtained Red Lake tribal council financial information, which we are currently in the process of reviewing. According to the documents that we have obtained, the tribal council overspent its fiscal year 2000 budget by $2,864,139. Most of the overspending was for unplanned development projects and salaries. They had to draw most of the money to cover the shortfall out of trust funds.

Now, they want us to accept the risk of their spending another $27 million dollars to expand the River Road Casino, including the water park. In addition, they want us to now go along with their spending another $8 million dollars for a new casino on the south boundary of the Red Lake reservation, when in fact the current casino is losing money. I think it's time for the Red Lake people to demand a full accounting of our financial condition.

Press/ON will be carrying more information regarding Red Lake financial information in the next several editions, as we are able to analyze and review these documents. I still haven't received any reply from the Red Lake Tribal Council to review the closing documents for the $27 million loan for the River Road Casino.

Red Lake Economics & the Trickle-Up Effect.

Chapter VIII: Introduction to Indian Gaming.

Since the days of subjugation, poverty and dependency have persisted on America's Indian reservations. Bill Lawrence believed Federal Indian policy is to blame and has had a most disastrous effect on the lives of Native people.

In 1988, in an attempt to enable tribal populations to achieve greater self-reliance, the United States Congress enacted the Indian Gaming Regulatory Act (IGRA), in Lawrence's view, another ill-conceived plan by the federal government.

The creation of Indian gaming was expected to be the new "buffalo," i.e. a chance for Native peoples to maximize the marginal lands they occupied, build wealth, rehabilitate their cultures, and restore dignity and self-sufficiency to the tribes.

Casinos would create jobs and thereby, eventually, raise standards of living and promote financial independence for tribal members. It is unfortunate but that scenario has not developed. The casinos have definitely produced new wealth, but it has not often been distributed equitably. Kleptocracy and secrecy are *modus operendi.*

The Congress did not expect that Indian gambling would be lucrative. With the small expectation of Native wealth to be derived from gaming, no stringent controls were put in place. And neither the Congress nor the states have addressed this situation.

Inadequate regulation and few reporting requirements of gambling proceeds have made it possible for unscrupulous tribal officials to make themselves the almost exclusive beneficiaries of the casino windfall. It is not uncommon for some tribal authorities to operate their casinos without disclosing any financial data regarding casino operations.

Thomas L. Friedman in his 2008 book, *Hot, Flat and Crowded,* articulated a premise about oil rich nations that has a surprising relevance for Native America. About petro rich countries, he observed, "there must be a correlation ... between the

194

price of oil and the pace, scope and sustainability of political freedoms ... When one went down the other went up."[1]

His statement applies as easily to Native American tribes, especially those that operate casinos. While it is especially true for tribes operating casinos, non-gaming tribes experience similar occurrences in connection with monies appropriated to them by the federal government.

Friedman sees this phenomenon occurring in "petrolist states," which he defines as, "authoritarian states (or ones with weak state institutions) that are highly dependent on oil production for the bulk of their governmental income. In virtually every case," he says, "these states accumulated their oil wealth before they established sound and transparent institutions of governance."

Native American tribal governments meet Friedman's definition of petrolist states. Many are authoritarian, with all power resting in the hands of tribal officials. Most tribes have yet to develop sound, transparent, accountable and representative governments, and are dependent on federal grant funds or casino proceeds. Many tribes have formal constitutions, but few of them provide for separations of powers, checks and balances, an independent judiciary, and civil rights protections or guarantees.

Mr. Friedman's observations create a useful analogy between what has recently been newsworthy in the world and the not-so-well known circumstances on America's reservations, where individual freedoms have steadily decreased. Substitute "casino revenue" for "oil wealth" and the analogy is complete.

Tribal officials, strengthened by access to casino revenues (or having unilateral control over government appropriated funds) have become increasingly reluctant to be accountable and to act within the bounds of lawful activity. As tribal officials avail themselves of the tribes' revenues, their prerogatives and living standards rise and the rights of individuals and the welfare of the group declines.

Finally, Tom Friedman asserts that, although many nations have realized sudden wealth as a result of successfully drilling for oil, the social and political situations of the people remain dismal. The same undesirable conditions also exist for Native communities with regard to casino revenues. Even with the influx of millions of dollars from casino gambling, Native Americans still hold the lowest socio-economic position in the country and too many are denied the constitutional protections they are entitled to.

Minnesota Appellate Court Judge R.A. "Jim" Randall in a published opinion has advocated that in order to bring accountability to Indian gambling that tribal governments be permitted by federal and/or state legislation to reorganize reservation governments into state regulated municipalities.

He states, "We have never had the decency and concern for Indian people to ensure that when we granted monopolistic gaming franchises to Indian tribes, those franchises were accompanied by necessary state and federal regulations needed to guarantee that funds received and funds distributed were accounted for and the intended beneficiaries fully protected."

Randall further stated,[2] "Until there is the same accountability that all municipally-owned business entities are subject to, Indian gaming will continue to be a cancerous sore..."

Bill Lawrence persistently called for and supported proposed amendments to the Indian Gaming Regulatory Act. To his regret and, despite hundreds of lines of copy urging it, that did not happen during his life time.

[1] Friedman, Thomas. Hot, Flat and Crowded. New York: Farrar, Straus, Geriox. 2008. J
[2] Randall, Judge James R.A. Dissent. Cohen v Little Six. . . State of Minnesota Court of Appeals, 8th District. December 18, 1995.

It's Time for Some Sunshine in Indian Gaming.
August 13, 1993.

In last week's edition of *Press/ON*, we ran an AP article titled, "Negotiators fail to meet deadline for Indian gambling deal." Considering that those attempting to make the deal were representatives of governors, state attorneys general, and tribes, and the fact that they had only been meeting for a month, no big deal.

What should be a big deal to Indian people is the fact that, at the direction of Chairman Dan Inouye of the Senate Indian Affairs Committee, the negotiations have essentially been conducted in secrecy and the participants muzzled. Considering the importance of gaming to Indian country and the current lack of accountability, this certainly doesn't send a very good message to those of us who think that Indian gaming is badly in need of some sunshine. We simply would like to know where all of our gaming funds end up.

In view of the fact that, back in the late 1980s, Senator Inouye, and most of the committee, labored through two years of investigations into Indian Affairs and came up with a call for a "New Federalism for American Indians," they are explicitly aware of the half democracies that exist on reservations.

To hold secret meetings on an issue that is so vitally important to Indian people, and exclude their participation, is nearly tantamount to passage of the recently enacted Deficit Reduction law without informing the American people.

Perhaps, Senator Inouye has been reading too much about tribal sovereignty and has become our new sovereign.

In contrast to the secret negotiations on amending the National Indian Gaming Act, Senator Inouye and members of the Senate Indian Affairs Committee went through the process of conducting field hearings around the country to solicit the views of all interested Indian people in amending the Indian Religious Freedoms Act.

Why can't he and the committee do the same for the Indian gaming law? Is it that the large amount of money involved in gaming makes it too important for the committee to seek the input of all interested Indian people?

*   *   *   *

It appears that the year and a half federal investigation into Minnesota Indian gaming and other tribal government activities is about to bear fruit. According to reliable sources the first indictment as a result of this investigation will come down next week. The indictments will serve as the opening salvo in the long process in cleaning up the corruption that permeates some of our Indian gaming in Minnesota.

Unfortunately, the axe will probably fall on the little guys that those in control have used. Those calling the shots have had over three years, and the use of a lot of Indian gaming dollars, to cover their tracks. They have plenty of funds to hire expensive lawyers to fight the charges. It will be interesting to see who the little guys hire to represent them come next week.

In any event, we should get some insight into the personalities involved in ripping off casino/tribal funds and, at least the first part of, the feds game plan in prosecuting the culprits.

Where was our trustee?
June 3, 1994.

Last Sunday's nearly three page article in the Minneapolis *Star Tribune* on Mafia ties to casinos owned by four Minnesota Chippewa tribal governments* (Boise Forte, Grand Portage, Leech Lake and White Earth) isn't exactly news.

We carried articles written by Susan Stanich of the Duluth *News Tribune* over two years ago. The articles won Susan a Premack writing award and nearly got her fired. Seeking her unemployment was a delegation of nine officials from the Minnesota Chippewa Tribe (MCT), led by the Chairman and a prominent tribal lobbyist, who met with the editor of the Duluth *News Tribune*.

The *Star Tribune* and its staff reporters, Chris Ison and Lou Kilzer,* should be recognized for doing all the research and writing that an article of this dimension takes. Timing of the article couldn't have been better in view of the upcoming Minnesota Chippewa tribal elections, and the ongoing federal investigation into alleged fraud, theft, mismanagement and mob influence at several of the tribal casinos. The *Star Tribune* article indicates that they have developed new sources of information which should be helpful in tracking down those responsible.

The one common thread through the Stanich/Ison/Kilzer articles is the involvement of a former Leech Lake and Minnesota Chippewa Tribal Attorney, who started out his law career as a legal aid attorney on the Leech Lake Reservation. He has been described, by knowledgeable tribal members, as the "godfather" of the Leech Lake Reservation.

According to a report prepared by the Inspector General of the Department of the Interior, released in December 1992, the Bois Forte band probably paid an exorbitant $6.4 million to lease video gaming machines rather than buying them. The report found that at least $12 million had been diverted from tribes through theft and mismanagement. How much more has been diverted since that report was prepared almost

199

two years ago? With all that cash changing hands every day, that $12 million is only a fraction of what has been ripped off at our casinos.

What the report didn't say is that the Interior Department, through the Bureau of Indian Affairs (BIA), is supposed to be the lead agency in carrying out the trust responsibility of the federal government to Indian tribes. Naturally the BIA uses the excuse that they didn't get funding to regulate the Indian Gaming Regulatory Act (IGRA). This is why we only have *reports* on fraud and mismanagement of our gaming industry, and not *indictments*.

If there is blame to assess for this situation it is with the Congress. It is hard to imagine that the Congress, with all its 'infinite wisdom and good intentions,' could enact an Indian gaming law without any means for policing it. Was it naiveté, or just plain ignorance of Indian affairs, that led them to pass a law without any mechanism for tribal members to enforce accountability of tribal governments for gaming funds?

Hopefully, the new amendments to IGRA will include a provision to require accountability of tribal governments to their membership.

Come to think of it, our trustee was busy at the casinos utilizing the contributions that later led to his early retirement.

* Chris and Lou Kilzer, "Mafia associates had ties to five casinos," Minneapolis *Star Tribune,* reprinted *The Native American Press/Ojibwe News,* June 3, 1994.

Indian gaming—unregulated and unaccountable.
August 23, 1996.

With the debate over amending the National Indian Gaming Act (NIGA) currently raging in Washington, a lot of rhetoric is emanating from all vested interests.

Unfortunately, and as usual, those of us who are supposed to be the beneficiaries of this piece of legislation have not been consulted for our views by any of the vested interests be they tribal, state or federal.

This is discouraging because probably around 90% of the Native American population in Minnesota has never seen a nickel or any kind of benefit from Indian gaming. We only see our tribal councils utilize casino monies as a gigantic slush fund, primarily benefiting themselves or their families or friends.

In an attempt to determine how our casino is operated and how our casino funds are spent, I made the following effort: Over the past two years as an enrolled member, I decided to make a concerted effort to obtain audited financial statements from our casino operations. This attempt has included numerous written requests to tribal chairmen and a lawsuit in tribal court.

With the tribal council in control of our tribal court, my suit got nowhere. My efforts have also included Freedom of Information Act (FOIA) requests to the National Indian Gaming Commission (NIGC) and Data Practices Act requests with the State of Minnesota. Both of these requests were summarily denied on the grounds that tribal casino financial information is confidential and not available to me, even as a member of the band. I decided against legal challenges to these denials because neither the NIGC or the state of Minnesota had obtained copies of the audited financial statements.

Tribes are required to submit copies of the audits to the NIGC within 120 days after the end of each fiscal year of the gaming operation. According to all tribal-state compacts, the audits are to be made available to the state upon request. It didn't appear that either the NIGC or the state had sought or received copies of audits from any of the tribes.

Not being able to obtain an accounting of our tribal casino operations, the question arose in my mind that if I, as a tribal member, can't monitor it, just who is looking over the shoulders of some of our less than trustworthy tribal officials?

Knowing the feds aren't doing any regulating and, according to the NIGA under the tribal/state compacts, the state is responsible for regulation of tribal casino operations, I sent a request under the Data Practices Act to find out just how much regulating the state of Minnesota was doing in this sea of cash that has been changing hands for the past couple of years. My request was sent to the Director of the Gaming Enforcement Division of the Minnesota Department of Public Safety in St. Paul.

According to the information furnished by the Director's office, I learned that he has a staff of three investigators and one clerk to do the background investigations of over 10,000 persons employed by the state's tribal casinos. They are also responsible to test more than 11,000 video machines at the 17 Indian casinos in the state. To date only one casino has been inspected with minor violations reported.

The state receives $150,000 from the tribes for gaming regulation. It is questionable if that entire amount is spent on tribal gaming enforcement activities.

In all fairness to the Governor, he did request $500,000 in his 94-95 biennium budget to be used to help regulate Indian gaming. This amount was approved by the State Senate but was defeated in the House of Representatives.

From my conversation with the Director of Gaming Enforcement, it is obvious that the state's tribal gaming enforcement activities are nothing more than a paper shuffling operation, with no meaningful regulating taking place. In fact, the only action the State's Gambling Enforcement Division can take against violations of the compact are written notifications to the involved tribal chairman. Considering the integrity of some of our tribal chairman isn't that comforting to know?

If you think your tribal council is any different from the one in question here, just go on in and ask your tribal chairman for a copy of the latest audited financial statement. Let me know what answer you receive. I hope that you get better results than I have gotten in my two-year quest for this information.

I think that in most cases you will agree that it is time for some regulation and accountability in our respective casino operations. Anyone who thinks that some of these Indian tribal governments are capable of, or have any intentions of, regulating and accounting for their gaming operations, unless forced to do so by law, is either naïve or also on the take.

*   *   *   *

In addition, don't forget that your congressmen and senators will be home soon for the 4th of July recess. It would probably be a good idea to let them know how you feel about the situation at your local casino. Let your congress person know you expect something to be done to correct this situation.

Corruption casts shadow over gaming.
May 16, 1997.

It looks like the $400,000 in political campaign contributions paid last year by the Minnesota tribal gaming interests only bought a few more months of the Indian gaming monopoly. The money would have been far better spent, and a much better sell with the Minnesota public, had they invested it in the needs of the urban Indian communities, rather than sending most of it off to Washington [as political contributions or lobbying fees]. [1]

As it now stands, the genie appears to be out of the bottle as far as the Minnesota public's willingness to support any expansion of gambling, be it for a stadium, Canterbury Park, poor Indians or what have you.

With only a few thousand Indians in the state benefiting from a $4 billion industry, how can you blame them?

It is the greed and unaccountability that has caught the public's attention. It is the fallout from Finngate and Chippygate [2] that has cast dark shadows over all of Indian affairs in Minnesota. It is the clandestine operation of the Minnesota Indian Gaming Association that raises doubts about gaming in Minnesota. It is the discriminatory and even vicious employment practices at some casinos that have caused the public to lose confidence in Minnesota Indian gaming. It is the ongoing practice of hiding behind sovereign immunity to escape responsibility as business owners and employers that has cost tribal gaming the public's support.

This is a bad sign for an industry that is so public dependent for patrons and employees. It is truly a house of cards. With the Minnesota legislative session scheduled to end on Monday May 19, and the Senate Majority Leader ... running interference, tribal gaming appears to have escaped this time. But the smell of money is in the air. If, as appears likely, the tribal gaming monopoly is broken, tribal leadership has no one to blame but themselves.

[1] In recent years, the amount has increased substantially. The National Indian Gaming Commission indicates that Indian gaming revenues amounted in 2010 and 2012 to nearly $30 billion.

[2] Refers to federal investigation and prosecution of two tribal officials, Harold "Skip" Finn and Darrell "Chip" Wadena, for tribal corruption

Redirect gambling revenues to meet needs of the poor.
February 13, 2004.

The big news stories of the week deal with discussions of proposed legislation to expand gambling and possible renegotiation of the gaming compact between the State of Minnesota and the 11 Minnesota Indian tribes. This issue raises the question as to what will happen to gambling in the state, and what changes are warranted.

There are several issues that this topic suggests. One is monitoring of the industry; a second is equity among all citizens of the state. Lastly, it may be time to reassess exactly how much good gambling is doing for anyone. Let's look at each of these issues.

Since Indian casino gambling was authorized, there has been no state money and limited authority to regulate what is actually happening. There has been no effective mechanism for requiring specific behavior from the tribes. The state hasn't requested an audit since 1995; there is no accounting or auditing staff to handle this responsibility in the Department of Public Safety that is charged with monitoring Indian gaming activity. This is a situation that should end.

It has been *Press/ON's* position from the beginning that regulation of Indian gaming, whether at state or federal level, has been a big joke, a farce.

Minnesota legislators have openly admitted they didn't know what they were doing in regard to negotiating the compacts. They were constructed by an entirely DFL (Democratic Farmer Labor) administration. Democrats controlled both houses of the legislature and occupied the governor's and the attorney general's offices as well. As far as state citizens are concerned, it has been described as one of the poorest compacts.

There has never been a legislative appropriation in support of a monitoring process. In mid-1990's Governor Arne Carlson included money in his budget for this purpose, but the Democrat-controlled legislature failed to accommodate his request. By now tribal PAC monies are beginning to direct the show.

Renegotiation of the compacts is long overdue. Equity is one of the issues: there should be a percentage going to the state. A recent study indicated there is a direct correlation between the presence of a casino on a reservation and increased social costs. It's estimated there has been an 8% increase in crime and a 9% increase in violent crime in counties throughout the nation that have a casino within its borders. Further, and for every $1 of casino revenue produced, there is a $2 social cost attached.

Indians who have never benefited from gaming also need to be considered. It is time the tribes who receive enormous gaming revenues, due simply to their location, be required to share their largess with those who live in more isolated regions. The opportunities and the benefits of the bounty that is gambling should be shared. Let those who support the vice provide the virtue of meeting tribal needs.

Lastly, one needs to ask, "How much good has actually been accomplished through Indian gambling anyway? A look at the Mille Lacs band of Ojibwe gaming revenues may be informative. Over the last dozen years, it is estimated the tribe's reported net income from gambling has amounted to about three quarters of a billion dollars. (This information is derived from 1991-95 copies of the annual casino audits that the tribe submitted to me pursuant to the lawsuit filed by the tribes to prevent me from getting this data, plus other audits and financial information I've received from other sources).

Additionally, the tribe has received, on average, approximately $10 million a year from federal programs. That is an enormous sum of money to spend on the needs and services of the slightly more than 1,000 tribal members living on the little over 4,000-acre, Mille Lacs reservation. Admittedly, there are about 2,000 additional tribal members living off the reservation, but services and benefits go primarily to those individuals who actually reside on the reservation.

When you consider the social conditions on the reservation, it's hard to see many benefits from the money that has been produced at the Mille Lacs casinos. There has been some improvement in the reservation infrastructure, but there doesn't seem to be effective progress in the handling of social problems. Benefits to education from the influx of dollars seem to be limited to two new school facilities. Test scores and numbers of graduates produced by the system have improved just slightly.

Problems stemming from the presence of a casino on the reservation, such as crime, gangs, drugs, and alcohol have actually increased rather than abated since the money has been available. This situation was a major concern in the State of the Band speech given recently by the Chief Executive.

It's going to be an interesting session to see how the governor, the legislature, the tribes and the people deal with the issue of expanded gaming. It's my opinion the whole issue of gambling should be submitted to the people through a referendum to decide by constitutional amendment whether and how gambling should be expanded.

It's time for adequate regulation of our Indian gambling
August 27, 2004.

It's always gratifying to have one's own comments taken seriously and have them be substantiated by another objective, respectable source. That happened this week when an article on Indian gaming appeared in the Wall Street Journal (WSJ).

The article is rehashed on page one of this edition. The issues are the same as I have been talking about since as early as 1993 with my editorial entitled "Indian Gaming is unregulated and unaccountable."

Issues in the WSJ that have relevance here in Minnesota are:
1. Regulation of casinos. The fox is guarding the hen house.
2. Insufficient funding for gaming regulators to do an adequate job. In Minnesota, Tribes contribute only $150,000 to the state for regulatory functions. This amount hasn't increased since 1993 and it was an inadequate figure then. This means there is almost no monitoring of pay out figures and serious question as to whether background checks of prospective and current employees is adequate or effective in screening personnel.
3. The magnitude of the industry. The number of casinos and the amount of revenue nationwide and here is rising dramatically. Minnesota Indian gaming produces a significant amount of money, has expanded substantially since its modest beginnings and is fraught with debt, mismanagement, unaccountability and maybe downright theft of tribal funds.
4. Politics - campaign contributions. State officials accept large contributions from tribes and protect the casinos from strict regulation, often hiding behind the veil of 'tribal sovereignty.'

Let's look at each of the issues individually.
1. Regulation. Tribal gaming grew out of the Indian Gaming Regulatory Act of 1988. Its purpose was to provide for the operation of casinos with the intent that such activity would promote tribal economic development, self-sufficiency and strong tribal governments. The tribes have consistently been resistant to regulation from the outside, claiming tribal

sovereignty protects them from scrutiny. And, in fact, the compacts between the state and the tribes are vague and tend to support the 'hands-off' policy.

However, the compacts were drawn up at the conception of Indian gaming, at a time when the future of gaming was unknown and whether there would be much in the way of revenue was as yet undetermined. To insist on retaining the same details of the compacts forever is like trying to wear the same pair of pants today that you wore when you were a child. You've grown up and require more material. Gaming has also come of age and requires objective regulatory oversight to assure revenue benefits the tribe and to prevent wrongdoing by insider tribal officials.

2. Insufficient funding for gaming regulators is at a ridiculous figure. What other budget number has remained unchanged for over ten years? How could anyone realistically say Minnesota has a regulatory system. We've heard that so few machines are inspected to verify pay out and reliability that the number does not even constitute the equivalent of a random sampling. Pay out is such a secret figure in Minnesota, no one has even begun to ask about it. And what about background checks for employees? Or drug testing? It is probably safe to say that neither of these two checks are used anywhere and most certainly not in elected officials that govern tribal casinos.

3. The magnitude of gaming in Minnesota as well as elsewhere is impressive. As the WSJ article pointed out, gaming revenues have nearly doubled in five years and some casinos produce more money than many of the larger Las Vegas establishments. The Indian gaming industry has grown from its first year's revenue of nearly $100 million to one that currently exceeds $14.5 billion.

Who would ever have imagined such an outcome? Indian casino revenues will likely exceed national gambling averages in four years. With operations of such magnitude, it is imperative that effective regulations are in place. In Minnesota, I estimate the 2003 gross revenue to be at $1.965 billion with a net revenue of $772 million. Most of the tribes have experienced major casino expansion projects. The issue is, of course, how is the revenue utilized? Does it go to the benefit of the tribes?

What about the gambling public? Who looks after their interests? Traditionally gambling has been closely regulated in this country. It's no doubt safe to say the average bettor thinks the same regulations hold for the Indian casinos. Nothing, it appears, could be further from the truth. With gaming at such a volume in this country (and in Minnesota), it is vital that regulatory oversight be wide spread, objective and have the teeth to enforce conformity to well-established gaming rules.

4. Politics. We learned that the California Attorney General has received hundreds of thousands of dollars from California tribes.

Tribal contributions became a campaign issue in the last, special election, gubernatorial race. We've reported consistently in the past on the extent of tribal campaign contributions in Minnesota. Contributions for the last campaign year from tribes were overwhelmingly slanted toward Democratic Farm Labor (DFL) candidates. The big money went as follows: $449,250 divided between the DFL House Caucus, the DFL State Central Committee and the Senate DFL Majority caucus.

In contrast, $66,650 was distributed to the House Republican Caucus and the Minnesota State Republican Party. Those figures should tell you something.

The focus of the California gaming news is the Governor's signing compacts allowing for new casinos. In exchange, the state receives $1 billion in upfront money and promises of as much as $400 million more each year in revenue. The question remains however as to how the annual amount will be determined since tribes will continue doing business as usual and not be required to disclose financial information.

Minnesota needs to do something similar, but with tighter regulation. The discussions of the last two legislative sessions indicate pretty clearly that the State is not interested in continuing the tribes'

211

monopoly in gambling unless they are willing to pony up more of the revenues than they have in the past. It is only fair that the tribes contribute substantially to the fund [the state budget] that supports so many of the programs that benefit reservations as well as pays much of the social costs associated with the presence of a casino in a community.

It is only realistic to expect also that they be required to show that tribal casinos are operated in a legitimate fashion, follow traditional business practices, disclose their financial data and provide reasonable protections and pay outs to their betting clients.

We have been in court three and a half years trying to get tribal casino audited financial statements, which I have always held to be public information under the Minnesota Data Practices Act. It appears that the case, which several tribes filed to prevent the state from giving me the records, is nearing conclusion. This has been an example of the difficulty individuals, even tribal members, face in getting the tribes to disclose information that should be public knowledge.

With or without adequate oversight, we've often said there is no "organized crime" in our tribal casinos. What's been abundantly clear however is a strong presence of "disorganized crime." This situation has become flagrant, abuses are everywhere, and it's time for a clean-up.

Gambling externalities cost Minnesota taxpayers an estimated $375 million a year.
February 11, 2005.

Three years ago, in January 2002, we reported in *Press/ON* that there were seven gambling bills pending in the Minnesota Legislature, including one that would establish a tribal/state casino in the metro area. We further reported on the 1996 work, titled "Casinos, Crime and Community Costs," by two economists, Earl L. Grinols and David B. Mustard.

The 1996 article documented the negative impact on crime in U.S. counties that hosted casinos. In September 2004 Grinols and Mustard revised the earlier article. The conclusion is still the same: "crime increases over time in casino counties and that casinos do not just shift crime from neighboring regions, but create crime."

Professor Grinols is with the Department of Economics at the University of Illinois. Professor Mustard is a member of the Terry College of Business faculty at the University of Georgia. The two widely published economists state that their "analysis of the relationship between casinos and crime is the most exhaustive ever undertaken in terms of the number of regions examined, the years covered and the control variables used." They indicate that there is still little comprehensive research into the gambling industry. The few studies that have been published are flawed, due in part to the small samples examined, or the contradictory results that were produced. Further, the studies weren't controlled for variables and/or were agenda driven, i.e., sponsored by special interest groups.

Their study examined casinos in every one of the 3165 U.S. counties and was academically oriented, giving it a large measure of objectivity. Their work is valuable, giving well-researched, credible information at a time when important decisions regarding gambling expansion in Minnesota are being considered.

Casino industry growth has been rapid in recent years, increasing by 203 percent (from $8.7 billion to $26.3 billion) between

213

1990 and 2000. To give a reference point, Gross Domestic Product increased 201 percent during the same time frame that casino revenues increased 660 percent.

Another factor is the growth of lobbying efforts and the practice of making campaign contributions in order to influence legislation and policy. The most recent figures indicate that from 1992-1997, $100 million was paid "in lobbying fees and donations to state legislators." These dollars have no doubt had a substantial impact on the industry.

While industry growth and outside influence have grown, the crime rate has also grown.

The changes in data from 1996-2004 are instructive. In 1996 the Grinols/Mustard study indicated, "between 3 and 30 percent of the different crimes in casino communities can be attributable to casinos."

The 2004 revision indicates the estimates rise to "between 5.5 and 30 percent of the different crimes in casino counties can be attributable to casinos." In 1996, the researchers say, "overall 8% of property crime and 10% of violent crime ... was due to the presence of a casino." By 2004, those figures had increased to "8.6 percent of property crime and 12.6 percent of violent crime was due to the presence of a casino."

The costs of casino-related crime have risen dramatically. Until 1984, they were $1.10 or less per adult per year; through 1988, the costs were between $5 and $9; by 1990, the costs had risen to $33 and by 1995, were $65. The 2004 revised article states that crime in casino communities now costs "the average adult $75 per adult per year."

Grinols and Mustard present conclusively that the problems associated with the presence of a casino grow substantially as the enterprise continues. Violent crimes such as rape and robbery have a negligible impact during the first few years after opening. But by the fourth and fifth years of business, a higher rape rate (6.5-10 [more] incidents per 100,000 population) occurs. For robbery, "the first year there were about 35 more incidents per 100,000 people, which increases to over

60 three years after opening. Despite increased law enforcement, robbery increased by 20%.

Larceny, a property crime as opposed to a violent crime, increases from zero in the second year after a casino opening to 4.1 incidents in the third year. By the fourth year, the number increases to 185 and then to over 600 occurrences in the fifth year.

Burglary estimates in the fourth year stand at 64; by the fifth year after a casino opens, the figure jumps to 325.

Their study indicates that by the fifth year after the opening of a casino, county crime rises as follows: robbery-136% higher; aggravated assault-91% higher; auto thefts-78% higher; burglary-78% higher; larceny-50% higher; rape-21% higher.

In an earlier interview, Professor Grinols said, "Gambling is a loser from society's point of view... The costs exceed the benefits 1.9 to 1 and that is a conservative estimate." This return means that for every dollar of revenue a casino produces, it creates $1.90 in unintended social costs.

The report is lengthy and punctuated with statistical analysis that substantiates the data presented, but challenges the average citizen's understanding of the method.

Even so, many startling and significant bits of information immerge. The following is a random sampling of such information: Gamblers Anonymous (GA) chapters have experienced enormous growth since the advent of casinos. A governmental report, the National Gambling Impact Study (NGIS), stated that the numbers have risen from 650 chapters in 1990 to 1328 in 1998.

Conversely, restricting gaming reduces the number of GA chapters. "South Carolina banned slot machines.... six months later, the number of GA groups dropped from 32 to 11 and the attendance from a typical size of about 450 to as few as one or two."

"One indication of the different clientele casinos attract is the large increase in pawnshops that occur when casinos open. Other tourist areas do not experience similar increases."

"Many law enforcement officials have testified that prostitution increased dramatically after casinos opened."

"Casinos may attract visitors more likely to commit rape or to be its victims."

"Pathological gamblers generally commit crime to generate money or to deal with their debts or to gamble... [In Illinois] communities ... have documented a significant increase in casino-related embezzlement, theft, and burglary, much of it committed by professionals like teachers and lawyers."

The number of problem and pathological (P&P) gamblers grows as the distance to a casino lessens to 50 miles or less. "Research conducted for the National Gambling Impact Study reported that the population percentage of problem gamblers rose from .3 percent to 1.1 percent when the distance to the nearest casino fell from more than 250 miles to less than 50 miles."

The report says that crime rates are likely to be influenced by the actions of P&P gamblers. Pathological gamblers, and to a lesser degree problem gamblers, "are identified by repeatedly failing to resist the urge to gamble, relying on others to relieve the desperate financial situations caused by gambling, committing illegal acts to finance gambling, and losing control over their personal lives and employment."

At this time there are a variety of gaming expansion bills before the Minnesota Legislature. While debate continues on the question of a tribal/state casino, it seems to center only on the obvious issues e.g. profitability for the participants. The State wants a new source of funds to balance the budget. The tribes are divided on the question, some seeing the expansion of gambling as a potential windfall to give their members a per-capita payment. Others opposing the proposition believe that insufficient benefit would come to them as a result of the increased debt associated with the development of such a casino.

Citizens Against Gaming Expansion (CAGE) was formed to resist any expansion of gambling and, in light of the information presented in "Casinos, Crime & Community Costs," their approach may be the wisest action.

It's high time for everyone involved to be thinking about what the two economists call "externalities," i.e. the costs associated with the casinos. Grinols and Mustard have simply demonstrated these costs, giving hard facts about the negative consequences and applying dollar figures to concretely illustrate their points; e.g., the cost associated with the presence of a casino to every adult for each year is $75. That's something everyone can understand and relate to.

If you take the approximate number of Minnesota citizens to be 5 million, the total externality costs associated with gambling would amount to $375 million a year. If you factor in the lottery and pull-tab operations, the figure could conceivably rise to $500 million a year. These amounts are what it is costing right now. Add another casino in the Twin Cities and the dollar figure would rise again.

The Governor wants a cut of tribal casino revenue to offset the substantial budget shortfall. If the externality costs of gaming were eliminated, the shortfall would be significantly reduced. Once again, it's time for some "out of the box" thinking.

This study seems to be the most extensive and unbiased report available to date. It behooves all decision makers and opinion leaders to become familiar with the information and be guided by what they see.

Note: the report is available at
http://www.terry.uga.edu/%7Edmustardlcasinos.pdf

Long overdue change coming to Indian gaming.
October 7, 2005.

A trip to a full-scale Indian casino is like an intensive look at the set of a Hollywood movie. The general impression is favorable. You will immediately notice an impressive façade. There may be columns, flying buttresses, fountains, and bas relief designs.

There certainly will be bright lights and an inviting aura. It's not as gaudy as Las Vegas, but it's pretty clear that big-time gambling has had an influence on these establishments.

Inside you will see a lobby tastefully decorated with just the right touches of Native American artifacts. You may see plush carpets in rich colors with images of moccasins, or representations of Indian floral motifs woven in. The walls will be adorned, depending on the locations, with historic implements, weapons, articles of clothing, etc.

There may be a "fine-dining" restaurant. There will often be a hotel, complete with the glittering gift shop. The design is usually tasteful, displaying just the right degree of allusion to Indian culture.

These facilities seem to be testimony to competent management. Staff looks smart in their uniforms. The public areas are clean and well groomed. The properties appear to be prosperous.

One would guess that Indian gaming is fulfilling its charge, delineated in the 1968 Indian Gaming Regulatory Act (ICRA), to "Provide a statutory basis for the operation of gaming by Indian tribes as a means of promoting tribal economic development, self-sufficiency, and strong tribal governments."

Unfortunately all that we see is sham.

The Indian Gaming Regulatory Act is in the news again. Everyone has known for quite some time that the Act was not doing what it was intended to do. People have been increasingly outspoken in their criticism of gaming, and the problems associated

218

with gambling have grown just as fast as the industry itself has grown.

Twenty years ago there was no such thing as an Indian tribal casino. By 2001, there were 196 tribes operating 309 gaming facilities. Revenues exceeded $10 billion.

In 2005, approximately 225 tribes were operating casinos. Revenue had grown to $19 billion. Another 227 groups were seeking Congressional recognition as tribal entities so they too could open and operate tribal casinos. There is also great interest on the part of tribes to expand their gaming activity *beyond* the reservation boundaries.

Anti-gaming groups and individuals alike are gaining strength in their protests concerning the social evils and costs associated with gaming, i.e., the crime and violence, the abuse and fraud by tribal officials, the lack of accountability and lack of regulation of the industry.

Labor unions, civil rights groups, federal agencies and the courts have all become involved in the disputes. Most recently the National Labor Relations Board ruled that they hold jurisdiction over tribal businesses that employ "or affect" non– Indians.

A District of Columbia federal judge has ruled that the National Indian Gaming Commission does not have authority to regulate Class III gaming activities.

The Department of Justice announced proposed changes to the Indian gaming law. If the changes are adopted into law, tribes will find themselves facing stricter limits on the kinds of games they can offer.

These events--the public clamor, the National Labor Relations Board's decision, the court decision and the Department of Justice announcement--have created sufficient energy to attract congressional attention.

Senator John McCain (R.AZ), Chairman of the Indian Affairs Committee, has scheduled hearings, the intent of which is to amend the 1988 Indian Gaming Regulatory Act.

Senator Byron Dorgan (D.ND), Vice Chair of the Indian Affairs Committee, has been quoted to say the growth [of the Indian gaming industry] demands renewed scrutiny by Congress.

And about time too.

McCain is entirely accurate when he says, "Ninety-nine percent of the patrons of these Indian gaming facilities are non–Indians. So we have an obligation to non-Indians, as well as Indians, to make sure that these gaming activities are honest, straightforward and adequately regulated." He also points out that the industry employs tens of thousands of non-Indians.

The regulation of Indian gaming has, like most federal Indian policies, always been a very flat and sad joke. Tribes have never been required to be accountable for their activities, not to their membership nor to the state that is supposed to be overseeing their operations.

National Indian Gaming Association leadership, predictably, takes issue with the National Labor Relations Board ruling and the federal judge's decision. The president of the National Indian Gaming Association said, "In our view, the National Labor Relations Board has tipped 30 years of decisions of law on its head." He added, "The National Indian Gaming Association disagrees with the decision. Until the Board revises its regulations or a court of competent jurisdiction orders changes in the scope of its regulations, it will continue to conduct business as usual."

I find it entertaining, even laughable, that the Indian hierarchy is calling for protection under the rule of law. Throughout the country, tribal officials are ignoring, are avoiding, or are simply defying the rule of law. Now they want the law upheld.

They don't seem to understand that the law is multifaceted, all-encompassing, entirely nonselective and, at least ideally, unbiased and fair. They can't reasonably expect observance of the law only when it is for their own protection and, at the same time, condone or at least disregard flagrant abuses of law in regard to their own members.

As early as 1993, we at *The Native American Press/Ojibwe News* pointed out the lack of regulatory authority for the Indian Gaming Act and the lack of interest on the part of the state to provide oversight.

A miniscule amount, $150,000, and three positions were allocated for Tribal Gaming Enforcement. This ludicrous effort was intended to regulate more than 10,000 tribal casino employees and 11,000 video machines throughout the state.

Since then many, many individuals have called to report incidents of theft. There have been reports of tribal officials walking out of the casino vaults with thousands of dollars in their pockets. Pilfering by both officials and employees is common.

Very few individuals have ever been prosecuted for these actions.

There have been efforts in the past to amend or correct this situation, including early efforts led by Senator McCain. These initiatives have all failed, however, probably stopped or pigeonholed due to the influence of campaign contributors, mostly those with big gaming interests.

Gambling has not been the solution to tribal unemployment or economic development that it was intended to be. Gaming has added to the already high level of societal dysfunction. Instead of solving the problems, unregulated gambling has created more. Kids are not being educated. Crime, addiction, drugs, gang activity, fraud, abuse, and domestic violence are all on the rise.

Reservations are on the verge of imploding because of the weight of social and political problems.

"Unregulated and unaccountable" is how we described the Indian gaming industry in our 1993 editorial. Hopefully the initiatives by regulatory agencies and/or judicial interests signal the start of true reform.

Indian Gaming Regulatory Act amendments may still see light of day.
January 20, 2006.

The Jack Abramoff scandal has opened a Pandora's Box of troubles for Washington politicians. It has exposed the corruption that is possible under the existing lobbying system. Today, an editorial in the *New York Times* states that Washington politicians "are staging a fire sale on promises to clean up the lobbying and influence-peddling abuses rampant on Capitol Hill." The article indicates that free meals, gifts and travel will likely be prohibited in any proposed legislation.

The editorial reminds these newly anointed reformers of a loophole that exists in the campaign finance legislation that would permit politicians to continue to accept such perks even if prohibited under lobbying regulations.

This issue is an important one for both Washington and the State of Minnesota. But, as important as this, the Abramoff scandal has also been the "open sesame" for renewed efforts to amend the Indian Gaming Regulatory Act of 1988 (IGRA). Senator John McCain introduced amendments to the IGRA in November that, in his words, "reflect the need to re-evaluate what constitutes appropriate regulation of this vastly changed enterprise."

Specifically, the legislation, acknowledging a federal court decision that ruled the National Indian Gaming Commission (NIGC) did not have authority to regulate Class III gaming, would give the agency the authority to regulate "minimum internal control (MICS) standards for class II gaming and class III gaming activities." McCain, in his introductory remarks said, "This amendment makes clear that NIGC continues to have the authority it has exercised until now to issue and enforce MICS, including the ability to inspect facilities and audit premises in order to assure compliance." The bill also gives increased authority for NIGC to inspect "all types of gaming contracts, development agreements and revenue sharing deals."

Tribes definitely do not want the National Indian Gaming Commission [NIGC] to have this authority. The National Indian Gaming Association (NIGA) pleaded with McCain not to propose the new amendments or to make his proposals simply "draft discussions" of the bill. McCain refused, but Representative Richard Pombo (R-California), Chair of the House Resources Committee, did bow to tribal demands in calling his proposed IGRA amendments "draft discussion."

This week *indianz.com* announced that "The Bush administration is moving forward with its controversial gaming legislation despite overwhelming opposition from Indian Country.

After limiting the comment period to three meetings, the Department of Justice has moved the proposed legislation back for review and search for a sponsor. An attorney for the Department's criminal division said, since Senator McCain has given the DOJ the task, he didn't see that finding a sponsor would be a problem. The administration bill could be introduced as early as March or April.

Tribal leaders at the Western Indian Gaming Conference last week claimed the bill would harm the Indian gaming industry and the jobs and revenues created by Indian casinos. Tribal leaders and the NIGA have been tremendously influential in keeping proposed changes to the IGRA off the table. They see the proposed legislation as enhancing states' ability to tax tribal gaming proceeds.

One Indian gaming commissioner said the bill "will help states extract more money ... from the tribes." He continued, "this [is] not about justice but about the State Governors' Association trying to get one hand up on Indians in Florida, California, Oklahoma and in all those states where we use Class II gaming."

Government officials have claimed the legislation is simply about clarifying the difference between Class II games that can be operated without any state control and Class III games. Class II games might include bingo while Class III games include slot machines and must be operated under the terms of tribal/state compacts.

Phil Hogen, chairman of the NIGC, expressed concern that the distinction between the two classes has become blurred by advancements in electronic games. Some games that in the past have been considered as Class II games have passed the bounds of that classification and are closer in character to Class III games. He maintains the bill is intended to clarify these concerns.

With huge tribal payoffs now exposed by revelations of Abramoff deals, Washington feels free to move forward with needed reform to the IGRA. I suggest it is also time for the State of Minnesota Department of Public Safety, Division of Alcohol and Gaming Enforcement, to do something similar and move off the dead space it has occupied since 1995, when the last tribal casino audit was requested.

Tribes have been reluctant to reveal their financial information. Tribal leaders have consistently criticized any attempt to change the original IGRA. Predictably they call "foul," characterizing any change as taking away from the tribes. They hint at racial discrimination. They hold up old treaty violations by the federal government. What they don't do is hold up their financial documents for review, not even to tribal members.

This strikes me as odd; it suggests the tribes are hiding something. There is a great deal of vested interest in secrecy. Published in today's issue is a chart of payments by tribes to lobbying organizations. The figure paid by the eleven Minnesota tribes or Indian communities during this past year is over $1.2 million.

This information should raise some concerns and questions. Is it mere coincidence that those paying the most were those most interested in stopping a tribal/state casino plan? Who was it that opposed the tribal/state casino plan, and why? Who can afford to pay huge sums to lobbyists and where does the money come from? Can you guess the answers from looking at the list of contributions?

There is also the matter of why the Minnesota Department of Public Safety (MDPS), Alcohol and Gaming Enforcement Division (AGED), has not requested copies of audited financial statements of tribal casinos since 1995.

When Governor Tim Pawlenty was in Bemidji last summer I had the opportunity to ask him why the State had not requested the audits. He replied he didn't know the State had the authority to do so. I told him it did and urged he make the request. Nothing has happened. Why?

I've requested copies of the audited financial statements of Indian casinos from the Department under the Minnesota Data Practices Act. The Department's response has simply been they do not have the information. It's obvious they have not requested the information. My question is a big WHY NOT?

Last week we reported on the former Leech Lake Police Chief's appointment as Director of the Alcohol and Gaming Division of the MDPS. While he is a qualified police officer, he is not an accountant. Is his appointment a tip off that the Department has no intention of looking into tribal finances?

Washington politicians are hastening to contribute any money received from Abramoff or his associates to charity. Headlines abound with such announcements.

Maybe it's time Minnesota politicians read the handwriting on the wall. The fallout could be just as incriminating and as many heads could/should roll. What's going on in Minnesota? By comparison the $1.2 million is not much compared to what Abramoff got. But by our standards, that's still a lot of money.

"Tribal Influence at the Minnesota Capitol." *The Native American Press/Ojibwe News,* January 20, 2006, page 5.

See Appendix for:
1.Total Tribal Principal Lobbyist Expenditures at the Minnesota Capitol 2007-2010.

State of Minnesota Campaign Finance Board, Total Tribal Principal Lobbying Expenditures at the Minnesota Capitol 2007-2010. Total expenditures for the period, $6,002,509.

State of Minnesota Campaign Finance Board, Total Lobbying Disbursements Reported for Lobbyists for Principals, <u>January through December 2016.</u> Total for Minnesota tribes for 2016, $1,594,137.

by INdoz HeeAMAHwPaN

Chapter IX: Introduction: Solutions.

The following article by Mark Boswell appeared in *The Native American Press/Ojibwe News,* January 3, 1990. As evidenced by the editorials that comprise this chapter, Publisher Lawrence regularly suggested remedial measures to improve conditions on Indian reservations.

The following list was originally Lawrence's campaign platform in his bid for Chairman of the Red Lake Tribal Council. It is comprehensive in coverage of that which needed to be changed or resolved and, although written in 1990, the proposed reforms are as needed today, for most tribes, as they were then. (See Annotated Bibliography of Current, Relevant Articles for substantiation of that statement.)

"Lawrence reveals platform for May elections.

"William J. Lawrence, publisher of *The Ojibwe News** and enrolled member of the Red Lake tribe, has announced his candidacy for the office of Chairman of the Red Lake Reservation.

"He has revealed a platform of sweeping reforms and restructure for Red Lake that would guarantee accountability and a proper voice for the members of that reservation.

"Lawrence provided a list of the reforms that he would work for if elected. It is as follows:

"1. Open tribal council meetings to full participation by the people.

"2. Have CPA audits completed for all tribal enterprises, programs, contracts and grants including Bingo and the Red Lake Builders. Make copies of these audits available to the people.

"3. Establish an independent and *elected* judiciary where fair and equal justice can prevail. Provide a legal services program to serve the needs of the people.

"4. Enact a tribal member employment preference policy based on qualifications and actively recruit qualified tribal members for all top management positions on the reservation.

"5. Eliminate all consultant contracts and review all attorney contracts for need and affordability.

"6. Protect treaty rights. Discontinue secret agreements with federal and state agencies and get the Department of Natural Resources out of our commercial fishing industry.

"7. Cut back all tribal employment and consultant travel to only that which is essential.

"8. Put an end to the wanton and reckless spending of our tribal funds.

"9. Develop the economy on the Red Lake Reservation by emphasizing the utilization of natural and human resources.

"10. Call a tribal constitutional convention to draft a new constitution for the people.

"11. Establish an activities and recreation program on the reservation with emphasis on fitness and chemical abuse education.

"12. Create a system where everyone is accountable to and responsible for tribal law and order.

"13. Take ownership of the problems on the reservation and address them as a tribe.

"14. Restructure the tribal organizational plan to make it more productive.

"15. Allow freedom of the press and speech to all on the Red Lake Reservation.

"16. Review and evaluate the Red Lake health care delivery program and redesign it to meet the health needs of the people.

"17. Initiate a campaign to protect the reservation environment and beautify our remaining lands by reforestation and other appropriate measures.

"Lawrence's platform includes many of the same issues stated time and again by Native American groups throughout the nation. He believes that the time is right to oppose the current government on the Red Lake Reservation and bring some of these important issues to the forefront.

"Opposition to the Chairman's decisions has surfaced recently when the Red Lake Tribal Council itself voted down a program that he supported. The resolution, reprinted in the December 20 [1990] issue of *The Ojibwe News,* represents *the only document not passed by the Red Lake Tribal Council in 32 years of the incumbent's tenure in office...*

"Lawrence has ... chosen *The Ojibwe News* as the vehicle for endorsing his campaign. 'As long as I'm paying the bills,' he joked, 'I might as well take advantage of this fine newspaper.'

"In closing," said Lawrence, "to my fellow tribal members, let us join together and turn out those policies of repression and secrecy that have run the reservation for the past 32 years. Let us join together to build a new community that is built on respect, honor of the individual, and a government that treats everyone as equals and accounts for all of our funds...

"Let us build a community that we can all be proud of, a community where we will all feel safe and secure, a community where the Chairman is not afraid to live among the people. [The then Tribal Chair had a luxurious home in the city of Bemidji.]

"Fellow tribal members, let's take that first step together. Vote for me and a new beginning for the Red Lake Reservation in May 1990."

*The newspaper was originally known as *The Ojibwe News.*

Voters should demand accountability and openness before supporting candidates.
March 20, 1998.

With 89 candidates running in the April 14th primary election for 18 tribal offices in the coming Minnesota Chippewa Tribe* (MCT) elections, you can bet that campaigning for those seats is getting real serious. Those 18 offices comprise 60% of the total elected offices of the six member bands of the MCT. As such, this election could have a profound effect on the future of the combined Minnesota Chippewa tribe[s].

Let's hope that tribal voters take that into consideration when deciding whom to vote for in this election. Due to the intensity of discord at Bois Forte, Leech Lake and White Earth, the rhetoric on those reservations is bound to increase dramatically over the next three weeks. Throw in the dollar value and power of the jobs on their respective reservations, and you can understand just why people so earnestly seek these positions.

It would be a good idea for tribal voters, this time around, to extract several promises from the candidates as they come to your doors or appear at various forums asking for votes.

One suggestion would be to make the candidates address the issue of accountability and explain just how they would deal with the current lack thereof if elected. One simple solution would be a requirement that all tribal and casino financial statements be published in the media like other entities of government and publicly owned businesses. This would eliminate a lot of the corruption and the need for secrecy on the reservations.

It would also give us a better tool to judge performance of our elected officials. Right now we have no way of judging and verifying just how the councils are managing our money and resources.

Voters should also extract promises from their candidates that all council meetings will be open to the membership and that meeting notices, with agendas, will be posted in all reservation communities or published in the media in advance of the meetings.

Other considerations should include redistricting of the reservation to insure that all our votes count equally. In addition, due to the large number of tribal members that now live off the reservations, off-reservation representation should be provided and the one-year residency requirement should be lifted.

If these changes mean that our tribal constitutions have to be amended, so be it. It is time that we bring our tribal governments into the 20th century, screaming and kicking if necessary, before we enter the 21st.

This election is our golden opportunity to do just that, so let's have at it. Perhaps it is not too late for us to save our reservation from the current level of mismanagement.

* The Minnesota Chippewa Tribe (MCT) is composed of six of the seven bands of the state's Chippewa (Ojibwe*). The six members are: Bois Forte, Fond du Lac, Grand Portage, Leech Lake, Mille Lac and White Earth. The Red Lake Band is not a member. The MCT is federally recognized.
The Tribal Executive Committee is composed of the Chair and the Secretary Treasurer of each of the six member Chippewa tribes.

*Anishinabig, Chippewa, Ojibwe, used interchangeably.

Recall ordinance necessary first step in making RLTC accountable. October 12, 2001.

This week's vote of the Red Lake Tribal Council to establish a Recall Ordinance is probably the most significant step that they have taken to restore some power to the people since the Constitution was passed in 1958. This is a welcome, and necessary, first step.

What is really needed is the rewriting of the Red Lake Constitution, providing for full separation of powers; redistricting of the reservation to ensure "one person, one vote;" guarantees of civil rights, open government, and accountability of the Tribal Council. This first step has taken almost 43 years to the day.

It used to be that our financial affairs were taken seriously, and held nearly sacred. In fact, I can remember that monthly income and expenditure reports were prepared and submitted to the Council by the Tribal Treasurer. Today, I understand that these reports aren't even prepared, let alone filed with the Council, and that our financial affairs are manipulated like a personal business by our current Tribal Treasurer.

If anybody knows how much we're indebted, how much we're going in the hole every day, they're sure not telling. But, it doesn't take a genius to figure out that with the denominations of the 374 slot machines they have at the River Road Casino, it would take extremely steady use of those slot machines, and fewer payoffs, in order for the casino to possibly make the kind of money it would require to pay off the ever-increasing debts.

It just seems like the present mentality of some Tribal Council members is that they are operating our tribal businesses for their own personal benefit, rather than out of a fiduciary responsibility for the benefit of the people. Some Tribal Council members are getting carried away with their own self-importance, throwing money around, giving out freebies and perks, for instance cars and bonuses, and they do not seem to be concerned about who these businesses actually belong to: the Red Lake people.

Reports are that the former gaming manager is still on the tribal payroll, and still has a tribal car. Other former tribal managers have apparently retained their tribal cars as a part of their "severance package" for mismanaging our affairs. There seems to be no plan, and little interest in trying to recover these cars, or in trying to get back the money that is "missing."

This apparent apathy is costing the Red Lake band hundreds of thousands of dollars. The Tribal Council's enterprises are overstaffed, and too many members of the staff on the tribal payroll are overpaid and underworked.

There are reports that every time one of our tribal businesses gets a project, they have to run to the tribal government for a letter of credit. Some of these businesses, like the Red Lake Builders and the Modular Home Plant, have been in business for years, but they are still not able to obtain credit on their own, without guarantees from the tribal funds. They have not built up financial reserves, and they have not established basic levels of business credit with financial institutions.

The blame lies squarely at the top. We do not have effective leadership. Tribal Council Members are off serving their own self-interest, or are too wrapped up in their own self-importance. The Chairman is travelling too much, flying around the country promoting his own political agenda at the expense of the Red Lake people.

What we need is a full disclosure of all travel accounts of all Tribal Council members; and we need audits of all tribal businesses and expenditures of tribal funds by an independent auditing firm. The council should prepare to take appropriate action if there has been culpable conduct in the management of our business affairs.

I think that a petition to force the council to disclose their travel expenditures, and the financial position of the tribe, should also be undertaken by the tribal membership if we are ever to get to the bottom of this, find out where we are [financially], and start picking up the pieces. We cannot afford to wait until next year's election.

It was good to see so many tribal members concerned and involved, not only at the recent Tribal Council meeting, but also through the numerous contacts we have had at *Press/ON*.

Special commendation should go to the Tribal Secretary for taking the initiative: preparing the draft recall ordinance and introducing the motion for adoption of the recall ordinance at last Tuesday's council meeting. Thanks also to the representative who seconded it, as well as to the other Tribal Council members who also voted for it.

It appears that our $53.5 million land settlement has become lost in the shuffle because of the war on terrorism, in addition to the current distractions created by the financial chaos engendered by certain members of the present Tribal Council. It would seem that the $10 million that was allocated for per-capitas will obviously never be disbursed according to the original plan, which called for payment on December 15, 2001.

Since the economy needs a boost on the reservation and in the surrounding areas, it would seem that preparation for making per capita payments should continue. I think that Congress would be willing to act in providing an economic bolstering of the tribe and local economy. I don't think that we should have to wait and do nothing, as was suggested at the most recent Tribal Council meeting.

There is no reason that just because the Council has other problems, the membership should have to wait for the [Land Settlement] per-capita payments. Congress has no legitimate reason to evade appropriating money for long overdue compensation. A part of the Tribal Council's mandate to the people is to continue making preparation for payment as scheduled, or give us a new schedule.

There are also reports that the new Law Enforcement Center is going to cost about $3 million dollars more than the $10 million appropriated by the Justice Department. The Tribal Council is going to have difficulties coming up with that money, as well as with operating funds.

The real problem is the system within which the Tribal Council and its tribal programs operate. The Tribal Council gets involved in projects, like the bottled water plant, the farms, the resorts, the expanded retail shopping area, but they don't have a feasibility plan, a well-researched marketing plan, a completion plan, or even a clear idea of what it's going to cost to finish and operate their projects. This is indicative of poor management, mismanagement and the people, who ultimately pay for it, are the tribal membership as a whole.

It was said at the Council that the tribe has $50 million in investments in businesses. What was not mentioned on the council is: what is our return on investments [ROI]? This is a crucial factor in investing, and unless an adequate ROI is in place at the outset, you don't make the investment.

Despite the financial chaos at home on the rez, the Tribal Council was down at the BIA on Wednesday, October 10, talking about taking over Individual Indian Money accounts. In view of their management experience to date, the people to whom the money belongs should be deeply concerned that the Bureau of Indian Affairs is even considering this.

As one individual, I can't do much about the way that the Tribal Council is running tribal businesses into the ground other than calling members' attention to the problems. But, I sure would not want the current Treasurer, [Dan King] or the 'fab four,' Tribal Council members, to have anything to do with my personal money.

Resolving Red Lake crime problems will require sustained community action.
October 4, 2002.

Nine Red Lakers were charged, indicted, or pled guilty this week to violations of the Federal Major Crimes Act. This has to be some kind of abysmal record at Red Lake, one of the worst weeks in Red Lake's history. As I recollect, even after the 1979 Revolution there weren't nine people charged with violations of the major crimes act in one week.

Think of what that does, not only to the lives of the people who are charged with these crimes, but also to their families, the victims and their families, and the community.

It's too easy to blame an influx of inner-city "gangs," and to cry for even more federal funding. Instead we need to look at what's actually happening at Red Lake. Instead of assigning blame, or getting caught in cycles of self-destruction and re-victimizing ourselves by using our community's problems as fodder for even more ineffective federal programs, it's time that we rethink where we're going, and then take the necessary actions.

Where do we, as a people, really want to be in the future? We have to honestly and seriously begin to build a society where people feel safe again, so that all of us have real rights, genuine responsibility in our government, and involvement with our community.

I think that the only way we can do that is to restructure tribal government by drafting an entirely new Tribal Constitution with real separation of powers, constitutionally protected rights, and workable mechanisms of justice built into it.

Rather than just hammering out a few dents in the Bureau of Indian Affair's old boilerplate constitution, we need to begin by having some serious discussions about what it means to be Red Lake Ojibwe people, and how we can work together to create a government that's an integral part of a viable, healthy community.

If we want to survive as a people and create the possibility of a decent future for our children and grandchildren, we must break away

237

from the outsiders' agendas. We must create our own definitions and governmental structures. We need to eliminate the "revised" constitution, government programs, and our own uncritical acceptance of the priorities and values imposed on us by others. We have been seduced by federal funding, economic dependence on gambling operations, and "big box" economic development schemes.

It's time that we started addressing our own problems and allocating our own money to do it. We can't depend on others because the foundations of our community are too important to let these problems fester any longer. We have the money to fund far less important things, like powwows, sporting events, and campaign donations.

We have reached the point where we must make it our priority to spend our money on improving our government and rebuilding our own society, and leave nonessentials to somebody else.

As detailed in a front page article, the schools at Red Lake are failing; our children are being cheated out of an education and deprived of the skills that they are going to need in order to survive and thrive in the 21st century.

We have to start dealing, not only with the drug and gang problems which are tearing our community apart, but also to convince our children that that's not the way to do things. We have to have more respect for each other, and to dispense some "tough love" to our children. All of us tribal members need to work together in carrying out our responsibilities to each other and to our community.

We have to get back to respecting nature. We've used up almost all of our resources. It's time to reinvest, replant, restock, and restore the natural environment that is the foundation of who we are as Indian people. We have to get away from plundering and abusing the environment for a "quick buck," and find a way to regain the harmony that's been ignored and eroded over the past several generations.

Our economic future depends on our resources that are here. We cannot continue to rely on the "quick fixes" that have gotten us into our current financial problems.

Recently we have shown that when we act together with a common purpose, put aside our differences and unite for the sake of our community, we can make change, as in the enactment of the recall ordinance and the recall of the former tribal treasurer, and in our election of six new tribal council members. It's time we act responsibly.

Hopefully June 11th will lead to positive changes.
June 7, 2002.

On June 11th the political campaigns on the six Minnesota Chippewa Tribe (MCT) reservations will culminate in tribal elections determining six reservation Secretary/Treasurers, and eleven committeemen and district representatives. This is an important election for the members of the MCT.

The balance of power on several reservations will shift when newly-elected tribal officers and reps are seated on the Reservation Business Committees (RBC) of the several reservations. The significance of these changes has been reflected in hotly-contested elections, as well as in the heavy debate on this paper's opinion pages during the past weeks.

As in many past elections, voters are concerned about the ethics of some candidates and about candidates' abilities to handle the challenges of running multi-million dollar tribal budgets and tribal businesses.

The tribal constitutions currently controlling tribal governments on MCT reservations are structurally almost unchanged since the Bureau of Indian Affairs (BIA) brought them to Minnesota reservations during the Great Depression more than sixty years ago as a part of the "Indian New Deal" under the Indian Reorganization Act (IRA).

Power in the RBCs remains tightly concentrated. The lack of constitutionally mandated checks and balances in tribal government means that the ethics and managerial abilities of people elected to serve in tribal government is far more important than it is for elected officials in the state and federal governments. When the IRA was written and enacted, tribal government was subordinate to the overarching and paternalistic administration of reservations by the BIA.

Prior to the creation of the Reservation Business Councils in the 1930s, Indian reservation governments were not the "sovereigns" they have become under court-created doctrines. They did not manage millions of dollars in state and federal program funding; they had little or no control over the BIA's courts of Indian Offenses or the BIA's Indian

240

policy, and there were no multimillion dollar tribal enterprises to be managed by the RBCs.

Conditions on Indian reservations and the context of the broader society surrounding reservations have changed since 1934. The MCT and its constitution need to be reformed and updated. It's not enough to depend on honorable people being elected to tribal office, not enough to rely on people remaining honest in the face of multi-million-dollar temptations and, on some reservations, an entrenched legacy of corruption.

The MCT, and member reservations' constitutions, must be rewritten to guarantee constitutionally mandated separation of powers in reservation government. The constitutions also have to be amended to properly authorize Indian law enforcement and tribal courts. And, most importantly, Indian constitutions must be amended to extend the civil rights provisions enjoyed by all other U.S. citizens and guaranteed in the Bill of Rights, to reservation residents and tribal members.

So far, past efforts at constitutional reform have not led to any meaningful results in Minnesota. The June 11th election is an important election for the MCT. Hopefully the newly elected officers and reps will work toward these ends, and hopefully tribal members will exercise their rights, and every eligible voter will turn out to vote and participate in their government. The June 11 election is an important election for the MCT.

New Red Lake council generates positive vibes.
August 16, 2002.

It not only looked good, it felt good to see the new council members being sworn in at Red Lake. As they begin their new terms, it appears we have a council that not only can work together, but that will be more in tune with the concerns of membership, and that will be more open and accountable to us.

Our first priority is getting back on a solid financial footing, and the best way to start is to complete the forensic audit, and to do it with as wide a scope as is necessary. It's far better to pay the money "up front" and find out exactly what's happening, than it would be to have to deal with hidden problems later.

The new Chairman and the Tribal Council have a large task in front of them. They deserve the support of the people as they begin the massive effort that it will take to rebuild our economy, and to contend with the chaos that has plagued the council and the band for the past three or four years.

The Chairman's inaugural remarks were brief but included the remark, "I'll do the best job I can."

We all have to work together to do the best job we can in order to ensure our future as a people. The events of the "outside world" are having, and will continue to have, significant effects in Indian country.

The days of the free-spending "war on poverty" are gone. On almost every reservation, Indian people are faced with federal and state budget cuts, as well as declining gambling revenues and, quite possibly, competition from non-Indian casinos whether run by the state or by private enterprise.

Red Lake is like almost every other reservation in that we are also confronted with serious social problems, including increasing rates of drug abuse, crime, and other violence. We have to figure out ways to deal effectively with these problems, which aren't going to go away by themselves. We also have to think seriously about constitutional reform and address the problems arising from defects built into the Indian Reorganization Act-based systems of reservation government.

We were a proud and self-sufficient people once. We need to find ways to become so again. To the new tribal council: congratulations and good luck!

Recent shootings at Red Lake calls out for change.
January 16, 2004.

The shootings of the last two-weekends are just the latest incidents of ongoing acts of violence at Red Lake. These acts of violence against each other seem to crop up every few years or so, going back as far as the riots of 1979. They recur with disturbing regularity.

The community must come to terms with this issue in some kind of a real way. Only the symptoms are being treated and the actual problems remain unresolved. There are many relevant questions rising from these incidents: Are we failing to instill proper values in our children? Have we failed to teach respect for our fellow human beings, for property, for law and order and ourselves? Where has the system broken down? What can be done to restore our reservation to peace, order and productivity?

A friend of mine with whom I regularly discuss these matters has suggested several times that a visioning process may be in order. Corporate America regularly turns to such a process to create or revise its mission and guide its problem-solving efforts. It works because everyone involved has input. Everyone has the opportunity, and responsibility, to give information, to participate meaningfully and honestly to the solving of problems.

The reasoning is this: If everyone who is affected is involved in stating the problem and envisioning a solution, the chance for success is greatly enhanced.

A version of this occurred in 1997. In June 1997, I attended one of a series of three meetings held in Redby in response to a stabbing death, shootings of three individuals and a severe beating. About 75 persons attended the meetings. What impressed me at the time was the vitality and commitment of the community to get something done to end the violence.

At that time I published the list of suggestions that the attendees came up with. The suggestions were: Establish a community watch program. Contact parents of juvenile curfew offenders. Reform and reorganize police procedures. Provide more training for police, dispatchers. Charge juvenile repeat-offenders as adults.* Hold individuals accountable for any damage done; cover the cost of damages by per capita withholding. Create emergency services. Provide more street lighting. Change Tribal Court; separate powers of Court and Tribal Council. Publish outstanding arrest warrant list. Assure that the public receives more information in a reliable manner. Community pledges to support the court system in prosecution of cases. Community supports banishment for major crimes.

At that time I concluded that reform could only occur through separation of the Court from the influence of the Council. Additionally, the Council must be responsive to the electorate rather than to their political supporters.

The suggestions of the people were right-on and they have been, to some degree, implemented. It is time for that energy and will to reappear. The community has an opportunity to do that on Wednesday, January 21, 2004 at a meeting scheduled for 7 p.m. at the Red Lake Community Center. The purpose of the meeting is to deal with the incidents of violence that have occurred.

How many members will show up to discuss the problem? How responsive will our Council be to the suggestions that the community might make? Are we all churned up enough to make another effort to put our community back together?

*Screen juvenile repeat offenders for fetal alcohol syndrome disorder.

Tribal Court Evaluation could be start of something good.
June 4. 2004.

The cover story in this week's issue is an account of an independent study of the Tribal Court authorized by the Red Lake Tribal Council. The evaluator, Judge Mary Pearson, is well qualified to make judgments about the system and stated her opinions in a clear and objective manner. I was impressed with the report even though I didn't agree 100% with all her findings. Nonetheless she offered the Tribe a true picture of its problems as well as a blueprint for making needed changes.

She didn't make comment on what created the problems and that might have been appropriate. The fact is that the Red Lake Nation Tribal Court [and many other tribal courts] has a long and shameful history of not meeting its community needs, of denying or ignoring civil rights and of being incompetent, biased and ineffective.

As far back as 1972, I stated in the *North Dakota Law Review* that the Red Lake Indian Court "in practice ... is ineffective in enforcing its judgments and ... most band members receive little or no satisfaction in bringing civil cases before the court."

Then, as now, "the greatest shortcoming and most basic criticism of the Court is its nearly total disregard for due process... The court is notorious for giving improper notice. There have been numerous cases in which judges have failed to allow parties to present testimony and evidence on their [own] behalf."

According to the independent study done by Judge Pearson, not much has changed. She related stories of battered women being berated by the judge, or of the police telling the victim that she would be taken into custody if she called in with another complaint.

She spoke of the high incidence of truancy on the Reservation that has not been addressed properly by the Court. She declared nothing less than, "The Red Lake Nation is losing an entire generation of youth to lack of education." She goes on to say, "In a few years this lack of education will have serious impacts on the Nation."

A cascload of 5000 cases a year is excessive by anyone's standards. It is especially so when one takes into account the fact that there are approximately 5000 individuals living on the Reservation. That's one per person per year. Clearly not every person at Red Lake is creating an offense. That makes it even worse to realize that the offenders are repeat offenders.

The high incidence of juvenile crime was discussed in several ways: truancy, alcohol/drug related crimes and violent crimes. The statistics given indicated that half the crimes committed by juveniles are violent or drug/alcohol related crimes. Pearson states that alcohol/drug and violent crimes are expected to rise to 48% of the total number of offenses in 2004. She states, "These numbers indicate that the Red Lake Tribe has a serious problem with both juvenile alcohol/drug related offenses and violent offenses."

It is too bad we need to hire an outsider to come in and tell us the obvious. It is no secret that crime, alcohol and drug abuse, gang activity, truancy and general disrespect for the law and the community are rampant at Red Lake.

The criminal activity is all interrelated, and much of the blame lies directly at the feet of the justice system. Judge Pearson spoke of the need for additional judges and/or training for judges, clerks, prosecutors, advocates and law enforcement personnel in all areas but especially in domestic violence cases.

Court personnel were unaware of the protection offered women under the Violence Against Women Act and the concept of "victimless prosecution." She explains that "this is an accepted form of investigating, prosecuting and trying both child abuse and domestic violence cases." Under the concept, victims are not required to testify. This is done in recognition of the very real danger that a woman and her children face if she comes forward and makes charges against an abuser. Judge Pearson strongly recommended training in these areas as well.

Why did the Tribe authorize the study and expenditure of roughly $15,000 to accomplish it?

The Red Lake community needs a competent, impartial, independent Court. Member dissatisfaction with the Court becomes consistently more evident. The high crime rate, the violence and abuse, the huge caseload, and backlogged cases all demand attention and resolution. The present Court is a model of dysfunction. Pearson's report revealed that somewhere between 15-16,000 police reports have been ignored by the prosecutor's office. Pearson says this bears immediate investigation. I agree.

Pearson's statement, "In a few years this lack of education will have serious impacts on the Nation" is not exactly accurate. The fact is, the impact of lack of education is being felt right now and this is a fearful situation.

The report contained at least one inaccuracy I want to correct. Early on she refers to Shirley Cain as having been terminated as Chief Judge. The fact of the matter is she was pushed out by a group of individuals who have a vested interested in maintaining the status quo.

This group will be the biggest obstacle to Court Reform now that the results of the study are in and the community expects some things to improve.

Regretfully, Judge Pearson made a case for appointment of judges by the Tribal Council. Her reasoning for this was the Council should be trusted to appoint a "qualified" judge. She opined that voters might elect an individual who was not qualified.

This shows an unconscious disrespect for the voters of Red Lake. After all, these same voters picked the Tribal Council members, so why shouldn't they also pick the judges? As a way of guarding against the eventuality of an "unqualified" judge being elected, Tribal Council can establish criteria/qualifications that candidates must meet to be candidates for election to judgeships.

All in all, the report has merit. The Council should be commended for taking the necessary action to study the Court. This is the first time the Council has taken such an initiative and it is an important step in making needed reforms. The big question that remains is this, will the Tribal Council have the will to adopt and implement the suggestions made in the report?

Unfortunately, the Council has a history of paying for advice and not following it. I sincerely hope that this expenditure will have been wisely made. The proof of this will be in the follow through by the Council.

Wrongful termination suit: Another test of the rule of law at Leech Lake.

December 3, 2004.

Something important has happened today. Eleven people have come forward to challenge the tribal government at Leech Lake. This is significant because it is another attempt to resolve a dispute following the rule of law. It's also important because people are beginning to realize the power of law and their responsibility to stand up and be counted on the side of peaceful and orderly resolution of problems.

The eleven people are all seeking redress through the Court for what they believe was wrongful termination of their employment by the newly elected administration at Leech Lake. The Plaintiffs seek reinstatement to their jobs and/or compensation to sustain them until they can find other employment. They point out that stable employment is the foundation of stable families and communities, and they are right. They are also motivated to seek legal action to correct past civil rights violations and to set precedence to guide future employment case law that will protect an individual's dignity and rights.

It's true that this legal wrangle will be costly and keeps the embers of discontent with tribal government glowing. However, on the positive side, it is another step toward acceptance of the rule of law as the guiding principal in resolving conflicts and gives every citizen/member the right to have a grievance addressed by an impartial, competent third party.

This system is decidedly an improvement over the older ways of dealing with contentious issues. From ancient times to this day, the victor of the battle (or the election) won all the goodies. In ancient times that meant wealth in the form of territory that provided abundant fish, game, water, shelter, etc. It also meant tribute to the victors in the form of slaves, horses, and other things that were valuable to a culture. And it also meant the demise of the opposing leadership.

Today we ostensibly live in a democracy where, in theory, every person has inalienable rights. It's true that democracy is an imperfect construct, but it still seems to offer the most beneficial system of governance. We expect our particular model of democracy, like the national form our tribal government is patterned after, to provide for guarantees of civil rights. The means to do this lies in the fundamentals of the rule of law and separation of powers.

After a victory, which signals a change in leadership, we have also come to expect an orderly and humane turning over of power to the victors. No retaliation or punishment of the vanquished, simply a changing over to reflect the new principals chosen by the people in the form of the power of votes. This change of power exists at all levels, from the National presidency down to the city council and the local school board selection in this country.

We acknowledge this pattern, at least nominally, on our own reservations as we have demonstrated by the adoption of the U.S. and tribal constitutions. Although we have subscribed to the concept, we have failed on our reservations to achieve the ideal of the democratic process. We have failed to achieve an orderly, bloodless, change of power. We still, figuratively, demand tribute in the form of power to make political appointments and, figuratively, to demand the severed heads of our opponents.

This situation is not in itself different than what goes on at the federal and state levels. A change of administration means a change in political appointments. Every department head and appointee (whether nationally or locally) understands that the position rests on the foundation of political power as evidenced by success in an election. At every level, following a change in leadership, political appointees graciously submit their resignations in recognition that their jobs exist "at the pleasure" of the leader. This is an accepted and honored tradition everywhere.

Not so however on the reservations. There heads roll on the pattern of the war lord-conqueror. We have, for the most part, accepted orderly elections and try hard to assure the integrity of the election process. The experiences of past reservation elections shows we have yet to understand how to effect an orderly and humane transfer of power. We have not seen an orderly transfer. What we've seen more closely resembles a looting and pillaging.

The eleven plaintiffs are protesting this lack of a dignified and honorable transfer of power. They are not (presumably) protesting the end of their jobs so much as the way in which it was handled. They are protesting the lack of due process and the denial of an appeal. They object to the defamation of character they experienced, and the callous treatment they received at the hands of the newly elected.

In a culture that values human rights, transition is handled in a fair way, with care shown for the protection of an individual's dignity and worth. The contribution an individual has made to the society while occupying an appointed position is acknowledged and appreciated.

The present administration appears to have abandoned the pretense of behaving in an honorable fashion. They have apparently abandoned their campaign pledges to deal with people forthrightly on the basis of fairness, preserving individual rights, and respecting individual differences. It looks like they reverted to a retaliatory "hacking up" of political enemies and a refusal to abide by the rule of law. They have demonstrated this by their refusal to accept court decisions and their failure to recognize the authority of the court.

What we've seen is contempt for the Court. This is unusual by itself since, unfortunately, the Court also sits at the pleasure of the Administration. This is evidenced by the Chairman's frequent assertion that the Court does not have the jurisdiction to make decisions (that are unfavorable to the administration), and by the failure of the Administration to abide by Court orders.

The authority of the new leadership was not won in a bloody battle. It is a gift bestowed by the vote of the people and, as such, requires behavior of a higher nature than we've observed.

On the positive side, I see the rule of law gaining momentum. It may be the last stronghold of those vanquished in the election but, nevertheless, it represents the proper way to express dissatisfaction with those in office. It also appeals to a higher, objective authority for resolution of differences.

Another positive is the Leech Lake Tribal Court itself. It is probably the most highly respected tribal court in the state. This is in large part attributable to the Judge. Under her leadership the Court has performed in a competent and impartial manner. The Judge's personal qualifications add to the credibility and respect of the Court. She is law trained and a member of the Minnesota Bar. This is an important element. Members of the Bar are held to a high standard; the expectation is that all decisions are reasoned and based on case law, not on personal preference or opportunity for gain. Any action taken by a member of the bar must be consistent with and guided by the tenets and principals of the oath of office.

Albeit it is with reluctance, but all parties have deferred to the legal system to resolve their differences. This fact is the single most promising piece of evidence that some progress toward a real, working democracy is taking place on the reservations. When we finally see true rule of law used to resolve our disputes; when we see a separation of power between the policy making, administrative branch of government and the legal system, we will truly have made an important stride forward in assuring all our members/citizens have the protections and rights we believe inherently belong to every person.

Press/ON **to publish financial information on twelve Minnesota tribal entities.**
March 31, 2006.

With the spring elections coming up soon, we at *Press/ON* feel it is important that members of the twelve Minnesota Indian tribes and bands know as much as possible about the financial status of their tribal government.

We have obtained copies of the Single Audit Reports for each of the twelve Minnesota tribal entities from the federal government. The most recent information is from 2004 since 2005 information is not yet available. Nonetheless, the information contained in the audits will reveal general trends and practices of the various tribal governments.

The Single Audit Reports have been obtained under the Freedom of Information Act from the Office of the Secretary of the Department of Interior (DOI). When the DOI sent the reports to me, the tribal governments were informed that the reports had been sent.

We have also obtained budget material and other information from some of the various Bands. We will be studying the individual reports and will publish analysis and information contained in the reports, in order to inform the memberships of the respective bands as to how their tribal governments have utilized federal and other funds. The data we present will be helpful in formulating questions for tribal members to ask of their individual candidates.

We will begin next week with discussions of financial data from Red Lake, Leech Lake and the Minnesota Chippewa Tribe. The Minnesota Chippewa Tribe primary election will be this coming Tuesday, April 4, 2006, and the general election will be June 13.

The Red Lake band has not yet announced their certified candidates. Their general election is May 17, 2006. If no candidate has a clear majority in the general, Red Lake will hold a run-off election later in the summer, usually mid to late July.

We encourage candidates to obtain budget information on their own by asking their tribal governments for data.

We invite all candidates to submit information they obtain for publication. We will be happy to publish questions raised by any candidate or carry comments on financial information from the candidates. We urge all tribal members to exercise their right, and responsibility, to vote.

**Anishinabe! Elections approach Take up your burden, choose wisely.
August 15, 2007.**

The general public in the U.S.A. has rolled along fat, uninformed and happy for too long. For the most part, Americans are secure in their jobs, have safe investments, adequate housing and their children are in public schools learning to become citizens like their parents.

Although there is a scale, published daily, informing us of the risk of terrorism, most people go blithely along through the details of their lives. There is little awareness that the quality of those lives could change dramatically for the worst with almost no notice--911 remains America's most dramatic example.

The bridge collapse in Minneapolis [1] is an example, and global warming hovers on the not too distant horizon.

For that matter, credible scientists predict a meteorite could fall from the heavens and obliterate the planet. If that should happen tomorrow, the rest of what I've written here would be irrelevant. But in the event that we are allowed to continue in our earthly existence, I offer these words.

Americans have placed unwarranted faith in their public officials and in the system which is, of course, only as good as our elected officers. The majority of Americans [remember the phrase, the silent majority?] persist in non-participation and are, for all practical purposes, non-judgmental about their government. In general, as a nation, Americans have paid little attention to who's minding the store. As a result, the country is suffering from a severe and potentially lethal deficit in leadership.

People need to accept the responsibilities of citizenship if they expect to reap the benefits of a life in a free enterprise democracy.

The same can be said of our Indian reservations. Good government (the kind that inspires, creates and maintains a society that protects, nourishes and flourishes its members) is the result of dutiful and vigilant citizens.

Americans have another opportunity to change this unfortunate situation in the upcoming elections. Politicians have been in gear for many months now.

The question is, will our citizens wake up to the evidence everywhere of a compelling need for citizen scrutiny of public officials and their acts?

The national situation represents the macrocosm. Indian reservations are the microcosm. The national is the society of the whole; the reservation system is a smaller version of the whole. In vague imitation of national activity, we are starting to discern the beginnings of political activity on our reservations that will culminate in tribal elections. Individuals are assessing their chances as candidates. Special interests are choosing and grooming people they can trust to do their bidding.

Tribal members, however, are disinterested and uncaring in regard to who is proposing to run the show. Unlike the dominant society, Indian reservation citizens do not enjoy things like job security, reliable health care, social services, civil protections under the law, and the usual freedoms guaranteed by the Constitution. The strongest thing Indian society has in common with the dominant society is lack of interest and disinclination to get involved in politics.

About an equal percentage of each society votes, that is only about 50 percent or less. And far fewer than 50 percent of the populations give any heed or thought to whether a candidate truly possesses the qualifications to do a good job, the integrity to lead based on common ideals, or the altruism to do a good job for the sake of the people. The too obvious, and completely neglected, assessment of whether or not the candidate is, in fact, simply honest escapes the majority of both populations.

Dominant society needs to wake up before all the good stuff-- democratic freedoms, national and personal prosperity, sustainable and reliable economies with the accompanying jobs and personal securities-- is lost. Indian peoples need to rise up and take control of their governments to assure they will begin to get some of the good stuff.

Their job will be a great deal more difficult. The traditional fixes, like more money, public works, educational reform, have not been effective. Don't dismiss this as mere melodrama. The ability of Indians to even continue existence on reservations in this country is at stake.

Indian societies are in a far more advanced stage of decay than is the dominant culture. There are many reasons to explain why Indians are 700 times more likely to die of alcoholism, 400 times more likely to die of diabetes and 500 times more likely to die of accident or injury than is any individual in the dominant culture.

The why of these "inconvenient truths" is irrelevant at this point. The how is paramount. How can they be saved? The answer to this question rests exclusively with Indians themselves. They once fought vehemently to save their disappearing way of life. The situation has degenerated now to a more basic concern---how do we save Indian lives?

The only answer is systemic reform of tribal governmental systems. Tribal leadership must be committed first of all to restoring health to the governmental process and to the people themselves. The spiral that created the despondency, the loss of faith in personal and tribal ability must be unwound.

Indian tribal government is like a cancer. For that matter, the analogy works as well for the dominant society, although the advance of the disease in Indian Country has been slower and less obvious. Tribal government is composed of cells that resemble ordinary ones that for a long time operated in the same way. But they have somehow gone wild. They have mutated into ugly, greedy and insensitive beings, intent on obtaining personal wealth at the expense of the people who elected them and who they pledged to help.

The end result is what you see on our reservations, dysfunctional individuals, families, government. Violence, crime, disharmony, distrust, fear, hopelessness. You also see infirm individuals, families, government, fetal alcohol syndrome, suicide, drug and alcohol addictions, diabetes, with its accompanying heart disease and obesity.

258

Like a body or an organ that is attacked by cancer, Indian government must submit itself to a serious plan of restoring health, a rigorous resistance to the attack and the rebuilding of strength and viability. For in the end, the cancer cells also perish when their invasion has completely overcome its host.

The remedy is painful. The odds of success are doubtful, but most affected bodies want to make the effort, and do not simply sit down and wait for the disease to advance to the point where it has consumed all healthy, life supporting tissue.

The state of Indian cultures is abysmal. Fifty to seventy-five percent of reservation families are involved or at least very affected by drug use, addiction and drug traffic.

On our closest reservations, one chairman is said to be the minion of the drug crowd, and on another the chairman is reputed to be a cocaine addict. The drug culture and government corruption go hand in hand. One supports the other.

In the past I have encouraged the people to rise up and take back their reservations. Nothing has happened on our reservations except that the downward spiral has lengthened and deepened, taking up more people, destroying more lives, and creating more havoc.

People, wake up. Take your own inventory: 1. Where are you? 2. What time is it? 3. What condition are you in? 4. Do you want something better?

I can supply answers for the first two questions: you are here and it is now.

To say the situation is critical is to gloss over the glaring, scary reality of life on Indian reservations.

If you don't find an easy answer for 3. - What condition are you in? Look at the list of existing situations on our reservations that is published below.

You know all the details already. I doubt however if any of you [and especially not those individuals who wish to govern you] have ever sat down and made such a list. It's important to study this one and use it as a basis for filling out your own list of desired outcomes. Then fold it up, put it in your pocket, and have it handy to use as a reference when candidates approach you for your support.

Make those candidates aware of the fact that you have done an inventory and that you find the existing circumstances unacceptable, and ask how any one of them proposes to change those realities.

Only you can answer 4. - Do you want something better? And unless enough people do want to do something to create a better reality, the only advice I can offer is to ask the last person leaving the reservation to shut the door and turn out the lights.

Inventory: **Existing conditions on our reservations**:

-Tribal Government is ineffective, unresponsive to members, operates in secret and is generally unaccountable.

-Ongoing violations of human rights, no protections or guarantees.

-No balance of power; no checks and balances to control power.

-Tribal Councils control of law enforcement and courts.

-Jurisdictional problems.

-Large tribal debt load; undisclosed financial conditions.

-Misuse of tribal resources, mismanagement and fraud.

-Big fees going to outsiders, i.e. lobbyists, lawyers, etc.

-Unqualified governmental officials, i.e. lack of education, etc.

-The myth of Tribal Sovereignty and how it allows repression.

-Casino and tribal resources do not benefit general membership.

-Self-serving officials and appointees.

-Fraudulent election practices are tolerated.

-No plan for a better future.

-A dysfunctional society dominated by violence, crime, addictions.

-Apathy, despair and depression are prevailing emotions.

-Loss of youth to drug use, violence, crime.

-High incidence of brain-damaged children through alcohol use.

-High crime associated with drug traffic, drug abuse.

-Gang activity, juvenile criminal activity and records.

-A populace heavily burdened with poor health—obesity, diabetes.

-Poor life style choices, e.g. alcohol, diet, inactivity, smoking
-Limited tribal services, e.g. addiction treatment, health supports.
-Inadequate and insufficient housing.
-Economic Development is impossibility.
-No ability to attract outside investors.
-No rule of law to insure contracts, sustain business dealings.
-Investors are wary of Tribal Sovereignty and its misuse.
-No sustainable economy.
-Inhospitable business climate due to the above.
-Inept leaders, corruption, fraud, mismanagement of resources.
-Failed enterprises and tribal businesses through mismanagement.
-Tribal resources allocated on basis of nepotism and favoritism.
-Jobs allocated to family members and political cronies.
-Federal funds poorly administered, i.e. Indian Health, HUD, Grants.
-Spotty services allocated on basis of favoritism.
-Availability of services limited while need is great.
-Failed Educational system.
-Schools not producing responsible citizens.
-Reservations have the lowest, or among the lowest test scores.
-Lowest graduation rates.
-Highest school dropout rates.
-Highest incidence of truancy.
-Graduates are unprepared for employment.
-Graduates are not self-sufficient.

* This list is not intended to be a comprehensive or exhaustive assessment. It is simply a snapshot of observable conditions on Indian reservations.

[1] Highway I-35W Minneapolis Mississippi River Bridge collapsed August 2, 2007. Thirteen persons died; 145 were injured.

Leech Lake Leadership To Do List:
1. Reorganize under rules that will serve and protect the people.
January 15, 2009.

"Letter to editor raises questions about actions of Leech Lake Reservation Business Committee (LLRBC)."

Following a few paragraphs of introduction, we have published the full text of a letter sent to *Press/ON* for publication. This letter came with documentation to back up its claims. The documents were: 1. Copies of completed Leech Lake Band of Ojibwe Single Source/Sole Source Justification Forms, and 2. Quoted material from the Minneapolis *Star Tribune*, April 20, 1996. The letter demands we investigate.

There seems little to check out. Presumably anyone could simply go to the sources, look at the original documents, and make an assessment as to their validity. Any interested reader can view the copies that were sent to us at the *Press/ON* office.

We could not find out who wrote the letter so we cannot know what his/her motivation might have been for sending it to us. What we can do is publish the letter and invite anyone with an interest or information about the allegations, including those accused of wrong doing in the letter, to come forward to support or contest the truth of the matter.

I believe the culture of corruption has ruled tribal governments for so long that many acts that are improper are not regarded as such, because they have been standard operating procedure for such a very long time.

Press/ON's justification for being is this: to be the voice of the people and to publish any and all information that keeps the people informed as to what their tribal officials are doing. In that spirit we offer up this letter:

"Leech Lake: Rebuilding a Native Nation, a letter to the editor. In 1996, [a tribal official] was convicted of conspiring to steal a million dollars from the Leech Lake Band of Ojibwe and resigned from his position as Chairman.

"In 2008, shortly after [a new candidate] was elected Leech Lake Chairman, the convicted chairman's pockets were once again being filled from Leech Lake's coffers: this time not from an insurance scam, but in the form of no-bid, high dollar, make-work contracts that were not approved at any Tribal Council meeting recorded in the *DeBahJiMon* [the tribal newspaper.]

"In the spirit of healing and moving forward as a nation, I have already forgiven the convicted chairman for the misdeeds he has done to our Reservation and our people. I hold no bad feelings toward the man personally. However, if we are ever going to move out of a corrupt system and "Rebuild" our "Native Nation," as the propaganda paper [*Press/ON]* is so fond of, we cannot afford to take steps backward into secrecy, misappropriation and corruption by allowing these individuals back into the decision-making process.

"Yet that is exactly what has happened here. [The three newly elected tribal officers] were sworn into office on July 4, proclaiming Leech Lake's new found freedom from tyranny, trumpeting a return to the rule of the people, and heralding transparent and open government.

"Eleven days later on July 15, without notice to the people and behind closed doors, [the three newly elected officers] gave the convicted former chair a contract for some $19,180 to be a "political adviser" to the Reservation Tribal Council (RTC) since there were "2 new Tribal Council members who have little experience in government operations," according to the Sole Source Justification.

"Then, on October 8, without further justification other than "additional services provided," [the former chair] was given an extra $4,000. It has also been further alleged that [this person] was given some $40,000 to advise the RTC on the Nelson Act Settlement issue.

"The point remains that misappropriation, secrecy, and corruption are alive and well at Leech Lake. I call on the *Ojibwe News,* in the interests of objective, balanced reporting, to investigate this matter to find out why this contract was needed. And if it was needed, why it was not placed for public bid and approved at a properly scheduled Tribal

Council meeting. I call on [the new] Chairman ... to live up to his campaign pledge of operating an open government and release any pertinent information regarding this matter. I call on [the new] Secretary/Treasurer ... to fulfill his campaign promise and start immediately printing every check that bears his signature in the *DeBahJiMon* so Band members can become informed of exactly where our money is going. I call on [the new district representative] ... to stop pushing for raises for himself. At the Twin Cities meeting during the campaign he told us he was going to keep his 'working man's' salary. Now $80,000 isn't enough for him; he wants a minimum of $105,000.

"I call on the Tribal Council to start standing up for our programs, especially our Tribal College, which is a shining jewel of Native accomplishment in the northland. Stop bickering and work together to solve the problems rather than creating new ones!

"Most importantly, I call on us, the People of Leech Lake, to hold these leaders accountable for their actions, not in hatred or vengeance or anger, but out of a deep-rooted concern for the well-being of our community and the future of our people. Equay."

We printed the letter because it was well written, respectful, repeats rumors that have been circulating, and raises issues that need to be resolved if the current administration is to have much success. It calls into question the actions of the current Leech Lake Reservation Business Council, three of whom have promised to be guided by the principals contained in the book, *Rebuilding Native Nations*.

The writer asks them to abide by their promises and to move forward in adopting nation building practices. Most importantly, the letter writer asks the people of Leech Lake to, respectfully, do their civic duty and demand accountability of their leaders.

As we pointed out in the last editorial, the rebuilding process will be slow and painful. Many will resist reform, some because they benefitted from the old way of running the tribe. Some will resist because shaking up the status quo is always uncomfortable, and that makes it seem wrong. And some will be upset when their standard operating methods are identified as "corrupt."

I have always been a critic of high salaries for...tribal officials. Officials, who sincerely wish to make needed change, will need to be careful that they are not doing business in the old—unacceptable—ways. Tribal governments everywhere need to develop "Corruption detectors," because much of what has passed for "business as usual," in the past, is simply corrupt practice.

Vote buying is a corrupt practice. Secrets of any type, with the possible exception of trade secrets that protect lawful profits from tribal enterprises, have no place in government. Bid rigging, kickbacks, excessive political favors are all examples of common tribal practices. But such actions are all examples of corruption.

Because many tribal officials have not had the opportunity of learning exactly what constitutes corruption, here's a tip. Tribal officials everywhere can identify right behavior over wrong behavior by simply applying the rule of open government, which essentially is: no secrets. If tribal officials feel like keeping an action from the public's knowledge, it is likely a corrupt practice. I believe that Leech Lake has begun an invaluable process that eventually, and I emphasize the eventual, will lead to improved conditions on the reservation.

Tribes that have decided to reform their systems will be rewarded with a safer, more prosperous, more responsive and responsible government. People will feel free to go about their business without fear of bodily harm. They will know their civil rights are guaranteed and protected. They will not fear speaking out against governmental wrong doing. They will have confidence that the rule of law will protect the community in every way. Economic development that will lead to more jobs, the reduction of poverty and the growth of prosperity for all will become reality.

The above letter raises important issues that the current Leech Lake Reservation Business Council needs to come to terms with. Are the allegations true or not? If they are true, what needs to be done to make things right? If needed, what can the accused do to make amends? If they are false, the accused are invited to explain their actions publically, as well as here within the pages of *Press/ON*.

Maybe acknowledgement and a reversal of any questionable activity would reassure people that their leaders have their interests at heart. Dialogue is important. Dialogue means that an exchange of information takes place between two or more parties, each having opportunities to explain and to question. The process is multi-dimensional, informative, and it is the only way misunderstandings can be cleared up and right action can be initiated. Government that follows a practice of responding to questioned activity is healthy and leads to a better life for its citizens.

Government need not be perfect, but it needs to conduct itself according to rules that the governed recognize and expects them to obey. Government that is self-serving, that ignores the needs and rights of the people, will not be successful.

It is therefore to everyone's advantage to work together to build a partnership between the governed and the governing that produces an environment where people can work together to build a better community. Governments who are guided by the will of the people and who operate in a transparent manner (that is without secrets), under an agreed upon rule of law, have every chance of success. That is what we have been hoping to see at Leech Lake.

I believe it is still possible that it could happen. It will all depend on how the Band's leadership answers its detractors, builds its credibility, and responds to the wishes and the needs of the people.

The letter writer was explicit in what s/he wanted the three newly elected Leech Lake RBC members to do. S/he asked the Chairman ... not to be a party to "secret" acts or agreements. S/he challenged the Secretary/Treasurer ... to publish the checks he signs. S/he seemed to disapprove of the pay raise that the RBC members voted themselves. S/he explicitly commented on how the Representative ... went against a campaign promise when he voted, as did the other RBC members, for a pay raise that seemed out of line.

The letter writer expresses thoughts that many Band members must also have. I suggest that the writer, and most of the Band members, would feel much better about conditions on their reservation if there were no more secrets in government operations.

When governments act in secret, it is easy to assume the people would not approve of what is going on. That is not healthy government. It would go a long way to eliminating suspicion as to what their government is doing with their money, if the Secretary/ Treasurer ... would do as he promised during the campaign and publish all issued checks. That would give a better idea of where their money is going. Most people handle check books but sometimes do not fully understand how to make sense of an accountant's balance sheet.

Lastly, given the comments about the executive salary increases, the best thing the Leech Lake RBC could do to restore the people's good will would be to rescind the pay raises they gave themselves. That single act would go a long way toward building credibility, respect and support from Leech Lake members. The difference between their salaries and the income of their members is a gaping chasm that shouldn't exist. It would be easy to point out that, in this economy with all the job loss, business failings and general hard times for everyone, the pay raises would be especially inappropriate.

But even if that were not the case, RBC members should not be giving themselves high salaries. Such action breeds distrust of government in the people.

I suspect the letter writer is a member of the disloyal opposition to the [new] administration. Nevertheless the questions raised have validity and need to be addressed.

If I am correct in my supposition, I want to remind our readers that the previous administration did everything in its power to prevent this paper from reaching the hands of the people. The former Chairman went

267

so far as to deny us distribution at the off reservation grocery and other places.

Press/ON has been in publication for over 20 years now. In regard to our being a propaganda paper, I point out it was *Press/ON's* investigation and publication of the facts that were instrumental in the prosecution of a half a dozen or more tribal officials for stealing from their tribes. Had we not made it public, it is possible the stealing would still be going on.

I acknowledge we have made a lot of enemies and I gain a certain self-satisfaction in counting them. I have made enemies, but corrupt officials are enemies of their nation. I do not regret helping to expose corrupt individuals. I will do it whenever I can regardless of who they are.

Chapter X: Introduction: Letters to the editor.

Although it was rarely used, *Press/ON* consistently invited rebuttals or objections to its articles or editorials. Lawrence "encouraged input in all forms." Letters to the editor, cartoons and rebuttals were favored features. The published letters were frequently unsigned. Lawrence's position was: "I am dealing with eleven governments that deny people basic rights, so I have to get in an advocacy role."

Writer critical of *The Native American Press* **article* on tribal sovereignty and gaming.**
October 11, 1996.

I almost always enjoy reading *The Native American Press,* but of late I am getting more than a little skeptical about the wisdom of your writing and thinking as they relate to Tribal Sovereignty and gaming.

I don't believe there is any doubt that many of your Indian readers share much of your concern about the management and assumed revenues from tribal gaming, and I don't doubt that equally as many feel that justice is sometimes not very well served under the protections of Tribal Sovereign Immunity, because it appears to be unequally applied and exploited as it relates to many of their tribal leaders.

The Native American Press may not have any roots or trust in tribal government or in the National Indian Gaming Commission or National Indian Gaming Association, and that may understandably prejudice your viewpoint and diminish your assessment of the damage that you do to the many tribes that operate responsible and trustworthy tribal government and gaming operations.

I have always believed that Indian people have enough known enemies in non-Indian people and institutions who have historically been critical and demeaning of 'Indianess' and tribal government, without having what are believed to be knowledgeable insiders undermining and diminishing the historic sovereignty that tribes were denied for some 500 years, and only now are learning to wisely assert and exercise for the benefit of their lands, resources and their people.

American Indian journalists with even a minimal sense of history would seem to understand this recent phenomenon throughout Indian country. On the other hand, if any Indian journalist operates some of the time, like many of their Indian

271

readers, driven by anger and resentment, it is easy to understand the lack of objectivity and wisdom that is being demonstrated lately in this regard by *The Native American Press*.

Indian people were dogged and oppressed many years ago by Indian Scouts for nothing more than a pittance for pay and for a little recognition by their white leaders and friends. It just seems totally inappropriate and totally out of context that Indian tribes should be subject to such a modern day version of Indian Scouts the likes of Indian journalists.

Respectfully submitted, [signed, name withheld.]

* This letter was in response to Lawrence editorial, "Corruption, Oppression—not reporting it jeopardizes sovereignty." October 11, 1996. See Chapter V. for copy.

Agree non-members take home tribal money.
March 7, 1990.

In the newspaper on Feb. 7th I read your Tribal Council Payroll. I noted how many people that are not tribal members that share the $707,000 payroll. That's right $707,000 in our tribal money gets paid in salaries. I also noted that $785,000 gets paid out in attorney contracts. That is a total of $1,492,000 almost $1.5 million. That is the sad facts we pay that much, mostly to non-tribal enrollees.

Our tribal enrollees for example make much less than [those who hold tribal office]. Maybe some tribal enrollees should have some of the high paying jobs.

With the non-enrolled members salary, and tribal bingo, and the trading post you would think we Red Lake members would be in for a hefty payment.

Keep up the good work on informing the people with the truth.

Name withheld
Red Lake, Minn.

Leech Lake Vote Buying.
March 4, 1993.

The Leech Lake Tribal Council has done their dirty work again. This has been going on much too long and it's about time this type of activity is stopped, once and for all. When are the Leech Lakers going to wake up? Only a handful are continuously trying to stop the mismanagement of our tribal affairs. We will be able to put an end to it only when EVERYONE gets out there and helps fight those who have the power and are abusing it.

The Leech Lake Tribal Council only wants "puppets" to work for them. They do not want anyone who can think for themselves and do good, for the whole tribe. When you see those puppets with their new cars, remember--it's your money that is paying for them. And when you see their wives and children shopping, remember--it's your money they're spending. Think about that while you're at the tribal office begging for something. So, if you stay home and don't do anything about this situation, then I think you deserve everything they do to you. And when you sell your votes to them, remember the hard times your friends and relatives are having.

This is how they maintain control of who wins seats on the tribal council and who doesn't. Some Leech Lakers sell their votes for as little as $100. Maybe that's okay if you can live on $100 for a few years until the next election, but I don't know anyone who can. Think about it. It's not worth it to sell out.

If we all get together and elect honest people who will be accountable to us, we can get a fair distribution of the casino money, and start feeling some benefit from the gaming on our rez. Leech Lakers, stand up and fight for your rights NOW! DON'T SELL OUT AGAIN!

Letter signed. Signature withheld for privacy.

Basic human rights not for all [Reservation residents].
August 8, 1994.

To the Editor:

On Saturday, July 30, at 6: a.m., my son, [name withheld for privacy], was attacked by three enrolled members of the ... band. They are: [names withheld]. These men attacked the [name withheld] home where my son was visiting.

One hit him with a baseball bat on the face below the temple. He was knocked out and then [a second one] tried to cut up his fingers with a knife.

At the time of the attack the [tribal] police were summoned, but they reported falsely, for the record, that "there was nobody around ... no one there," when they arrived.

I know the attack by the three men was with an intent to kill (a felony) so I went to the FBI. My son wanted to sign a complaint.

The [tribal] Judiciary has not responded so far to my requests and I do not believe they will. This denial of my son to equal protection under the law is a violation of the U.S. Constitution, but that is business as usual on the ... reservation.

I know the [perpetrator] will not be charged by the [Tribal] Judiciary for this crime because of who he is related to, just like when he was brought to court for molesting a four-year-old child. Evidence is suppressed and [the man] was free. The [Tribal] Judiciary protects those who have relatives in the tribal services.
Name given, but withheld by Editor.

Red Lake students hungry for nutritious meals.
June 5, 1998.

To the editor: Since I've been working at the Red Lake Elementary School, I've been appalled at the school lunches I've seen. Not only are they awful, but the quantity they give isn't enough to fill up anybody.

It's the same food over and over again. If the food isn't burned it's raw!

Sometimes it's burned and raw together. The kids get sick of the same food over and over again.

They never get salt or pepper. ON OCCASION, they get ketchup with their burned and raw French fries.

The kids are scared to ask for seconds, and they wouldn't get it if they asked anyway.

Aren't school lunches supposed to be nutritious? Shouldn't all kids go away from lunch being full, instead of still starving?

What about all this talk of the war on diabetes? Shouldn't that start in the school?

I know a lot of other employees who feel the same way. And parents should be concerned too. This is our future generation.
Name Withheld Upon Request.

Mr. Dill Lawrence, *The Native American Press,*
December 14, 2004.

My nephew is not an enrolled member and keeps being held in the tribal jail for trespass. I've filed a writ in Federal Court after having no luck talking to the tribe.

Since we have to go this far, I am filing a suit in Federal court against the Tribe for violation of his civil rights and denying me the pleasure of his person. The suit will be for 100 million dollars to wake the Tribe up to the fact that they "too" have to follow the law.

Everyone I talk to they're scared of the Council because of their use of Banishment Powers.

I am an Indian from another Rez and I don't live in such fear on Fort Belknap.   Signed,
Name withheld.

We have our own "Katrina" going on here.
September 23, 2005.

I was sitting at home thinking about that big storm in New Orleans and do I ever feel badly for the families and people. I am in no way making a joke out of what happened over there, but I thought it would make a point to the people on our reservation and to many other reservations.

We have our own "Katrina" going on here. Our native kids are killing each other. All the hate you see day after day. Everyone seems to hate their own kind. We see a lot of bad things happen here on the northern Minnesota reservations. My heart goes out to everyone...

I've seen a lot more of the younger generation pass away rather than the elders. We need to step up and do something for our people to show them hurting someone else is not what we're supposed to be doing.

We are natives. We're supposed to be brave, but in a good way. Have courage, but in a good way. Have pride, but in a good way.

I have seen kids have these, but use them in a bad way, which causes or starts a lot of problems. If you look at someone the wrong way they want to fight. If you act the wrong way, then it's on.

There are so many negative feelings for these young people. That's why I say we have our own storm going on and it's a bad one. But yet there is nobody here to care or to stop and see that we need help. Our kids need help. Everyone's dying left and right. We're burying our own kids and families.

I do not see anyone giving us any type of support with grief or with the bad things happening on our reservation.

A lot of families here don't have a home. Don't have anywhere to go. No place to eat or enjoy. Now does anyone care?

278

I always wondered what needs to happen? Do we need a big, big disaster to get the help we need here on our reservation? Why would anyone want that? We don't need that to happen. We have enough going on. Someone needs to come forward and take control and think about our families and kids and put aside the hostility and find a way to help our reservation. Mainly for our children that have seen nothing but hostility and fighting going on between our chairman and our [District] Reps.

So I suggest that you sit down and take care of our storm and I'm not the selfish type but please do not send our money to Katrina. We need it here for our reservation, our storm.

I thought for sure I would see our Chairman with the big check on the front page giving money away, which we don't have. I figured he would copy the other chairmen. That's usually how things go. Gotta look good, even though your reservation is hurting.

Think about it people! We love our kids, our families, our own natives. Let's start helping out more and saving ourselves from going through these hard times. Use your heart for something good! Don't use it to feel hurt and sorrow.

Take care – the Rez will Recover.
Name withheld.

The "Buck" stops here.
December 9, 2005.

This Chairman, Buck, is still lying to the American people. By that I mean all the people who read the Minneapolis Star Tribune, The Pioneer Press of Bemidji, the St. Paul Pioneer, as well as those who watch the state/local news on TV.

You can call a spade a shovel, or if you say stake, it could mean steak!

"GUILTY," is just what it implies, it can't be sugarcoated with fancy words as Buck is doing.

It was a "plea bargain," that Buck agreed to for his son, Louis, being a juvenile. Buck knows the system and how it works. The FBI and state prosecutors had him on two other charges, including "Conspiracy to commit murder."

By accepting the deal presented to them they would not have to go to trial to face the other charges. There was a lot more involved with Buck and the FBI. Buck wanted to get a resolution in the Council to limit the FBI's authority on our reservation. He was informed that was not a possibility.

So Buck did the next best thing in his mind. He fired the Criminal Investigator and Public Safety Officer for assisting the FBI in their criminal investigation and arrest of his son.

During Buck's reign of terror, excuse me, chairmanship, we have had the worst tragedy that can befall in the community—drug use and availability have proliferated. And for the first time, under his leadership, our school had to forfeit their football games for the season. Gangs in school are forming, emulating their leader, a role he played in Minneapolis before he was sent up here to take over.

Buck could go back down there and lead those people. We were OK before he became chairman and caused all this grief.

When Chairman "Butch" Brun took and held his meetings in Minneapolis, Buck cursed and berated the Elders. Those spirits

280

have answered him and are not through with him yet. **Signed: The "Buck" Stops here Committee, Ponemah, MN.**

Note: Chairman 'Buck Jourdain's son was accused, and subsequently plea bargained, in the shooting incident referred to in the next letter.

Father of slain Red Lake security guard responds to spurious remarks regarding death of son.
November 2, 2006.

I was shocked with disbelief and sadness when I was contacted by friends of my family... They informed us that an interview on CBC public radio and also rebroadcast on Minnesota Public Radio on October 10, 2006 denigrated my son Derrick Brun, who was one of the victims shot and killed at the Red Lake High School on March 21, 2005.

This interview on CBC Public Radio, "As It Happens" between Barbara Budd and Wisconsin State Rep. Frank Lasee, Republican congressman, dealt with HOW TO MAKE SCHOOLS SAFER. During the interview Rep. Lasee commented on the school shooting at our school in Red Lake.

He stated: "THE ARMED SECURITY GUARD DID NOT DO HIS JOB. HE RAN OUT THE OTHER WAY. THEN PEOPLE WERE SHOT AND KILLED. This was my son Representative Lasee was talking about.

My family and I were provided all the information regarding the death of my son, who would have been 30 years old on September 28th of this year. He stood his ground and confronted the troubled youth who took my son's life and the lives of eight other innocent victims, which included his grandfather and his companion. My son died a hero, and for Rep. Lasee to make comments critical of my son's action without knowing what actually happened is unbelievable and outright irresponsible.

Lasee's "Arm the Teachers" proposed bill may or may not have some merit, however, if he did not take the time to investigate all factual information and events that have occurred at schools throughout North America, arming teachers and administrators will not be the answer to the increasing violence and threats occurring at our schools.

The pain and grief of all families who have experienced the death of their family members in school settings will never subside. How can a legislator such as Rep. Lasee make unsubstantiated

282

comments in an interview that will retrigger the emotional and mental anguish one experiences when a family member is murdered?

My youngest son Derrick Brian Brun was hired as a temporary Security Guard in October, 2004 and was killed on the first day of spring, March 21, 2005. He was a police officer for our Law Enforcement Department for 6 years, and a job-related back injury prevented him from completing the Federal Bureau of Indian Affairs police academy training requirements needed to continue as a police officer for our police force. He was not a coward and would not run from any danger.

He was unarmed and, like some of our troops in Iraq, he had no body armor. He was shot twice in the chest area and the second gunshot to the heart must have killed him instantly. I miss and grieve for my son each and every day. Our love for him will never die. He is in our memories forever!

Sincerely, Francis "Chunky" Brun, Red Lake.

Bibliography: The Arrogance of Tribal Power.

ABC News. Casinos not paying off for Indians. January 26, 2018.

Administrator. State Government Finance Committee. Minnesota House of Representatives. December 2, 2011.

Allen, William B., Chair, "Statement. The Indian Civil Rights Act." United States Commission on Civil Rights. Clearinghouse: A Project of the Tribal Law and Policy Initiative. June 1999.

Annett, Kevin Daniel. "Hidden from History. The Canadian Holocaust: The Untold Story of the Genocide of Aboriginal Peoples." Vancouver: The Truth Commission and the Genocide. 2001.

Associated Press. "Apology to tribes." *Native Sun Times.* May 23, 2010.

Barberi, Susan. "An Enemy of his People." *Minnesota Magazine.* April 1999.

Barreiro, Jose and Tim Johnson. Editors. *America is Indian Country.* Golden, Colorado: Fulcrum Publishing. 2005.

Bartlett, Donald L. and James B. Stede. "Look Who's Cashing in at Indian Casinos. Hint: It's not the People Who are Supposed to Benefit." *Time.* December 15, 2002.

Beaulieu, Raymond. "Housing overpays tribal per diem." *The Ojibwe News.* May 24, 1988.

Beaulieu, Raymond. "Ojibwe News pulled from tribal store shelves." *The Ojibwe News.* June 1, 1988.

Bibeau, Frank. Leech Lake Reservation Tribal Council. Correspondence, editor's file. June 6, 2012.

Blair, Gary. "Former Minnesota Senator, Leech Lake Tribal Attorney, disbarred two years after conviction." *The Native American Press/Ojibwe News.* April 10, 1998.

Bordevich, Fergus M. "The Least Transparent Industry in America." *Wall Street Journal.* January 5, 2006.

Brody, Sam. "Before we were invisible: How Minnesota's most prosperous Indian Tribe became a powerhouse in Washington." MinnPost.com, November 20, 2017.

Brown, Curt. "Indian watchdog issues its final bark." Final edition. Minneapolis: *Star Tribune.* September 29, 2009.

Brown, Curt. "Watchdog journalist Bill Lawrence, 70, dies." Minneapolis: *Star Tribune.* March 5, 2010.

Brunswick, Mark. "Gambling monitors could use a hand." Minneapolis: *Star Tribune.* February 12, 2004.

Bryan, Susan Montoya. "Task Force eyes rural, tribal exposure to violence." *Native American Times.* February 2, 2012.

Capricciosi, Rob. "President Obama's Million Dollar Native Fund Raiser." *Indian Country Today.* February 20, 2012.

Center for Responsive Government. www.opensecrets.org/industries/totals. Accessed June 6, 2012.

Charles, Mark. "U.S. 'Apology' to Indian people goes unnoticed." *indianz.com.* March 12, 2012.

Cleveland, Harlan. "Leadership and the Information Revolution." Minneapolis, MN: The World Academy of Arts and Sciences of the United Nations University. 1997.

Daffron, Brian. "Bill John Baker, Policy-Maker: An interview with the New Cherokee Principal Chief." *Indian Country Today.* March 5, 2012.

Dennis, Tom. "Our opinion: Reservations need, deserve a free press." *Grand Forks Herald.* March 30, 2011.

Department of Justice Sues South Dakota Department of Social Services for Racial Discrimination." *Nativenewsonline.net.* November 5, 2015.

Egan, Timothy. *Short Nights of the Shadow Catcher: The epic life and immortal photographs of Edward Curtis.* Boston: Houghton Mifflin Harcourt, 2013.

Eisler, Kim Isaac. *Revenge of the Pequots: How a Small Native American Tribe Created the World's Most Profitable Casino.* New York: Simon & Schuster. 2001.

"Ex-Oklahoma tribal leader indicted for embezzlement." *News from Indian Country.* November 2011.

Facts About American Indians Today. www.infoplease.com. Accessed July 4, 2012.

Fairbanks, Robert A. Letter to Pulitzer Committee. January 24, 1997. Lawrence's personal file.

Fixico, Donald L. *Resilience and Rebuilding: Indigenous Nations in the Modern American West.* Tucson: University of Arizona Press. 2013.

Fogarty, Mark, "20 Billion: Total Support for American Indians,*" Indian Country Today Media Network.* October 25, 2015.

Fogarty, Mark, "2017 Budget Request of $21 billion for tribes." *Indian Country Today.* January 29, 2012.

Foreign Aid Assistance. beta.foreignassistance.gov. Accessed September 29, 2017.

"Former Seminole Councilman Guilty..." The *Florida Sun Sentinel.* April 14, 2012.

Friedman, Thomas L. *Hot, Flat and Crowded.* New York: Farrar, Straus & Giroux, 2008.

Friedman, Thomas L. "The Ben Laden Decade." *International Herald Tribune.* June 2, 2011.

Giago, Tim. "Freedom of the Press in Indian Country." *Nieman Reports.* Fall 2005.

Giago, Tim. *Notes from Indian Country. Volume I.* Pierre, SD: State Publishing Company, 1984.

Giago, Tim. *Notes from Indian Country, Volume II.* Rapid City, S.D: Giago Book Publishing Company, 1999.

Graves, Bruce. "Letter to the Editor." *The Native American Press/Ojibwe News.* November 9, 2001.

Gray, Christine K. *The Tribal Movement in American Politics: The Struggle for Native American Sovereignty.* Lanham, NY: Alta Mira Press. 2013.

Grinols, Earl L. "Gambling Economics: Summary Facts." www.texaspolicy.com. November 17, 2004.

Grow, Doug. "The mighty fall to Indian editor." Minneapolis: *Star Tribune.* May 17, 1996.

Haga, Chuck. "Minnesota journalist Bill Lawrence dies." *Grand Forks Herald.* March 7, 2010.

Hartman, Sid. "Gopher Frosh Boast Top Quarterback Crop."
Minneapolis: *Star Tribune*. Clipping, family scrapbook. No date.

Hayes, Robert G. A *Race at Bay, New York Times Editorials on
"The Indian Problem, 1860-1900."* Carbondale: Southern Illinois
University Press. 1997.

Heffelfinger, Tom. Quoted in "Losing a voice for American
Indians." Minneapolis: *Star Tribune*. October 3, 2009.

Holmes, Ernest. *The Science of Mind*. New York: Dodd, Meade &
Co. 1938. P.53.

Horwitz, Sari, "The Hard Life--and High Suicide Rate--of Native
American Children on Reservations." The *Washington Post*. March
9, 2014.

ICTMN staff. "Ex-Oklahoma tribal leader indicted for
embezzlement." AP. *News from Indian Country Today*. November
2011.

Indian Land Tenure Foundation. "The Allotment Act."
www.iltf.org/resources/land-tenure-history/allotment. Accessed
July 4, 2012.

Jawort, Adrian. "Blackfoot Man Jailed for Speaking Out." The *New
York Times*. November 26, 2013.

Jorgenson, Miriam. Editor. *Rebuilding Native Nations: Strategies
for Governance and Development*. Tucson: University of Arizona
Press. 2007.

Kantrowitz, Barbara. "How an Amazon Tribe Used Google to Save
Their Land." *Reader's Digest*. March 2012.

Kennedy, Todd. "Slots get little or no state review." Minneapolis:
Star Tribune. February 7, 2012.

Kershaw, Sarah. "Drug Traffickers Find Safe Haven in Shadows of Indian Country." The *New York Times,* February 18, 2006.

King, Lise Balk. "Native America Calling." January 5, 2012. www.nativeamericacalling.com. Accessed August 7, 2012.

Klobuchar, Jim. "It's time casinos stop using 'Tribal Sovereignty' as a shield." Minneapolis: *Star Tribune.* November 2, 1993.

Kristof, Nicholas D. "Poverty's Poster Child." The *New York Times.* May 9, 2012.

"Lawrence making good." Minneapolis: *Star Tribune.* Clipping, family scrapbook 1958.

Lawrence, William J. "A Warrior's Creed: Today is a good day to die." *The Native American Press/Ojibwe News.* September 1, 2009. Final issue of newspaper.

Lawrence, William J. Advertising Letter. June 6, 1991. Publisher's files.

Lawrence, William J. Affidavit. In RE: RULES OF PROCEDURE FOR THE RECOGNITION OF TRIBAL COURT ORDERS AND JUDGEMENTS. Minnesota Supreme Court. July 10, 2002.

Lawrence, William J. "Consider this..." *The Native American Press/Ojibwe News.* January 27, 1995.

Lawrence, William J. "Do Indian reservations equal apartheid?" *The Native American Press/Ojibwe News.* June 6, 2003.

Lawrence, William J. "King thwarted in attempt to derail recall petition." *The Native American Press/Ojibwe News.* January 11, 2002.

Lawrence, William J. Letter to advertisers. July 27, 1988. Publisher's files.

Lawrence. William J. "Post King." *The Native American Press/Ojibwe News.* January 22, 2002.

Lawrence, William J. "Reservation drug trafficking attracts coverage in The *New York Times.*" *The Native American Press/Ojibwe News.* February 24, 2006.

Lawrence, William J. Testimony. The Committee on Indian Affairs, United States Senate. "The American Indian Equal Justice Act, S1691." April 7, 1998.

Lawrence, William J. Testimony. "Tribal casinos must share the wealth." The Minnesota Joint House/Senate Tax Committee. St. Paul, Minnesota. April 30, 1997.

Lawrence, William J. "Tribal Injustice at the Red Lake Court of Indian Offenses." *North Dakota Law Review.* (Summer 1972).

Lawrence, William J. "Tribal Sovereign Immunity is the Single Biggest Factor Contributing to Corruption on American Indian Reservations." Presentation. American Indian Law and Policy Symposium. Norman: University of Oklahoma. March 21, 1998.

Lawson, Russell M. *Encyclopedia of American Issues Today.* Greenwood: an imprint of ABC-CLIO, LLC. 2013.

Lillihaug, David. Quoted in "Indian watchdog issues its final bark." Minneapolis: *Star Tribune.* September 29, 2009.

Loewes, James W. *Lies My Teacher Told Me.* New York: The New Press. 1995.

Lovett, Ian. "Power Struggle over Indian Tribe Splinters into Violence in California." The *New York Times.* February 28, 2012.

Marlantes, Karl. "The Truth About Being A Hero." The *New York Times.* August 20, 2011.

Martinez, David. *Dakota Philosopher: Charles Eastman and American Indian Thoughts*. St. Paul: Minnesota Historical Society Press. 2009.

McKinnon, John D. "U.S. Offers Official Apology to Native Americans." The *New York Times*. December 22, 2009.

Meister, Allen. "The Economic Impact of Tribal Gaming. American Indian Gaming: A State by State Analysis." http://www.americangaming.org. Accessed September 17, 2017.

Mengelkoch, Louise. "Blind in Red Lake: How the Press Made a Bad Thing Worse." *Columbia Journalism Review*. March/April 2006.

Mengelkoch, Louise. "Sovereignty and secrecy." *The Native American Press/Ojibwe News*. March 17, 2005.

Meriam Commission. "The Problem of Indian Administration." Report of a survey made at the request of the Honorable Hubert Work, Secretary of the Interior, and submitted to him February 21, 1928. www.Alaskool.org.

Meuers, Michael. "New Red Lake Nation College Takes Shape of an Eagle." *Indian Country Today*. March 28, 2015.

Meuers, Michael. "Red Lake Capitol Construction Ahead of Schedule. *Indian Country Today*. September 20, 2014.

Minnesota Historical Society Digital Newspaper Hub. newspapers.mnhs.org.

"Minnesota tribal watchdog dies at age 70." Associated Press. Minneapolis: *Star Tribune*. March 5, 2010.

Moquin, Wayne and Charles Van Dorn. Editors. *Great Documents in American Indian History*. New York: DaCapo Press. 1995.

Morlan, Cliff. "Three to go." *Bemidji Pioneer.* No date. Clipping family scrapbook.

Mosedale, Mike. "No Reservations." *City Pages.* Minneapolis, MN. June 20, 2001.

Moyers, Bill and Company. Episode 1, "Joseph Campbell and the Power of Myth." May 23, 1986.

Murphy, Sharon M. "Journalism in Indian Country: Story Telling That Makes Sense." *Howard Journal of Communications, 21:4.* 2010.

National Indian Gaming Commission. Gaming Revenue Reports. "Growth in Indian Gaming 2004-2013."

National Indian Gaming Commission. Gaming Revenue Reports. "Gross Gaming Revenue Trending Fiscal Year 2015."

National Relief Charities. Native American Reservation Facts, www.nrcprograms.org. Accessed July 4, 2012.

Nelson, Todd and David Hawley. "Judge due to block release of tribe's casino audits." *Pioneer Press.* Bemidji, MN. September 21, 2001.

"NIGC: Indian Gaming Revenue. 2016. $31.2 billion." nigc.gov.

Niiska, Clara. "Tribal PAC contributions for 2002 Minnesota elections total $261,300 as of August 19: Alleged campaign finance irregularities." *The Native American Press/Ojibwe News,* October 25, 2002.

Niiska, Clara. "What's the impact of a decade of Indian casinos?" *The Native American Press/Ojibwe News.* January 4, 2002.

Obama, Barack. Presidential Proclamation. "National Native American Heritage Month, November 2009 " *indianz.com*. October 30, 2009.

Obama, Barack. Presidential Proclamation. "National Native American Heritage Month, November 2014." *indianz.com*. November 2, 2014.

"Obituary: Joseph W. Lawrence." *Bemidji Pioneer*. June 14, 1944.

Overholser, Geneva and Kathleen Hall Jamieson. Editors. *The Press*. New York: Oxford University Press. 2005.

Owings, Alison. "The Declaration of Independence, Jefferson's 'Merciless Indian Savages'." *Indian Country Today*. July 6, 2017.

Oxford Companion to the United States Supreme Court. *Santa Clara Pueblo v Martinez*. http://www.answers.com. Accessed April 21, 2012.

Pember, Mary Annette. "The Quiet Apology to Indians." *Politics and Government*. December 13, 2011.

Pfanner, Eric. "G-8 Leaders call for Tighter Internet Regulation." The *New York Times*. May 24, 2011.

Pulitzer Prizes. www.pulitzer.org. Accessed June 26, 2012.

Randall, R.A. "Jim." Dissenting Judge. *Cohen v. Little Six, Inc., d/b/a Mystic Lake Casino*." State of Minnesota Court of Appeals Eighth District. December 18, 1995.

Rave, Jodi. "Challenges Natives and Non-Native Journalists Confront." *Nieman Reports*. Fall 2005.

Reilly, Hugh J. *Bound to have Blood: Frontier Newspapers and the Plains Indian Wars*. Lincoln: University of Nebraska Press. 2010.

"Remembering 'Bill' Lawrence, of *The Native American Press/Ojibwe News.*" *Bemidji Pioneer*. Bemidji, MN. March 18, 2010.

Rigert, Joe. "Casino wealth and wellbeing. Excerpts from a book by a former [Minneapolis] Star Tribune Reporter." Minneapolis *Star Tribune*. September 1, 2016.

Robbins, Catherine C. *All Indians Don't Live in Teepees [or Casinos]*. Lincoln: University of Nebraska Press. 2011.

Roberts, Michael J. "SWOyate. Information Poll. Results April 2010 to October 2011." SWOyate.com. Accessed March 2012.

Robertson, Dwanna L. "The Myth of casino riches." *Indian Country Today Media Network*. June 23, 2012.

Robertson, Lindsay G. "Native Americans and the Law: Native Americans under current U.S. Law." thorpe.ou.edu/guide/robertson.html. 2010.

Russell, Steve. *Sequoyah Rising. Problems in Post-Colonial Tribal Governments*. Durham, N.C.: Carolina Academic Press. 2010.

Schroth, Raymond A. "He Was All of America Talking to Itself." *On Second Thought: The Sevareid Issue.*" North Dakota Humanities Council. Bismarck, ND. Autumn 2010.

Shilling, Vincent. "And now there are 573! Six Native American Tribes get Federal recognition as President Trump signs bill." *Indian Country Today*. January 30, 2018.

Shilling, Vincent. "Native History We Are Never Taught in Schools." *Indian Country Today*. January 17, 2018.

Shilling, Vincent. "Senator Heitkamp Embraces 'Not Invisible # for Missing and Murdered Indigenous Women.'" *Indian Country Today*. December 6, 2017.

Shilling, Vincent. "The Biggest Federal Tax Overhaul in 30 Years: Native Tribes are not Included." *Indian Country Today.* December 14, 2017.

Siemens, Oliver J. "Native people deserve equal access to voting box." *Indian Country Today.* February 19, 2014.

Sontag, Deborah and Brent McDonald. "In North Dakota, a Tale of Oil, Corruption and Death." The *New York Times.* December 28, 2014.

Sorenson, Thomas. "Tribal Gaming and the Political Contribution Strategies of Native American Tribes." *Thesis.* Bemidji State University, Political Science. 2010.

Sortal, Nick. "Indian Gaming Surpasses Non-Tribal Casinos." *Tribal Business Journal.* 2018.

"Sovereign enemy." The *Brainerd Dispatch.* May 8, 1999.

Stannard, David E. *American Holocaust: Columbus, Christianity, and the Conquest of the Americas.* Oxford: Oxford University Press. 1992.

Strickland, Patrick. "Life on the Pine Ridge Native American Reservation." [Home of the Oglala Sioux Lakota] *Aljazeers.com.* November 2, 2016.

"Tex Hall No Longer in Chairman Race Amid Scandal." *Shale Oil News.* PBS. October 13, 2014.

"The Long Trail to Apology." Opinion. The *New York Times.* June 28, 2004.

The Natives. "Current conditions of Native Americans on reservations." http://wwwthenatives.com. Accessed March 27, 2016.

Toesing, Gale Courey. "Gaming appears to be recession-proof." *Indian Country Today.* April 4, 2011.

Tolocz, Kerri. "As Native American Casinos Proliferate, the Social Costs of the Gambling Boom Are Ignored." *Forbes.* September 25, 2013.

"Tribes' high-interest lending venture booms." AP Helena, Montana: *Independent Record.* December 27, 2011.

Trudeau, Justin, Prime Minister. "We need to get to a place where Indigenous peoples are in control of their own Destiny." Speech before Canadian Parliament. February 14, 2018.

"Twenty billion: Total U.S. Support for American Indians." *Indian Country Today.* October 27, 2011.

United States Census 2010. American Indian/Alaska Native Population. www.uscensus.gov.

United States Commission on Civil Rights Report. *A Quiet Crisis: Federal Funding and Unmet Needs in Indian Country.* Washington, D.C. July 2003.

United States Commission on Civil Rights Report. *Broken Promises: Evaluating the Native American Health Care System.* Washington, D.C. July 2004.

United States Commission on Civil Rights. *Discrimination Against Native Americans in Border Towns.* Briefing Report. Washington, D.C. November 9, 2007.

United States Government Printing Office. *Hearing: Tribal Sovereign Immunity.* Committee on Indian Affairs. U. S. Senate, 104th Congress. September 24, 1996.

United States Health and Human Services. Office of Minority Health. American Indian/Alaska Native Profile. http://minority health.hhs.gov.

Vizenor, Gerald. *Blue Ravens.* Middleton, CT: Wesleyan Press. 2014.

Vizenor, Gerald. *Survivance.* Lincoln: University of Nebraska Press. 2008.

Vizenor, Gerald. *The Everlasting Sky.* St. Paul: Minnesota Historical Society Press. 2000.

Vizenor, Gerald and Jill Doerfler, David E. Wilkins. *The White Earth Nation: Ratification of a Native Democratic Constitution.* Lincoln: University of Nebraska Press. 2012.

Watson, Ivan. Interview with Wael Ghonin. CNN. February 9, 2011. Reported on the Lede. www.nytimes.com. Accessed February 2011.

White, Byron. Justice U.S. Supreme Court, "Dissent: Indian Civil Rights Act of 1968. *Santa Clara v. Martinez*" (No. 76-683) May 5, 1978.

"White Earth Tribal Council salaries are public knowledge." Letter to the Editor. *The Native American Press/Ojibwe News.* April 15, 2008.

White House Tribal Nations Conference Progress Report. "Achieving a Better Future for Tribal Nations: Promoting Sustainable Economic Development in Indian Country." December 2011.

White House Tribal Nations Conference Progress Report. "Building prosperous and ... brighter future and progress and hope ..." December 2015.

Wilkins, David E. Introduction, *The White Earth Nation: Ratification of a Native Democratic Constitution.* Lincoln: University of Nebraska Press. 2012

Wilkins, David E. *The Navaho Political Experience.* 4th edition. Lanham, Maryland: Rowman and Littlefield. 2013.

Wilkins, David E. and Heidi Kiiwelinepinesiik Stark. *American Indian Politics and the American Political System.* Lanham, New York, Toronto: Rowman and Littlefield Publishers, Inc. 2010.

APPENDIX

1. Annotated Bibliography of Current Relevant Articles.
2. *Duhaime's Law Dictionary*: Definitions: Tribal Sovereignty and Tribal Sovereign Immunity.
3. Guest editorial: The Honorable Lloyd Omdahl, Former Lieutenant Governor of North Dakota. "It's time to look at reservation governance." The *Grand Forks Herald.* July 15, 2015.
4. Lawrence's achievements as Publisher of *The Native American Press/Ojibwe News,* 1988-2009.
5. Picture of Lawrence and Bea.
6. State of Minnesota Campaign Finance Board List of Native American political contributions for 2016.
7. Total Tribal Principal Lobbyist Expenditures at the Minnesota State Capitol: 2000-2010.
8. *The Native American Press* Fetal Alcohol Series. 2005-2008.

Annotated Bibliography of Relevant Articles from Recent and Current Publications, 2012-2018.

Black, Michael. Acting Assistant Secretary of Indian Affairs, U.S. Department of the Interior before the Senate Committee on Indian Affairs, addressing the significant challenges faced by children in Indian Country.

"Safeguarding to the Seventh Generation: Protection and Justice for Indian children and the Implementation of the Native American Children's Safety Act of 2016." April 21, 2017.

Brady, Sean. "Opinion: Audits find wide-spread corruption in Indian country.

"Native American tribes waste federal money on bills, personal trips, casinos.

"The federal government has revealed that several tribes have been mishandling, mismanaging, and misusing federal funds granted them by authorities... The tribal government has recently been exposed of corruption, misusing federal funds for their own purposes.

"... the surviving tribes have been pushed aside and hidden, suffering from severe poverty while the tribal governments have trouble creating an economy that allows them to live decently on the reservation... Now Native Americans have to deal with corruption. The federal government and private auditors have revealed widespread corruption among certain tribes ... with federal money directed toward [money] being pocketed to fund vacations, pay bills, and other personal business." *indianz.com*, October 8, 2013.

Brown, Matthew. "Auditors say tribes can't account for $3.5 million.

"... funds included money for a corruption-plagued water project...tribal leaders were unable to fully document how they spent the money or provided inadequate records to justify the spending." *Native Times.* October 3, 2017

"Chairman of Paskenta Band removes armed guards from casino." *indianz.com.* June 17, 2014. See also "Rival faction of Paskenta Band tries to shut down casino." *indianz.com*, June 10, 2014

Champagne, Duane. "Living and surviving on Native American Reservations." Topics include: High Unemployment Rates, Family Violence. *Indian Country Today.* September 27, 2017.

Childress, Sarah. "Where Tribal justice works."
"In 2011, a man in northeastern Oregon beat his girlfriend with a gun, using it like a club to strike her in front of her children.
"Both were members of the Confederated Tribe of the Umatilla Indian Reservation. The federal government, which has jurisdiction over crimes in Indian country declined to prosecute, so the tribe stepped in. The man was convicted in their court and sentenced to 790 days in federal prison...
"The Umatilla tribes had recently enacted new provisions from a federal law, the Tribal Law and Order Act, that allowed Native American courts to try their own people for felony crimes instead of relying on federal authorities." Frontline. PBS. April 3, 2013."

Daffron, Brian. "Bill John Baker, Policy Maker: An Interview with the new Chief Principal Chief.
"The citizens deserve to be heard, and so we are letting them be heard. One of the first policies to change was that we

would allow employees to speak to the Tribal Council. There had been a policy in place that said you'd be fired if you talked to the Tribal Council." *Indian Country Today.* March 12, 2012.

DePalma, Anthony. "Canada's Indigenous Tribes Receive Formal Apology." The *New York Times,* January 8, 1998.

Donovan, Lauren. "Three Affiliated Tribes' Chairman Tex Hall says report 'smear campaign.'" *Bismarck Tribune,* September 16, 2014.

Eagle, Kevin. "Ten from Pine Ridge indicted on drug charges.
"Rapid City. According to U.S. Attorney Brendan V. Johnson, 10 individuals from Custer, Pine Ridge, and Rapid City have all been indicted by a federal grand jury...
"All 10 defendant appeared before U.S. Magistrate Judge John E. Simko on Monday, May 30, 2014, and pled not guilty to the indictments." *Native Sun News,* June 10, 2014.

Eagle, Kevin. "Tex Hall ousted in North Dakota tribal primary.
"The incumbent president of the Mandan, Hidatsa, and Arikara tribes of North Dakota, Tex Hall, was ousted... After months of investigation called for by members of the Three Affiliated Tribes...
"The court documents allege Hall ... demanded $1.2 million from oil and gas company, Spotted Hawk Development, before he would sign its development plan. The documents also claim he used his position as Chairman to secure more that $580 thousand in payments for a water hauling company..." *Native Sun News.* September 26, 2014.

"Editorial: Hits and misses. "Miss: Another inflammatory press release in the Tehama County Indian war.

"Unlike the cowboys vs Indians ... the latest squabble is intramural, with one part of the Paskenta Nomlaki tribe feuding with another. It is something that happens pretty darn often when casinos and the revenue that they generate are involved, and it is almost impossible for someone from the outside to figure out what is happening as tribes are sovereign governments, answerable to themselves.

"What we know here is that two segments of the tribal leadership have ousted each other, and the ... [one] faction ... has brought in armed guards to protect [the casino].

"The [other] faction has hired former Tehama County Sheriff Clay Parker as tribal police chief, an appointment not recognized by the group ensconced in the casino... nothing new about this.

"Parker, this week, issued a press release stating that without federal intervention, the situation could truly turn violent." *Chico Enterprise Record*, May 31, 2014.

"Editorial: Lawlessness on Indian Land." Opinion. "Violence and crime rage unchecked in Indian country, yet the federal government, the primary law enforcement on reservations, is investigating and prosecuting fewer violent felonies, and reducing financing for tribal courts and public safety programs. That is a scandal.

"According to Justice Department data the Navajo reservation ... with 180,000 people had more reported rapes in 2009 than did Detroit, a city of more than seven million...

"The Pine Ridge Reservation in South Dakota covers about 3500 square miles. It has 49 tribal officers now, nine fewer than in 2000.

"Crime has been a problem on reservations for generations, because of federal neglect and lack of money, but also because of a spaghetti tangle of jurisdictions that hobble effective law enforcement. A crime can be a federal, state or tribal matter, depending on where it is committed and whether the suspect or victim is Indian...

"The Tribal Law and Order Act, signed by President Obama in 2010, was supposed to increase prosecutions and give tribal police more authority to enforce federal laws. But its reforms require public support that has not materialized...

"The worsening plague of crime in Indian country is a moral atrocity. The Obama Administration and Congress need to keep the federal government's failed promise to give tribes the resources they need to maintain law and order." The *New York Times*, November 21, 2012.

"Editorial: Online poker a bad gamble for California.

"Santa Rosa. The tribes see a lucrative new market, and they don't want competition from off-shore companies.

"California tribes are among the biggest donors to political campaigns and, not coincidentally, law makers tend to be very responsive to the tribes." *Press Democrat*, June 11, 2014.

Egan, Timothy. "Science and Sensibility. In Indian country today, a man with a head full of rage can knock his wife or girlfriend to the ground, kick her, cut her, sexually assault her and expect to walk away untouched by the courts or cops." [Discusses opposition to the Violence Against Women Act.] The *New York Times*, February 28, 2913.

Eligon, John. "Anger Over Plan to Sell Site of Wounded Knee Massacre.

"... the massacre site, which passed into non-Indian hands a generation ago, is up for sale.

"The land is believed to have gotten into non-Indian hands sometime after a process of allotment began in the late 1800s in which the federal government divided land among the Indians and gave some parcels to non-Indians."

The owner "moved away in 1973, after the violent occupation of Wounded Knee by ... the American Indian Movement left much of the town destroyed... [the owner] said he had been trying to sell the land to the Oglala Sioux for about three decades, and he blamed the tribe's internal disorder for his inability to do so. 'They never could agree on anything,' he said." The *New York Times*, March 30, 2013.

Estes, Nick. "Racist City, S.D.: "Life is Violent and often Deadly in Rapid City.

"... raped citizen, native population living in poverty, the rates higher than many reservations.

"... 50% of the city's natives live below the poverty line. The poverty rate is higher than any other urban demographic.

"More than poverty, however, afflicts native residents. Living in Rapid City, South Dakota, is violent, often deadly." *indianz.com*. September 5, 2014.

Estes, Nick. "You Try to Live Like me—Looking to Understand Albuquerque's Homeless Natives." *Indian Country Today*. September 12, 2014.

Fogarty, Mark. "2017 Federal Budget request of $21 billion for tribes. A 77% increase over 2016." *Indian Country Today*. January 29, 2017.

"Former Chairman of the Chippewa Cree Tribes plans to plead guilty to theft and bribery charges.

"[He] was accused of accepting a $25,000 vehicle from a Havre businessman as a reward for past dealings.

"... latest conviction in a sweeping corruption investigation that has targeted misused federal money on the Rocky Boy Reservation... The probe already has netted guilty pleas from multiple tribal officials and the consultants and companies awarded contracts to work ... on a fifty-mile water pipeline to repair flood damaged buildings on the reservation." *indianz.com,* September 25, 2014.

"Fraction of Revenues go to fight gambling addiction." Assoociated Press, November 24, 2017.

"Gun Lake Tribe announces full revenue–sharing payments: The State of Michigan will be receiving over $1.7 million." *Aljazeers.* November 2013.

Haga, Chuck. "Tribal Judge says court, social workers see kids' safety as top concern.

[The tribal court Judge Shirley Cain,] "a member of the Red Lake Band of Ojibwe Indians in northern Minnesota, served earlier in other tribal courts, including as chief judge on her own reservation. She left that position after a few months in 2003, however, following a dispute with tribal officials over what *The Native American Press/Ojibwe News,* published in Bemidji, called her efforts to reform the tribal court system and make it more independent of the tribal council." *Grand Forks Herald,* April 8, 2013.

Hall, Kip. "Oil dealings prompt investigations of North Dakota tribal chairman."

A former U.S. attorney will lead an investigation into the dealings of a tribal chairman [Tex Hall] thought to have been the target of a North Dakota oil speculator with ties to a man shot dead on Spokane's South Hill." *Spokesman Review*, March 5, 2014.

Hollenbeck, Brian. "Mashentuckets' Treasurer Steve Thomas quits, will plead guilty to theft." *indianz.com*, October 2, 2013.

Hudetz, Mary. "Slow-moving justice for women in Indian country.

"Even with the law now passed, legal loop-holes remain in the wait for justice for Indian women continues... Tribes must have implemented a series of steps that many might not already have in place and could pose large legal costs.

"One of those steps, for example, includes insuring tribal judges have appropriate credentials they might not already have..." *indianz.com,* June 16, 2014.

"Hundreds at Memorial for boy found burned, buried." *News from Indian Country,* August 1, 2012.

"Indigenous peoples cite victories, map future on seventh anniversary of United Nations Human Rights Declaration." *Indian Country Today*, September 13, 2014.

Jawort, Adrian. "Blackfeet man jailed for speaking out... "Although [Brian] Farmer's actions are protected under the 1968 Indian Civil Rights Act, locally, the Blackfeet tribe deemed it a violation of the Blackfeet Ordinance 67, which protects tribal members against libelous 'or misleading statements meant to harm, injure or discredit' them. Farmer's attorney, David Gordon, writes, 'They're basically saying if you criticize the tribal council, you are going to go to jail and that is frightening.'" *Indian Country Today,* November 26, 2013.

Jensen, Elizabeth. "Family Secrets, Bared on Camera. Robin Charboneau, an Oglala Sioux [decided] that she needed to open her mouth...

"So she let the documentary filmmaker David Sutherland follow her for more than three years as she struggled to raise her family as a single mother while confronting her alcoholism and the scars of being sexually abused as a child.

"What she didn't know was that her decision would temporarily cost her custody of her two children in tribal court, or that her teenage daughter would disclose that she too had been sexually abused—by her own father...

"Now, ... his [Sutherland's]work can be seen as something of an Exhibit A in explaining why the Federal Bureau of Indian Affairs took control of the social services on the Spirit Lake [ND] Indian reservation last year, citing concerns that tribal mismanagement had led to abuse of children there." The *New York Times,* March 22, 2013.

Kristof, Nicholas D. "Poverty's Poster Child. Pine Ridge [reservation in South Dakota] is a poster child of American poverty and of the failures of the reservation system for American Indians in the West. The latest Census Bureau data was that Shannon County here had the lowest per capita income in the entire United States in 2010. Not far behind in that Census Bureau list of poorest counties, are several found largely inside of the Sioux reservations in South Dakota: Rosebud, Cheyenne River and Crow Creek...

"Unemployment on Pine Ridge is estimated at around 70 percent and virtually the only jobs are those working for the government or for the Oglala Sioux tribe itself...

"Half the population over 40 on Pine Ridge has diabetes, and tuberculosis runs at eight times the national rate. As many as two-thirds of adults may be alcoholics, one-fourth of children are born with fetal alcohol spectrum disorders, and life expectancy is somewhere around the high 40s—shorter than the average for Sub-Saharan Africa. Less than 10 percent of children graduate from high school...

"... [One] reason businesses don't invest is that ... companies find it difficult to recruit dependable workers... A second is that reservations are often structured in ways that discourage private investment ... and tribal law means that outside investors cannot rely on uniform commercial codes and may have no reliable recourse if they are cheated." The *New York Times*, May 9, 2012.

Lawrence, William J. "Department of Public Safety caves in to tribal gambling interests." *The Native American Press/Ojibwe News.* June 9, 2001.

Lawrence, William J. "Everything you ever wanted to know about 'Finngate' but were afraid to ask." *The Native American Press/Ojibwe News.* March 17, 1995.

Lawrence, William J. "Finn's $449,944. Reservation Risk Management (RRM) dividend." *The Native American Press/Ojibwe News.* March 22, 1996.

Lawrence, William J. "'Finngate' defendants guilty on 16 counts." *The Native American Press/Ojibwe News.* April 21, 1996.

Lawrence, William J. "*Press/ON* celebrates thirteenth anniversary."

"It is satisfying to note that this edition of *Press/ON* concludes thirteen years of continuous publication... I am proud of the fact that we have been able to give a voice to the people so that they can express their views, and to present accurate information so that they can make informed decisions about issues that affect their lives...

"I am most gratified that we have been able to do this on our own-without having to accept funding from any government or foundation sources.

"*Press/ON* has remained independent, and as far as we know, we are the only independently-owned, weekly native owned newspaper in the country... Without your support, this would not have been possible." *The Native American Press/Ojibwe News.* May 25. 2001.

Lawrence, William J. "Supreme Court says Tribal documents not exempt from Freedom of Information Act." *The Native American Press/Ojibwe News.* March 9, 2001.

Lockwood, Denise. "Wrongful death lawsuit filed against Potowatomi Hotel and Casino.

"The family ... filed a wrongful death lawsuit against the casino alleging that employees failed to help a man after he had a heart attack... The complaint alleges that after the heart attack left him sprawled over two chairs, a group of employees passed by him without offering assistance. Only when a casino guest found him unresponsive ... and notified a security officer, did he begin to receive medical attention." *Milwaukee Business Journal*, September 24, 2014.

Lustgarten, Abraham. "Land Grab Cheats North Dakota Tribes out of $1 Billion, Suit Alleges.

"And, the suits claim, the federal government facilitated the alleged swindle by failing in its legal obligation to see that the tribes got a fair deal.

"This is a story as old as America itself...

"In 2011, a team of elders audited the tribal council's activities. They found widespread financial inconsistencies that they said indicated systemic misconduct. 'We saw millions of dollars going out and hardly anything coming back to the Three Affiliated Tribes,' said ... a forensic auditor who chaired the team. 'We're not just talking about cash. It is rooms, food, travel, donations, and it is only a handful of people that can get all this stuff.'

"[Tex] Hall, the tribe's current chairman, had previously held the post from 1998 until 2006. He didn't deny that there had been corruption, but said that since he came back into office in 2010, he has focused on reform and on making sure the oil revenues benefit the broader tribal community. He said he had formed tribal entities to directly control a pipeline and refinery project, set up a $100 million trust fund for the tribes, and began to sign lease agreements that are favorable to Native Americans on the reservation." *ProPublica.* February 23, 2013.

"Many Pine Ridge residents say that they have been forgotten by mainstream society, abandoned by politicians, and neglected by state institutions." The *New York Times*, December 28, 2014.

Meuers, Michael. "New Red Lake Nation College Takes the Shape of an Eagle.

"A more than $10 million USDA loan will be used to build a 27,400 square-foot tribal government center next to the college...
"... in the process of being built are huge twin buildings in the shape of Migizi (bald eagle) ...

"The twin college campus and tribal government center buildings' Eagle design symbolize the culture, strength, power, and perseverance of the Red Lake Nation.

"In addition to the new buildings, the project will include new powwow grounds, walking trails along the lake and a Veterans Park honoring all Red Lakers who have served in the U.S. Armed Forces. The park will feature black granite monuments for inscribing names of living and deceased service personnel..." *Indian Country Today*. March 28, 2015.

Meuers, Michael. "Red Lake Capitol Construction ahead of schedule.

"Construction of the new buildings will be a source of pride to the Red Lake Nation...

"The new buildings will increase educational opportunities and be an accredited school...

"With high unemployment rates and numerous social and health issues, the Red Lake Tribal leadership feels that higher education is one of the best long-term solutions for community development. *Indian Country Today*, September 20, 2014

Editor's note: Dan King, the project manager in the above cited articles was once the Red Lake Tribal Treasurer. He was the subject of many *Native American Press/Ojibwe News* editorials and articles that cited financial irregularities in the Band's financial affairs. Under his financial leadership, the tribe became overly burdened with huge debt because of ill-advised construction projects. During his tenure, despite a feasibility study that indicated a new casino would not be viable, the tribe, under his direction, went ahead with the building.

Although King resigned before a recall election in March 2003, the tribal council voted to proceed with the action because, according to the Red Lake Constitution, if a person is recalled, s/he will be barred from ever holding tribal office again (*Native American Press/ Ojibwe News* story March 8, 2006.)

It is interesting to note that he continues to serve in high position, as President of the Red Lake Nation College, in the Red Lake government. [See *The Native American Press/Ojibwe News*, 2004: January 20; February 6, 13, 20, 27; March 5, 12, 19, 26; April 4 for a series of articles disclosing questionable construction practices and financing decisions by the Red Lake Band under King's advice/guidance.

"Montana tribal members fight for voting rights.
"It was mid-April and Montana was gearing up for this year's primary election...
"People ... could head to the courthouse to sign up [for absentee ballots].
"But for Ed "Buster" Moore... It wasn't so simple. 'I couldn't afford it,'" Moore said.
"Moore's situation isn't unusual. There are measures that curtail minorities' voting rights, such as stringent ID requirements and limited voting time...
"The challenges Native Americans face when they go to the polls have never been on the national radar. In the second decade of the 21st century, nearly 50 years after the Voting Rights Act of 1965 outlawed discriminatory voting practices, American Indians are still working to obtain more voting rights." *Indian Country Today.* June 10, 2014.

Murray, David. "The Crisis in our Backyard: Montana's reservation Housing. Homelessness, Overcrowding and Black Mold... tribes struggling with decades of housing neglect." *Great Falls Tribune.* March 31, 2015

"NIGC* reportedly sends investigators to check on the Paskenta Band Casino.

"The National Indian Gaming Commission sent investigators to the casino owned by the Paskenta Band of Nomlaki Indians in California.

"The NIGC previously sent the tribe a letter on April 21 that questioned who was in charge of the ... casino.

"'It's becoming clear that laws are being broken and money is being mishandled... at the casino, leaving the tribe in jeopardy of being robbed of millions of dollars...'

"... one faction ... issued a closure notice to the casino. But the facility continues to operate under the chairman ... who claims his rivals have been removed from their seats by the council.

"Both sides have made allegations against each other, with [the chairman] claiming that a group of tribal members have stolen more than $10 million." *indianz.com,* May 24, 2014.

*National Indian Gaming Commission.

O'Donnell, Lara Escobia. "Supreme Court upholds tribal immunity against state in casino law suit.

"In Michigan v. Bay Mills Indian Community ... the U.S. Supreme Court affirmed the lower court's ruling that tribal immunity barred the State of Michigan's suit against Bay Mills ... for opening a casino outside of Indian Lands." *Association of Corporate Council,* September 22, 2014.

Owings, Alison. "The Declaration of Independence, Jefferson's 'Merciless Indian Savages,'" ... *Indian Country Today.* July 6, 2017.

Risen, Tom. "Left Behind: For Some Native American Communities Facing Water Problems, Hope Circles Down the Drain.

"Nearly 30% of Native Americans and Alaskan Natives living in poverty in 2014 – Approximately double the nation's overall poverty rate." *U.S. News.* June 16, 2016.

Sanchez, Mary. "Justice for Native Americans rests in restoring relationship with the land, not in reparations.

"We tend to simplify native people while ignoring the massive poverty and alcoholism on reservations. Not every tribe is operating a successful casino.

"It's as if America prefers professing romanticized idolatry in place of understanding, much less acting on, a more nuanced view of justice." *Kansas City Star*, June 16, 2014.

Schwarz, Alan. "Overcoming addiction, Professor tackles perils American Indians face.

"Doctor David A. Patterson, ... 49, has devoted what he considers his second life to studying the quicksand [of alcohol abuse] that just about swallowed him, and that continues to imperil American Indians more than any other ethnic group..." The *New York Times*, May 11, 2013.

Siemans, Oliver, J. "Native people deserve equal access to the voting box.

"Good citizens of Montana, please tell your Secretary of State and the election officials of Rosebud County, Blaine and Big Horn Counties to stop wasting hundreds of thousands of dollars, eventually maybe millions, fighting Native American voting rights." *Indian Country Today,* February 19, 2014.

Sontag, Deborah and Brent McDonald. "In North Dakota, a Tale of Oil, Corruption and Death."

Tex Hall, "... a once seemingly untouchable leader, was under investigation by his tribal council because of his connection to an Oregon man who would later be charged with murder for hire in the two deaths." The *New York Times*, December 28, 2014.

Strickland, Patrick. "Life on the Pine Ridge Native American Reservation [Home of the Oglala Sioux Lakota]."
Excerpts: "... use of car batteries and generators for a few hours of electricity each day ...
"80-90% unemployment.
"Public health has suffered. More than 80% of the residents suffer from alcoholism... A quarter of children are born with Fetal Alcohol Syndrome.
"... per capita income ... is about ½ that of the U.S. average.
"... poverty rate is around 3x higher." www.*Aljazeers.com*, November 2, 2016.

Tasker, John Paul. "Liberal Government to back up Indigenous Rights Bill, demand full implementation of the United Nations Declaration of the Rights of Indigenous People." *CBC News,* November 21, 2017.

"Tex Hall no longer in chairman race amid scandal.
"Tex Hall is the current tribal chairman, having won the tribal election in 2010, as well as previously from 1998 to 2006. Hall is no longer in the race as of September 16th, amid a scandal involving his 'unethical business deals' associated with the oil and gas industry. Yesterday members of the tribe protested outside of the tribal administration building... The protestors demanded more transparent government, citing years of allegations of impropriety by the chairman." *Shale News. BPS.* October 13, 2014.
[Tex Hall rose to the presidency of the National Congress of American Indians. He served two terms in that position.]

"The Natives "Current conditions of Native American Reservations." Discusses: Employment, Suicide, Education, Housing, Disease Blog/2016/3/27 http://www.thentvs.com March 27, 2016.

"Tribes get $11.3 million in federal grants to combat chronic disease." *Indian Country Today*, September 26, 2014.

U.S. Foreign Aid Assistance: Department of State. $27.4 billion planned in Foreign Aid for FY 2019. http://foreignassistance.gov/.
[U.S. allocation to American Indians is $20 billion.]

Volz, Matt. "Families from two reservations charged with theft.
"Members of two families are charged in separate indictments ... a part of a long-running investigation into corruption on Montana's Indian reservations.
"... accused of forging checks ... accused of forging the signature of [the city of] Brockton's mayor ...   [the family] was charged with wire fraud, theft ... and aggravated identity theft. They were indicted in U.S. District Court.
"In a second indictment ... [two others] who worked for Stone Child College ... are accused of taking more than $242,000 from a construction company that ... worked at the Rocky Boy Reservation. [One individual] was the president of the college and [the other individual] was its facility manager between 2010 and 2012 when they accepted payments from a company implicated in other corruption indictments." *Great Falls Tribune*, September 22, 2014.

Wikibooks.org/wiki/American_Indians."American Indians today have the highest rate of infant and child mortality, domestic

violence, rape, child abuse and neglect...highest rate of suicide..."
Discusses: Jobs, Exploitation, Environmental destruction, Lack of education and Poverty, e.g.

"Among all ethnic groups...the American Indians have the highest school drop out and lowest life expectancy (55 years)." Accessed November 11, 2017.

Wilkins, David E. *The Navaho Experience.* 4th Edition. Lanham, Maryland. Rowman and Littlefield Publishers, Inc. 2013.
"The Navajo Times, like 95 percent of the newspapers in Indian country, was, until 2003, owned by the Navajo Nation government.

"Most of the 300 reservation publications serve largely as newsletters touting their tribal government's accomplishments. In other words, most tribal newspapers are organs or instrumentalities of the governing body of the tribe..." p.173.

Williams, Timothy. "Child Abuse at Reservations is Topic for Three Lawmakers.
"Residents have complained that the Bureau of Indian Affairs and federal prosecutors have done too little to stop child abuse, which officials acknowledge is commonplace on Spirit Lake [reservation in North Dakota] and has reached epidemic levels, whistle blowers say.
"North Dakota's Senators and a Representative are expected to attend the meeting. The Federal Government took over the tribe's social services in October, and in one month federal officials say they had investigated 100 cases of reported child abuse." The *New York Times,* February 15, 2013.

Williams, Timothy. "Officials see Child Welfare Dangers on a North Dakota Reservation." The *New York Times.* July 7, 2012.

Williams, Timothy. "Pine Ridge Reservation Votes to end Alcohol Ban." The *New York Times*. August 14, 2013.

Williams, Timothy. "Psychologist Who Wrote of Abuse is Punished." [This is follow-up to "Officials see Child Welfare Dangers..."]" The *New York Times*. July 30, 2012.

Williams, Timothy. "Quietly, Indians Reshape Cities and Reservations. "... she is part of a continuing, and largely unnoticed mass migration of American Indians, whose move to urban centers over the past several decades has fundamentally changed both reservations and cities.

"Though they are largely associated with rural living, more than 7 of 10 Indians and Alaska Natives now live in a metro area according to Census Bureau data released this year, compared with 45 percent in 1970 and 8 percent in 1940." The *New York Times*. April 13, 2013.

Williams, Timothy. "Task Force to Study Crime on Indian Reservations." The *New York Times*. November 14, 2013.

Williams, Timothy. "U.S. Says it Pursues More Prosecutions on Indian Lands." The *New York Times*. May 31, 2013.

Williams, Timothy. "Washington Steps Back from Policing Indian Lands Even as Crime Rises.

"The federal government has cut the size of its police force in Indian country, reducing financing for law enforcement and begun fewer investigations of violent felony crimes, even as rates of murder and rape increased to more than 20 times the national average...

"[A] Justice Department report underscores a reputation for chronic lawlessness on Indian reservations, where unchecked crime has for years perplexed federal agencies, which are largely responsible for public safety on Indian lands." The *New York Times*, November 12, 2012.

Wood, Josh. "Oil-rich North Dakota reservation to get new leader.

"Chairman Tex Hall has been at the helm of the [Three Affiliated] tribes for much of the oil boom. He is the former [two-time] President of the National Congress of American Indians and served three terms as chairman of the tribes.

"Despite the benefits oil money has brought, many here question how the new found wealth has been spent by those in power and push for more transparency in tribal government." *Native American Times,* September 19, 2014.
[Should the allegations against Tex Hall be proven, he would be typical of the many tribal officials that Lawrence exposed.]

Woodard, Stephanie. "The missing Native vote in these times with Liberty and Justice for All." *Indian Country Today*, June 11, 2014.

Editor's Note: Citing these articles, in one way, may argue against the premise that Americans are ignorant of Indian Affairs.

Some articles could be classified as "local news," and therefore of interest only to persons of a particular region. Others are somewhat esoteric in nature and are not widely distributed.

The articles are cited to indicate that the problems Publisher Lawrence addressed have not been solved and America is in need of being educated about "the Indian problem" before "the problem" can be solved.

Duhaime's Law Dictionary

Tribal Sovereignty: Definition

(USA) A doctrine which recognizes Indian tribes' inherent powers to self-govern, to determine the structure and internal operations of the governing body itself, and exemption from state law that would otherwise infringe upon this sovereignty.

Related Terms: Tribal Sovereign Immunity

Tribal Sovereign Immunity: Definition

(USA) A doctrine that Indian tribes are immune from judicial proceedings without their consent or Congressional waiver.

"It's time to look at reservation governance."
By Lloyd Omdahl, Former Lt. Governor, North Dakota.
   (Editorial published in the *Grand Forks Herald*,
July 15, 2015)

   North Dakota's two U.S. senators have been taking a peculiar interest in the well-being and governance of Indian reservations, probably because of recent scandals in social services and foster care.

   This is dangerous territory because as soon as non-Indians start talking about reservation problems, the race card is played. Frank discussion is not necessarily racism, but calling it racism is one way to kill discussion.

   Senator Heidi Heitkamp, D. ND, has maneuvered the creation of a commission to study problems on reservations. The Heitkamp commission can be effective if it focuses on specific areas, such as education, social welfare and governance.

   Senator John Hoeven, R. ND, has gained approval of federal legislation that would require back-ground checks on participants in Indian foster care programs. This is an attempt to protect children from abuses too common in foster care.

   He also has pressed the federal government to do a better job of monitoring expenditures on reservations after the Government Accountability Office reported the misuse and loss of federal [Indian] funds.

   Hoven is right to be concerned about management and governance practices on reservations. The politics on some reservations is similar to the boss rule that prevailed in major American cities in the latter part of the 19th century, when favoritism and arbitrariness were ways of doing business.

   We need only look at the way the 'Fighting Sioux' logo issue was handled on the Standing Rock Indian Reservation. The chairman arbitrarily decided that he would not let the tribal members vote on the question. His decision killed the logo

324

because without Standing Rock's approval, the National Collegiate Athletic Association would not permit use of the logo.

This decision was made after the Spirit Lake, Sioux near Devils Lake, voted 2-1 in favor of keeping the logo. It is obvious that the Standing Rock chairman blocked the vote because he felt that his constituents would vote to keep the logo if they had the chance.

This sort of autocratic action indicates a serious weakness in the rules of governance on reservations. Obviously, the tribal members who wanted to vote had no established course of action to overrule the decision of the chairman.

Because there are no established rules of procedure, tribal members can become victimized by their leadership. Governing decisions can be made without regard to fairness or merit. Too many decisions can be made at the whim of one or two people at the top.

This brings us to the operation of the casinos on reservations. Casinos can exist only with approval of the governor. Unfortunately, we failed to require full transparency of casino operations as a condition for that approval. In view of the arbitrary nature that creeps into reservation governance, there is reason to wonder about the benefits of reservation gaming. Do all of the members get regular reports on the receipt and disbursements of revenues? Are all tribal members given an equal opportunity to be employed in the casinos?

It is naïve to assume that funds are handled scrupulously and fairly just because they are administered for American Indians by American Indians. The federal government monitors states, cities, and counties, so it isn't racism to ask for the same degree of integrity in reservation government and finances.

Here's hoping that Heitkamp's commission will give the procedures of governance and transparency high priority. The rights of the rank-and-file American Indians who are on the outside of the governing loop are being trampled too often by a governance system that is too loose and too arbitrary.

"The moral objective is that of saving a people, or person, or an idea. He is sacrificing himself for something. That is the morality of it. Now ... from another position [it] might be [said] that 'something' wasn't worth it, or was downright wrong. That is a judgment from another side. But it doesn't destroy the heroism of what was done. Absolutely not." [1].

Lawrence's accomplishments as Publisher of *The Native American Press/Ojibwe News*.

Publication of the consistent misdeeds of an autocratic 30-year tribal chairman resulted in his finally being removed from office through defeat at the polls.

Investigation and publication of information provided by tribal members.

Maintenance of pressure on the U.S. Attorney to investigate a reservation insurance scam resulted in indictment and sentencing of at least three tribal officials. A key player was the first Native American Minnesota State Senator. The investigation began in 1988 with receipt of a U.S. government memo, dated 1986, questioning costs of an insurance program. Ten years passed before the perpetrators were sentenced to federal prison.

Coverage of the insurance scam in *The Native American Press/Ojibwe News* inspired federal investigation into tribal corruption on other Minnesota reservations; indictments were issued. Several other tribal officials were also sentenced to federal prison.

Lawrence frequently requested financial documents under the Freedom of Information and the Minnesota Data Practices Act. He relentlessly pursued access to casino financial information. One of his requests for information to the Alcohol and Gambling Enforcement Division of the State of Minnesota provoked a lawsuit against the State by several of the wealthiest tribes seeking to prevent the State from releasing the information. The tribes contended the information should be kept secret.

Lawrence, at his own expense, entered the suit as a friend of the court. The proceedings stretched out over three years. The ruling, a precedent: The Audited Financial documents of tribal casinos are subject to the State Open Records Law. The tribes appealed and again were denied their position.

For his efforts in this and other cases, the St. Paul Chapter of the Society of Professional Journalists recognized him in 2003 with the Peter Popovich Award given for "Aggressive defense of the public's right to know and consistent support of the First Amendment."

After numerous reports of mistreatment of intoxicated individuals, including sexual assault of native women, by employees of the Hennepin County Detox Center, *The Native American Press/Ojibwe News* published thirty-eight stories on the subject and was instrumental in having the center closed and services transferred to an alternative organization.

A series of news articles on financial irregularities within the Indian Board of Health, Minneapolis, resulted in the Executive Director being found guilty of laundering money, falsifying the books and cronyism. The Executive Director sued Lawrence for libel. He successfully defended himself against the charge. He was exonerated. The Executive Director was fired. Altogether he was sued three times for libel, he successfully defended himself in each case.

The Native population consistently supported the newspaper by providing documents, photos, etc., that allowed Lawrence to publish the activities of corrupt officials. He championed the rights of reservation natives for over two decades. He instructed on what was due them as U.S. citizens; he encouraged them to resist tribal oppression.

He educated the people in innumerable ways, advised on how to counter injustice from tribal leaders, suggested solutions to chronic problems, informed about health issues, especially fetal alcohol syndrome.

In a series of articles, he discussed prevention, the advisability of early diagnosis and intervention of Fetal Alcohol Syndrome. He urged tribal officials to acknowledge the problem, something they have successfully avoided, as the first step toward amelioration.

As an Ojibwe and member of the Red Lake Band, he was a role model, both by example and by deed, for the people. He championed the rights of reservation residents for over two decades.

Lawrence ran for public office numerous times; he was elected to School Boards in Minnesota and California.

He was nominated in 1997 for the Pulitzer Prize in two categories: meritorious public service by a newspaper through use of journalistic resources; and for distinguished investigative reporting.

Over the years the mainstream media came to accept and depend on his expertise and spoke in praise of his bravery and good intentions. Local media didn't have access to the information he was privy to. Lawrence expressed doubt that if they'd had the information they likely would not have published it. Lawrence spoke many times during the years on behalf of freedom of the press, exposure of tribal corruption, tribal sovereign immunity and denial of basic civil rights to tribal members who, as U.S. citizens, are entitled to all the protections of the U.S. Constitution and the Bill of Rights, but who are frequently denied such benefits.

1972 Published Essay. "Tribal Injustice at the Red Lake Court of Indian Offenses." *North Dakota Law Review.*
1997 Testimony. The Minnesota Joint House/Senate Tax Committee. "Tribal Casinos Must Share the Wealth."

1997 Speaker, Participant. Investigative Reporters and Editors National Convention. "Investigating in Indian Country: Tribal Governments and the Agencies that Oversee Them.

1998 Testimony. The U.S. Senate Committee on Indian Affairs. "The American Indian Equal Justice Act."

1998 Speaker. The American Indian Law and Policy Symposium. "Tribal Sovereign Immunity is the Single Biggest Factor Contributing to Corruption on American Indian Reservations."

2002 Affidavit. State of Minnesota Supreme Court. "Rules of Procedure for the Recognition of Tribal Court Orders and Judgments."

2002 Statement. The Supreme Court Rules Committee regarding proposed "Full Faith and Credit Rule" as applied to tribal courts and judgments.

2002 Published Essay. "In Defense of Indian Rights." In *Beyond the Color Line.* Abigail Thernstrom and Stephan Thernstrom, editors.

2005 Addressed Convention of Foreign Award-Winning Writers acknowledged for their fearless exposure of wrong doing. World Press Institute.

2007 Written Testimony. "Discrimination Against Native Americans in Border Towns." United States Civil Rights Commission on Civil Rights.

Maintenance of an independent free press in Indian country for over two decades.

The Minnesota Digital Newspaper Hub [Minnesota Historical Society] has preserved the complete, twenty-one-year collection as an historic document that assures that his contribution will continue to be accessible to scholars.

[1] Episode 1. "Joseph Campbell and the Power of Myth The Hero's Adventure. The moral objective." Bill Moyers & Co. May 23, 1988.

Bill Lawrence and Bea, *Native American Press Office*

State of Minnesota Campaign Finance Board
[https://cfb.nn.gov]

Total Lobbying Disbursements Reported by Lobbyists for
Principals, January through December 2016
Found at "2016 Lobbying Disbursements Summary."

Principals with Disbursements over $250,000.

Mille Lac Band of Ojibwe	$350,000	p.31
Minnesota Indian Gaming Association	$280,650	p.31
Prairie Island Dakota Community	$269,752	p.32
Shakopee Mdewakaton Sioux Community	$260,000	p.32
	$1,160,404	

Disbursements Reported by Lobbyists January 1-December 31, 2016.

Reservations:

Bois Fort	$76,075	p.49
Fond Du Lac	$70,836	p.71
Grand Portage	$50,824	p.72
Leech Lake	$80,000	p.84
Lower Sioux	$40,000	p.84
Red Lake Ojibwe	$76,000	p.132
White Earth	$40,000	p.152
	$433,735	
	$1,594,139	

TOTAL TRIBAL LOBBYING EXPENDITURES AT THE MINNESOTA, CAPITOL 2007-2010*

Compiled from reports filed by tribal entities at the State of MN Campaign and Disclosure Board

Tribal Lobbyist				
Reported expenditure	2007	2008	2009	2010
Bois Forte	$120,000	100,000	125,600	120,000
Fond du Lac	$ 40,000	20,000	20,000	20,000
Grand Portage $40,000	40,000	60,000	60,000	
Leech Lake	$20,000	70,000	60,000	
Lower Sioux	$20,000	60,000	Unavail.	
Mille Lac	$340,000	320,000	410,000	430,000
MN. Indian Gaming	$340,000	300,000	310,000	280,000
Prairie Island	$360,000	280,000	240,000	280,000
Red Lake	$60,000		0	0
Shakopee Mdewakanton	$200,000	200,000	200,000	200,000
Upper Sioux	$40,000	40,000	40,000	40,000
White Earth		20,000	20,000	20,000
ANNUAL TOTALS	$1,516,909	1,420,000	1,555,600	1,510,000

$6,003,509, 2007-2010.

*Lobbying organizations were required by the State of Minnesota Campaign Finance and Public Disclosure Board to disclose their annual lobbying expenditures.

These figures do not include PAC contribution totals and expenditures spent by PACs affiliated with these tribal lobby entities. [Published originally in *The Native American Press/Ojibwe News*].

THE NATIVE AMERICAN PRESS/OJIBWE NEWS
SPECIAL SERIES:
FETAL ALCOHOL SYNDROME/SPECTRUM DISORDER

Made in the USA
Monee, IL
17 July 2023

39470925R00193